PERSUADING THE PEOPLE

BRITISH PROPAGANDA IN WORLD WAR II

DAVID WELCH

THE BRITISH LIBRARY

There are a number of individuals at the British Library that I need to thank. First, the publishing team Robert Davies, Jon Crabb and Sally Nicholls for making the production of this book such a joy. To Ian Cook for all his help, and especially Louis Allday for his generosity in providing material on the Middle East and for translating texts in Arabic. To my wife Anne for reading the manuscript and improving my poor grammar.

Finally, I would like to dedicate this volume to my mother Ivy Emily, who died in 2016. In World War II she served in RADAR and was part of an extraordinary, self-effacing generation, whose spirit and sacrifices I have endeavoured to capture in this book.

First published in 2016 by
The British Library
96 Euston Road
London NW1 2DB

Cataloguing in Publication Data
A catalogue record for this publication
is available from The British Library

ISBN 978 0 7123 5654 1

Designed and typeset by Will Webb Design

Printed and bound in China
by C&C Offset Printing Co., Ltd.

Contents

Preface

Among the Ministry of Information (MOI)'s varied duties during World War II was the responsibility for issuing 'national propaganda' to maintain morale at home and influence opinion abroad. Such propaganda was disseminated through a variety of media: films were produced, radio broadcasts were organised, exhibitions were curated, and a vast number of posters was issued. Parts of this work will be familiar. However the MOI's role as a major publisher is perhaps less well known.

Books, illustrated magazines, pamphlets, and postcards had assumed an important place in the MOI's pre-war planning. Indeed, in order to justify Britain's second declaration of war against Germany in twenty-five years, it had been agreed that a publication entitled *Why Britain is at War* should be one of its first examples of 'official' British propaganda. The pamphlet, which was eventually published as *How Hitler Made the War*, was nearly abandoned in October 1939, and W.H. Smith Ltd warned that 'nobody would want to buy it' after plans for photographic illustrations were abandoned by the MOI.[1]

As the embryonic MOI was being re-shaped to respond to the exigencies of World War II, books and pamphlets would ensure that 'official' messages, such as why Britain was at war, had an enduring impact. Unlike films, radio, exhibitions, and posters, such outputs were designed to last, and as a result they encouraged an increasingly professional approach to publishing and a businesslike relationship between the MOI and book publishers and distributors. This would require huge print-runs to satisfy demand, and a sensitive approach designed to appeal to audiences of all ages and tastes – especially in material aimed at overseas audiences.

A considerable amount of this largely forgotten aspect of British World War II propaganda can be found in the Central Office of Information (COI) archive held at the British Library.[2] There is an irony here, in that the COI would replace the MOI in 1946 once the war had ended. MOI publications can be found in the boxes marked 'PP'. These boxes are arranged in a sequence numbered 1–277 (although some numbers are spread across more than one box, and some numbers appear to be missing from the sequence). Boxes numbered 1–25 and 27 (26 does not appear) are marked '1940s', and are exclusively MOI publications. MOI publications are also spread through boxes with later numbering (all are marked '1940s–1970s'), and examples were found on the COI database up to box number 88. Some boxes contain multiples, including the same publication reprinted and translated in many languages. Frustratingly, many of the 'official' government publications, such as fold-out booklets and pamphlets, were not dated by the MOI. I have provided publication dates wherever possible, or approximate dates based on the historical context and the content of the publication. In order to provide a wider context, I have also cited examples of more familiar propaganda from outside the British Library's collection, including films, radio broadcasts, and officially commissioned paintings.

My aim is to provide an insight into the nature and scope of MOI propaganda produced during the war, including different types of propaganda messages. They range from the crudeness of some of the specifically anti-Nazi and anti-Japanese publications, and the defiant and even cheeky humour in some of the material depicting events that turned the war in Britain's favour, to the more light-hearted campaigns that discouraged citizens from gossiping – while at the same time encouraging them to savour the culinary delights and health-inducing qualities to be found by experimenting with versatile Potato Pete and Doctor Carrot. The sheer mass of publications is truly staggering, ranging from booklets demonstrating how well-known figures such as members of the Royal Family continued to demonstrate solidarity with their subjects to postcards showing inspirational figures such as Churchill, Monty, and 'Bomber' Harris. Different types of literature and visual propaganda showed women assisting in the war effort and how the colonies made their own substantial contribution in the fight against the Axis powers. To this end, I have included a section devoted to British overseas propaganda – this was largely sent to the British Empire, but also to areas such as the Middle East and even hostile territories. The MOI used the Royal Air Force for this purpose. The intended audiences for these campaigns and messages were equally diverse, so wherever possible, I have also tried to show how the Ministry pioneered social surveys and utilised secret wartime intelligence, partly in order to monitor the success or failure of its propaganda.[3] While I remain critical of the Ministry's bureaucracy and some of the censorship it imposed, and while it was often undermined by low self-esteem and a lack of political clout – especially prior to 1941 – one cannot fail to be impressed by the improvisation eventually shown by the MOI in handling social and political questions associated with national morale. The MOI experiment represented government propaganda on an unprecedented scale. By critically examining some of the major propaganda campaigns, I hope to provide greater insight into the mind and thinking of both government and people during World War II.

Notes

1 *How Hitler Made the War* is discussed in Chapter 2.

2 There is also an extremely exciting digital project funded by the Arts and Humanities Research Council being undertaken by the University of London, entitled 'A Publishing and Communications History of the Ministry of Information, 1939–45'. Further details can be found at: http://www.moidigital.ac.uk/ (accessed November 2015).

3 I have not discussed the theory and definitions of propaganda. However, in 2013 I co-curated a major exhibition, 'Propaganda, Power and Persuasion', held at the British Library. In the accompanying book I provided changing definitions of propaganda from the late nineteenth century to the present time (including my own working definition). These can be found in D. Welch, *Propaganda, Power and Persuasion* (London, 2013), 32–40, 201–5.

'I am encouraged by the opportunity of talking to the House (of Commons) about anything concerned with the Ministry of Information because the House has ceased to have any interest in our Department. We are now less exciting than the British Museum.'

BRENDAN BRACKEN

(MINISTER OF INFORMATION) SPEAKING (SARCASTICALLY) DURING A COMMONS DEBATE ON 5 AUGUST 1943.

CHAPTER ONE

Britain and
Propaganda
in World War II:
A People's War

The Ministry of Information

During World War II, authorities appropriated and controlled all forms of communication by means of strict censorship, in order to requisition them for propaganda purposes. In the totalitarian states such as Italy, Germany, Japan, and the Soviet Union this posed few problems, as the media – indeed the arts in general – had become part of the apparatus of the state. In the liberal democracies, on the other hand, the effort proved more problematic. Nevertheless, on the propaganda front Britain appeared to be better prepared than she had been for World War I. The first Ministry of Information (MOI) was established in 1918 and disbanded the following year. A new MOI came into being within days of the declaration of war in 1939, but when set up it was, to some extent, making up for lost ground. Morale would, obviously, be a crucial factor in enduring the bombing of civilians or a war of attrition, and the MOI would have to compete with totalitarian propaganda machines of the Fascist and Communist states that had already been in existence for several years. The new Ministry lacked authority in Whitehall and suffered from a difficult relationship with the press, which accused it of censoring and withholding news, and more generally of bureaucratic muddle. Nor, when it was first established, had the MOI any means of investigating or monitoring public opinion.

Interestingly the MOI commissioned the psychologist Professor Frederic Bartlett of the University of Cambridge to write a monograph on mass psychology and propaganda entitled *Political Propaganda*. Bartlett's ideas, published in 1940, were to inform the Ministry's thinking about the role that propaganda should play in a democracy engaged in 'total war':

> What is democracy? To this question all kinds of answers can be given. From the present point of view, however, one consideration overrides all others. In the modern world, political propaganda may be said to have been adopted as a weapon of State, but very nearly everywhere it has been adopted as the tool of a single political party within the State. This is precisely what cannot happen, except in a very incomplete way in a democratic country. A democracy differs from every other form of government in that it must always contain at least two main political parties, each treating the other with a very considerable degree of respect. Although each party may develop its own political propaganda, neither can violently suppress that of the other without destroying the spirit of democracy itself.[1]

In Fascist Italy, National Socialist Germany, or the Soviet Union, propaganda was to be controlled by the one-party state, but in Britain it was soon realised that if the MOI was to command the respect of the public it should not be seen as the exclusive instrument of a single political party. The first Minister of Information, Baron Macmillan, was a Tory peer – prompting the Labour leader Clement Attlee to remark that he 'was not satisfied that the Ministry of Information was not part of the Conservative machine'.[2] Following the formation of Winston Churchill's coalition government in May 1940, the perceived bias within the MOI was remedied.

In 1939 Britain appeared to be in a better state of readiness than she had been in 1914. The second Ministry of Information had been planned for some time and went into operation almost as soon as war broke out. However, appearances were deceptive. Planning for the conduct of propaganda can be traced back to October 1935, when a sub-committee of the Committee of Imperial Defence, chaired by John Colville, was appointed to draw up secret guidelines for a new Ministry in the event of war. In 1936, following the committee's recommendations, Sir Stephen Tallents, a civil servant who had been head of the Empire Marketing Board, was appointed as MOI Director General Designate. When the MOI was first partially mobilised on 26 September 1938, during the Munich crisis, it happened amid chaos and confusion. Tallents' problem was trying to make any kind of headway. Of the small group of Whitehall officials who knew of the Ministry's existence, few were confident of its ability to combat effectively the already tried and tested machinery of the Nazis' Ministry of Propaganda if war did break out. Tallents was eventually viewed as a troublemaker and sacked in 1938 after the Munich crisis,[3] when he began to push for greater clarity, and the Public Trustee, Sir Ernest Fass, was brought in. Fass had little idea of what he was doing. He lasted four months and then an equally inappropriate choice was made, the ageing former diplomat Lord Perth. Perth did not last long either, and the next choice was Baron Macmillan, an elderly Scottish barrister, who was in post when the war broke out.

The Munich 'dress rehearsal' provided the British planners with both time and opportunity to remedy the deficiencies exposed by the crisis. One of the most important lessons to be drawn was in the field of propaganda techniques. Before 1939 little attention had been devoted to various techniques of disseminating propaganda. British officials were far more preoccupied with constructing the appropriate structure and machinery. Using Lord Beaverbrook's model of 1918 as a blueprint for their new Ministry, the planners, led by Sir Stephen Tallents, had recognised an essential truth of propaganda in wartime, namely the connection between propaganda and censorship. The biggest difficulty the MOI would have to face would be that of news management: how could a nation which prided itself on freedom of speech and information become an overbearing censor, particularly if it chose to fight in the name of freedom? But they had too readily accepted that the methods employed during World War I could equally be applied to a war against Fascism and Nazism. Moreover, the planners initially failed to recognise that advances in communication technology in areas such as broadcasting and the cinema had widened the possibilities offered by propaganda.

Although Britain entered World War II relatively ill-equipped to conduct effective propaganda, it had made considerable progress during the final year of peace. As war became increasingly likely, the nucleus of the MOI was finally permitted to recruit the services of interested experts and outside organisations such as the Royal Institute of International Affairs (also known as Chatham House).[4] In June 1939 Chatham House commissioned an enquiry into broadcasting and propaganda that, it considered, would be of value to the planners of the embryonic MOI. The document contained eighty-six basic ground rules, and considerable attention was devoted to the question of propaganda methods and techniques, albeit rather late in the day. The ground rules appear somewhat basic, even naïve, too readily accepting the methods employed in World War I ('propaganda should fit pre-conceived impressions, e.g., a Chinaman thinks every foreigner a cunning person who is prepared to use a concealed gun should wiliness fail'). But, interestingly, they reveal that those who drafted the secret document were familiar with Hitler's view on propaganda published in *Mein Kampf* ('My Struggle'). Not only that, but they appeared to endorse some Hitlerite propaganda principles. For example, the document talks about appealing to the instinct of the masses rather than to their reason, and stresses the importance of building on slogans and the need for repetition.[5] It also had a section devoted to propaganda overseas. This was an important and often overlooked aspect of the Ministry's work, and I will return to this when discussing British propaganda directed at the Dominions and the Colonies and against the enemy.

Propaganda and Censorship

When World War II started, the British government decided not to take over the media or suppress editorial freedom, but rather to allow debate and interpretation. However, it would control the flow of information to the media. In spite of a number of eccentricities, the Chatham House blueprint formed the foundations of the basic principles of Britain's wartime propaganda. Initially, however, in October 1939, the Prime Minister Neville Chamberlain announced that a newly created Press and Censorship Bureau under the control of Sir Walter Monkton would conduct news censorship separately from the MOI. The experiment lasted just over six months. When Sir John Reith, the former Director General of the BBC, was appointed Minister of Information in 1940,[6] he laid down two of the Ministry's fundamental axioms for the balance of the war: that news equated to the 'shock troops of propaganda', and that propaganda was more effective when it told 'the truth, nothing but the truth and, as near as possible, the whole truth'.[7] The MOI handled propaganda intended for home, Allied, and neutral territory, and the Political Warfare Executive dealt with enemy territory. The programmes of the BBC earned Britain a powerful reputation for credibility that proved an asset long after the war ended. George Orwell later observed: 'The BBC as far as its news goes has gained enormous prestige since about 1940 … "I heard it on the radio" is now almost equivalent to "I know it must be true".'[8]

Reith would last only four months as Minister, and in April 1940 he fell victim to the end of the Chamberlain government. Yet at least he had some interest in and knowledge of propaganda after fifteen years' service at the BBC, and it was he who put the MOI on a more efficient footing. It was in that month that the MOI reabsorbed the Press and Censorship Bureau. Censorship had, frankly, been a farce. The censors were over-preoccupied with details and mechanical questions, while the press had become so contemptuous of them that editors frequently ignored their rulings, thus threatening the collapse of the 'voluntary' system and its replacement with straightforward compulsory censorship.

The incorporation of the censorship machinery of the Press and Censorship Bureau into the MOI (in contrast to the mistakes of World War I, when they remained separated) was an important organisational reform that reflected recognition of the need to integrate the control of news with the dissemination of positive propaganda. These principles were implemented so successfully that the press, the BBC and other organs of 'news' managed to maintain the trust of the British public at home and gained a reputation for Britain abroad for having even in wartime an honest, free, and truthful media, yet which gave practically nothing of significance away to an ever-vigilant enemy.[9]

Good relations continued with the BBC, which maintained the spirit of 'voluntary co-operation' established in wartime. After Brendan Bracken took over as Minister in 1941, organisational squabbling continued, but crucially, the MOI's censorship functions began to settle down to a coherent pattern. By 1941 the system was operating so effectively that most observers were unaware that a sophisticated form of pre-censorship was in force, even within the BBC. This explains why Britain's wartime propaganda gained its reputation for telling the truth when, in fact, the whole truth could not be told.

Propaganda and Public Opinion

How do we measure 'success' when it comes to propaganda? It is a recurring issue, and as the scale of mass communications has proliferated, so have the means by which governments have attempted to measure public opinion. The historian A.J.P. Taylor once famously said, in the context of World War I, that you 'cannot conduct a gallup poll amongst the dead'. Nevertheless, even during that war most governments did obtain some limited feedback on public opinion by means of police reports and letters to newspapers and magazines; but measuring public opinion was still in its infancy.

At the outbreak of World War II all the major belligerents had in place organisations providing detailed information on popular attitudes. In Britain, Mass-Observation worked for the MOI, which also used the Home Intelligence Reports, and in the United States the Office of Government Reports provided 'opinions, desires and complaints of the citizens' for the Office of War Information.

Although the MOI had been re-established relatively early in the war, it had no co-ordinated system of intelligence for discerning what the British public was actually thinking and feeling about the war and its impact. It quickly discovered an alarming gulf between government and governed which was exemplified in one of its first posters – 'Your Courage, Your Cheerfulness, Your Resolution WILL BRING US VICTORY' – which was widely criticised for its patronising tone.[10] The MOI responded by setting up its Home Intelligence Division in January 1940. In addition, it started a programme of wartime social surveys, the investigators being labelled by the public as 'Cooper's Snoopers', after Duff Cooper, Minister for Information between May 1940 and July 1941. Home intelligence reports recorded complaints from those who felt that the British state was 'becoming dangerously akin to the one we are fighting'.[11] The cost of such activities was also queried in Parliament.[12] Writing in the BBC's handbook for 1941, Harold Nicolson, the Ministry's Parliamentary Secretary, observed that the MOI was 'the most unpopular department in the whole British Commonwealth of nations', as a result of the public's 'healthy dislike for all forms of government propaganda'.

The Home Intelligence Reports were compiled every week between 1940 and 1944. They were drawn up on the basis of weekly submissions compiled from thirteen regional offices to help guide the MOI in its work by presenting 'an unbiased and objective picture of the state of British public opinion on matters connected with the war' and to assess 'as accurately as possible, the general state of public confidence'.[13] Intelligence officers were given special training to help them to record their observations impartially. The officers' work was based on a panel of voluntary contacts in the regions covering all classes and aspects of life in Britain. Each region had between 200 and 400 contacts, a proportion of whom were asked every week to submit reports about shifting moods – including both praise and criticism – on issues facing the Home Front such as food rationing and tax increases. When victory appeared certain at the end of 1944, the reports were discontinued.

The Ministry also had access to the information provided by the BBC's Listener Research Department, which recorded the reaction of the public to news and other programmes broadcast by the Corporation. Further information was provided by Mass-Observation, which had been founded in 1937 by the anthropologist Tom Harrison, the poet Charles Madge, and the filmmaker Humphrey Jennings in order to study British society. Mass-Observation was a fact-finding body that recruited a team of observers and a panel of volunteer writers to study the everyday lives of ordinary people in Britain and was commissioned by the MOI to carry out surveys on British public opinion on specific issues. Mary Adams, who was chiefly responsible for its redeployment, warned that Mass-Observation's methods were not strictly scientific and that care should be exercised in the interpretation of its findings.[14] She need not have worried on that score, as there was an inherent suspicion on the part of civil servants in the Ministry that the organisation leaned heavily towards the left. Indeed, Adams would often be obliged to defend it against such charges. Nevertheless, the MOI placed a heavy reliance on the work performed by Mass-Observation.[15]

Propaganda policy was formally constructed in two major committees. First of all, there was the Policy Committee consisting of the Minister and his senior executive officers. The Policy Committee's responsibility was to formulate and to approve departmental policy across the whole range of the MOI's domestic and overseas functions. Below it was the Planning Committee, whose task it was to work out the implementation of domestic policy handed down to them and to recommend action designed to sustain civilian morale. Both committees received information, ideas, and comments from a range of different sources; some came from within the various sections of the MOI, some came in the form of directives from the War Cabinet, while others were contained in 'feedback' reports of the Home Intelligence Division, the BBC, and Mass-Observation. Prime Minister Winston Churchill would, on occasions, interfere and criticise MOI policy, but generally speaking he took little interest in this aspect of the Ministry's work. The explanation for this may be that Churchill possessed a much greater faith in the people's determination than the MOI, who were – at least until the arrival of Brendan Bracken as Minister – frequently reading into the flimsiest of evidence the imminent breakdown of Britain's bulldog spirit.[16]

In his memoirs, Duff Cooper referred to the MOI as 'a monster … that no single man could cope with … Within the mind of the monster there lurked as much talent, as much experience, as much imagination and brilliance, and as much devotion to duty, as could ever have been collected in any one department of state … it was tragic to see so much ability, so much good will so nearly wasted.'[17]

Ministers were saddled with an additional problem of having constantly to reassure many backbench Conservatives, who looked on the MOI as a hotbed of socialism. There can be little doubt that the lack of political enthusiasm ensured that, when the Ministry was formally created in September 1939, there was no clear or agreed idea of its functions. As a result the MOI became the butt of satirists in its first incarnation. One of the most popular comedians, Tommy Handley, referred to it on his radio show *ITMA* ('It's That Man Again') as the Ministry of Aggravation. It was also mocked for overstaffing (999 at this stage of the war) by Fleet Street journalists, notably Cassandra of the *Daily Mirror*.

In spite of the initial hostility and setbacks, in July 1941 the War Cabinet had drawn up clearly defined objectives for the Ministry. They are worth quoting in full:

To publicise and interpret Government policy in relation to the war, to help sustain public morale and to stimulate the war effort, and to maintain a steady flow of facts and opinions calculated to further the policy of the Government in the prosecution of the war.[18]

I have borne in mind these objectives when choosing and analysing the mass of material produced by the MOI that has been included in this book. One of the most striking features of Britain during World War II was the extent to which the public was bombarded with appeals, exhortations, and instructions. Most of these campaigns – including 'Make Do and Mend', 'Coughs and Sneezes Spread Diseases', 'Careless Talk Costs Lives', and 'Dig for Victory' – are discussed in later chapters. But it is worth saying something about the process of dissemination. At the beginning of the war most departments submitted their proposals for publicity and campaigns to the MOI which, in turn, decided upon the nature and scope of the publicity. This would often involve bitter interdepartmental struggles with the Ministry, with departments fighting to maintain ascendency. However, this was to change in 1941 following a restatement of its functions by the Prime Minister, who instructed that department publicity should be conducted through the MOI. Furthermore, all public relations officers were to co-operate as a team under the direction of the MOI.[19] This placed the MOI, as the government's publicity agent, in a powerful position to act as a conduit between government propaganda and the people.

The MOI: Shifting Fortunes 1939–45

The story of the MOI for most of the war is one of repeated dismantling and rebuilding. These changes in structure and focus were often precipitated by the fluctuating fortunes of the war. Thus, as the war situation became more desperate for Britain during the summer of 1940, the MOI's attention turned increasingly towards home publicity; similarly, as the military tide turned in 1942, Brendan Bracken expanded the overseas division by adding a number of increasingly specialised sub-sections focused on particular geographical areas.

Between 1939 and 1945 the MOI's personnel grew from 999 to 5,310.[20] Its varied responsibilities, and the inevitable difficulties it faced, had encouraged the addition, removal, and restructuring of different 'groups', 'divisions', and 'departments'. For home publicity, for example, the Ministry dealt with the planning of general government or interdepartmental information, and provided common services for public relations activities of other government departments. The Home Publicity division undertook three main types of campaigns: those requested by other government departments; specific regional campaigns; and those it initiated itself. Before undertaking a campaign, the MOI would ensure that propaganda was not being used as a substitute for other activities, including legislation. The General Production division, one of the few divisions to remain in place throughout the war, undertook technical work, often at extraordinarily short notice, in order to respond to the exigencies of war. Artists were liable for call up for military service along with everyone else. Many were recalled from the services to work for the MOI in 1942, a year in which £4 million was spent on publicity, approximately one-third more than in 1941. Of this, £120,000 was spent on posters, art, and exhibitions.[21]

From the pre-war planning period until 1941, the MOI experienced shifting fortunes. 'It is ironic that the body charged during World War II with sustaining public morale and with maintaining confidence in the government should itself have suffered from chronic low morale and been the object of general ridicule.'[22] One of the most revealing aspects of the history of the MOI is the Ministry's constant debate within its own ranks on how its responsibilities should best be carried out. It was no coincidence that confidence improved vastly following Brendon Bracken's appointment – with Churchill's moral support. The MOI had discovered its role. This was reflected in the findings of a 1944 government audit, which noted that the MOI now enjoyed 'a thoroughness and solidity, combined with flexibility and enterprise which are the hallmarks of administrative efficiency'.

During this period the MOI produced an extraordinarily wide-ranging collection of propaganda material (although it would never openly acknowledge it was engaged in disseminating propaganda) which helped to maintain the morale of the British people, to acknowledge the incalculable worth of the contribution made by its allies, and to foster an unshakeable hatred of the enemy. Nevertheless, at the end of World War II (just as at the end of World War I), the Ministry's task was done. It would have no place in the post-war world. The MOI was replaced in April 1946 by the Central Office of Information, which would in future be responsible for conducting government public relations campaigns.

SUPPLIES TO RUSSIA

TO LOFOTEN

FOOD

SHIPS

GUNS

SHIPS

ELECTRIC POWER

TANKS

AIRCRAFT

COAL

LONDON

FOOD

SHIPS

SUPPLIES AND TROOPS TO AFRICA, MIDDLE EAST, INDIA, PERSIA, AUSTRALIA, ETC., ETC.

BOULOG

DIEPPE

BRUNEVAL

Railways

Gasworks

Troops

Airfields

PARIS

BREST

LORIENT

Railways

ST. NAZAIRE

NOTES

1   F. Bartlett, *Political Propaganda* (Cambridge, 1940), 16.

2   Cited by Sir John Reith in his memoir *Into the Wind* (London, 1949).

3   The Munich crisis is forever associated with a policy of 'appeasement' and British Prime Minister Neville Chamberlain's three meetings with Hitler in September 1938 attempting to avert a war by conceding to German demands regarding Sudeten Germans in the independent state of Czechoslovakia.

4   Chatham House, also known as the Royal Institute of International Affairs, emerged out of the Paris Peace Conference (1919) and came into existence in 1920 as a non-governmental organisation based in London, its mission was (and is) to analyse and promote the understanding of major international issues and current affairs.

5   TNA, INF 1/724. Memorandum by the British International Broadcasting and Propaganda Enquiry, 21 June 1939.

6   Reith had replaced Macmillan on 5 January 1940; he was replaced by Duff Cooper on 12 May 1940. Brendan Bracken replaced Cooper on 12 July 1941 and remained in office until 12 May 1945.

7   Reith, *Into the Wind*, 354.

8   Quoted in P. Lashmar and J. Oliver, *Britain's Secret Propaganda War* (Stroud, 1998), 19.

9   N. Pronay, 'The News and the Media', in N. Pronay and D.W. Spring (eds), *Propaganda, Politics and Film, 1918–45* (London, 1982), 174.

10 The poster drew the following comment from *The Times*: 'The insipid and patronizing invocations to which the passer-by is now being treated have a power of exasperation which is all their own.' Quoted in I. McLaine, *Ministry of Morale. Home Front Morale and the Ministry of Information in World War II* (London, 1979), 86. This remains an indispensable source. For examples of the Home Intelligence Reports see P. Addison and J. Crang (eds), *Listening to Britain: Home Intelligence Reports on Britain's Finest Hours* (London, 2011).

11 TNA, INF 1/264, 'Points from the Regions', 22 July. 1940.

12 *Parliamentary Debates (Commons)*, 5th Ser. Vol. 363, 31 July. 1940, cc. 1215–17.

13 Cited in *Persuading the People* (London, HMSO, 1995), 10.

14 TNA, INF 1/262, Mary Adams to Ivison Macadam, 6 March 1940.

15 For two excellent analyses of Mass-Observation, see N. Hubble, *Mass Observation and Everyday Life: Culture, History, Theory* (Basingstoke, 2010) and J. Hinton, *The Mass Observers: A History 1937–49* (Oxford, 2013).

16 See McLaine, *Ministry of Morale*, 138–9.

17 D. Cooper, *Old Men Forget* (London, 1957), 285.

18 Quoted in *Persuading the People*, 10.

19 TNA. CAB 66/17, Memorandum by Prime Minister, 26 June 1941.

20 T. Wildy, 'From the MOI to the COI – Publicity and Propaganda in Britain, 1945–1951: the National Health and Insurance Campaigns of 1948', *Historical Journal of Film, Radio and Television*, Vol. 6, No. 1 (1986), 3.

21 For a discussion of official war art and propaganda in World War II, see D. Welch, 'The Culture of War: Ideas, Arts and Propaganda', in R. Overy (ed), *The Oxford Illustrated History of World War II* (Oxford, 2015), 373–401.

22 McLaine, *Ministry of Morale*, see Introduction, 1–11.

'Although the summer holiday is still on, village schools have reopened as centres where the evacuated hordes from London can be rested, sorted out, medically examined, refreshed with tea and biscuits, and distributed to their new homes. The war has brought the great unwashed right into the bosoms of the great washed…'

MOLLIE PANTER-DOWNES

LONDON CORRESPONDENT FOR THE *NEW YORKER*, SEPTEMBER 1939.

CHAPTER TWO

Mobilising the Nation for War

Justifying War

One of the most significant lessons to be learnt from the experience of war in the twentieth century was that public opinion could no longer be ignored as a determining factor in the formulation of government policies. Unlike previous wars, World War I was the first 'total war' in which whole nations, and not just professional armies, were locked together in mortal combat. Although the Napoleonic Wars and the American War of Independence had foreshadowed this phenomenon through their level of popular involvement, the world wars of the twentieth century were markedly different. Total war was elaborated in the interwar period, reinforcing the view that future national wars would be fought between whole populations and not just the fighting services.

World Wars I and II both served to increase the level of popular interest and participation in the affairs of state. The gap between the soldier at the front and civilian at home narrowed substantially, in that the entire resources of the state – military, economic, and psychological – had to be mobilised to the full. This was the logic of the new circumstances of total war. The statistics alone are revealing. In World War I, where, for example, civilians had their first experience of aerial bombing, 14 per cent of war deaths were civilians. This increased to a massive 76 per cent in World War II (not including the Holocaust).

The outbreak of a new global war would see the belligerent states employing propaganda on a scale that dwarfed that of all previous conflicts. Both modern participatory democracies and totalitarian dictatorships had emerged from World War I, and the outbreak of hostilities in 1939 was – among other things – a testimony to their mutual incompatibility. There followed a total war even more all-encompassing than World War I, reflecting mass societies and ideological and racial conflicts; and once again propaganda was a significant weapon. It was also arguably, from the Allied point of view, a morally justified war, thus invalidating humanitarian 'protest' literature and art.

In Britain, partly as a result of perceptions shaped by official propaganda, World War II evolved into a 'people's war', and as Winston Churchill prophesied to the House of Common in May 1901: 'The wars of peoples will be more terrible than those of kings.'[1] Between 1939and 1945 civilians were in the front line as never before. Advances in the technology of war, particularly in aerial bombing, served to transform their experience of conflict. The scale of suffering and sacrifices that civilians were likely to experience persuaded the British government in 1939 that, although the war that Britain had declared against Nazism was widely acknowledged as being inevitable, it would still require justification and explanation. In the modern age, propaganda and warfare have become inseparable, and justifying war to an often reticent public has become one of the propagandist's most complex and important tasks. Accordingly, in the aftermath of Britain's declaration of war on Germany in September 1939, the Ministry of Information (MOI) put together a series of publications (translated into many languages) using official documents intended to show that Britain had done everything possible to avoid war. The first pamphlet was simply entitled *The Outbreak of War* and consisted of reproductions of speeches and radio broadcasts made by leading politicians and a 'message to his people' from King George VI.[2] The King started by reminding the nation that 'for the second time in the lives of most of us we are at war'. Bearing in mind the propaganda slogan prominent in World War I that the country was fighting a 'war to end all wars', this might appear to be an inflammatory statement. However, since Prime Minister Neville Chamberlain's policy of 'appeasement' of Nazi Germany in the years leading up to 1939 had failed, there was a mood of resignation to the inevitability of war within the country. The King, in his message, reiterated that the country had been 'forced into conflict' by a 'state in the selfish pursuit of power' that had 'disregarded its treaties and its solemn pledges'. He warned that the principles and the freedom of 'our own country and of the whole British Commonwealth of Nations would be in danger'. To this 'high purpose' the King called upon his people to make 'this cause their own' and to stand firm, calm, and united. He ended by alluding to the changing nature of total war and the sacrifices that would be required:

> There may be dark days ahead and war can no longer be confined to the battlefield. But we can only do the right as we see the right and reverently commit our cause to God. If one and all keep resolutely faithful to it, ready for whatever services or sacrifice it may demand, then with God's help, we shall prevail. May He bless and keep us all.

The second pamphlet in the series (Fig. 1) sets out, through a series of diplomatic documents released by the Foreign Office, to condemn Hitler in his own words.[3] It attempts to show how Nazi Germany reneged on its Pact with Poland, and the final chapter, written by Sir Nevile Henderson (the British Ambassador to Germany), is on Hitler and Hitlerism. It demonstrates that, in Henderson's words, Hitler 'has made this war' and should bear full responsibility. As it was an official document it contained no photographs or comments, but allowed the documents to speak for themselves. The title is simple and to the point: *How Hitler Made the War*.[4]

How Hitler Made the War.
(PP/17/25A)

Following the Nazi invasion of Poland, a consensus of sorts emerged that condemned Nazism as evil, with a 'worldview' which posed a direct threat to British democratic values. What this now-popular view of Fascism did was to present the arguments that had dominated the 1920s and 30s in a new light. British opinion was forced to choose between profound fear of what war might represent and a growing sense that if 'civilisation' was to survive, it would have to be fought for.[5]

Once it became clear that the war would not be over quickly and that the United States of America would initially remain neutral, it was imperative to remind the nation, both at home and in the trenches, of what they were fighting for. Moreover, the needs of total war required the mass mobilisation of people and the economy to provide fighting forces and the equipment necessary to sustain their efforts.

The major themes included a call to arms and a request for war loans, and efforts to encourage industrial activity, to explain national policies, to channel emotions such as courage or hatred, to urge the population to conserve resources, and to inform the public of food and fuel substitutes. The novel concept of the 'Home Front' had actually been introduced in Britain in 1915. It was based on government intervention, on a massive scale, in order to restructure the country's economy and society for war, with corresponding sacrifices from the civilian population. In order to achieve these objectives, British propaganda constructed a tableau in which the demands of total war were depicted as a series of 'battles' that had to be fought to achieve ultimate victory. Accordingly, propaganda created a series of narratives, or campaigns, around such themes as the battle for health, the battle of production/supplies, the battle for civilisation, the battles for the air and the sea, and so on. This required civilians to 'fall in' and fight.

The Battle for Health: Food and Rationing

Total war in the twentieth century provided a major spur for propaganda. During World War II governments employed propaganda for a wide range of objectives. While a stress on people's obligations towards their country in the 'Your Country Needs You' spirit was appropriate in times of war, governments were becoming increasingly conscious – partly as a result of the sacrifices made during these wars – of their responsibility towards their own citizens. In World War II propaganda came to have an important instructional role in conveying public information on issues such as health and hygiene.

Health campaigns figured prominently in official World War II propaganda. The wartime emergency meant that citizens had to be physically fit in order to fight, work in industry, cope with air raids, and endure the hardships caused by food and other shortages. In Britain, adequate food supplies were recognised as a key factor in the maintenance of morale. The British government mobilised a number of ministries in conjunction with the MOI to explain official policy and to stress the importance of good health for the successful conclusion of the war effort. The Ministry of Food was thus one of the largest spenders on publicity, issuing a constant flow of leaflets and press advertisements, as well as short films explaining the rationing system and providing wartime recipes and ways of making limited supplies last longer.

Before the war Britain imported 70 per cent of its food; this required 20 million tons of shipping a year. The country imported 50 per cent of its meat, 70 per cent of cheese and sugar, 80 per cent of fruits, 70 per cent of cereals and fats, and 91 per cent of butter. Knowledge of this would lead the Axis powers to hope that they could starve the British population into submission, by cutting off those food supply lines.

2
From the
'Dig for Victory'
leaflet series.
Growing food made
simple for the masses
(BL/ BS/3/98)

The Ministry of Agriculture was responsible for increasing the amount of land under cultivation in order to grow more vegetables. One of the most famous slogans of the war was 'Dig for Victory'. Britain's Home Front was encouraged to transform private gardens into mini-allotments. The slogan 'Dig for Victory' was also employed by the MOI to exhort agricultural workers in the British Empire to produce greater food yields

It was believed, quite rightly, that this would not only provide essential crops for families and neighbourhoods, but would also help the war effort by freeing up valuable space for war materials (rather than food imports) on the merchant shipping convoys. Over 10 million instructional leaflets were distributed to the British people. The campaign proved extremely successful and the number of allotments in England and Wales increased from 815,000 in 1939 to 1,450,000 by 1944. In addition, potential growing space such as front gardens and window boxes soon proudly sprouted rows of healthy vegetables or fruit. Fig. 2 shows a very small, pocket-sized pull-out leaflet that provides simple, step-by-step instructions on how to 'Dig for Victory' by transforming a piece of land in order to grow vegetables.

The *Kitchen Front* radio broadcasts (five-minute BBC programmes, aired at 8.15 am every morning) were concerned with using food efficiently, as well as with making use of what was readily available to mitigate shortages. In addition to the circulation of familiar Ministry of Agriculture 'food flashes', literature and poster displays, anthems were also introduced, including one under the slogan 'Dig for Victory':

> *Dig! Dig! Dig!*
> *And your muscles will grow big.*
> *Keep on pushing the spade.*
> *Don't mind the worms.*
> *Just ignore their squirms*
> *And when your back aches laugh with glee.*
> *And keep on diggin'.*
> *Till we give our foes a Wiggin'. Dig!*
> *Dig! Dig! to Victory*

During World War II, millions of people listened to the *Kitchen Front* programme. With the assistance of domestic science teachers, dieticians, school-meal-organisers, and hospital caterers, the Public Relations Division of the Ministry of Food gave the public guidance about new food sources and creative recipes for items which were not rationed. It also gave advice to people about the healthiest way to feed themselves and to make the best use of their rations. The *Kitchen Front* programmes were hugely popular, and the slogan 'Food is a munition of war: Don't waste it' appeared to resonate with the public.

From the summer of 1940 to the end of the war, the Ministry of Food and the MOI published weekly 'Food Facts' including recipes and tips on how to make food (and food substitutes) go further. The first Food Fact urged the population to:

> *Grow fit not fat on your war diet! Make full use of the fruit and vegetables in season. Cut out 'extras'; cut our waste; don't eat more than you need. You'll save your money, you'll save valuable cargo space which is needed for munitions, and you'll feel fitter than you have ever felt before.*

In 1943 these tips were collected together in a small booklet entitled *100 Facts About the United Kingdom's War Effort* (see Fig. 6). In addition to the posters and pamphlets, two of radio's most popular characters, Gert and Daisy (played by Elsie and Doris Waters) published a wartime recipe book, which, along with culinary tips and ideas, warned against wasting bread: 'So, if you ever forget, do what Daisy did. She chucked a bit of bread out of the window, suddenly remembered, and rushed downstairs and caught it before it reached the ground.'[6] This chimed with the government's 'Bread

Wise eating
in wartime

from the Ministry of Food's
KITCHEN FRONT BROADCASTS
4D

YOUR BABY'S FOOD *in War Time*

From the
Ministry of Food's
**KITCHEN FRONT
BROADCASTS**

into Battle' campaign. For example, Food Fact number 99 warned housewives that:

> … *too many crusts are being thrown away … What takes the lion's share of our shipping space? Even if the daily waste of bread is as little as half an ounce per head of the population: that means a waste of fifteen loaves a second, and thirty shiploads of flour in a year – a whole convoy! Bread into Battle? Yes indeed – that's why every half-ounce saved is half the battle.*

A pamphlet prepared in 1943 by the MOI and Ministry of Food, *Wise Eating in Wartime* (Fig. 3) contained fifteen of the broadcasts in the *Kitchen Front* series given by Dr Charles Hill, who was known to millions of listeners as 'the Radio Doctor'. Because rules of that time prevented members of the medical profession advertising, he could not broadcast under his own name, and so was known simply as 'the Radio Doctor'. His distinctive rich voice helped make an impact. Dr Hill offered homely advice spiced with populism to a nation undergoing food restrictions. Stressing the need for a varied diet, his first talk noted that 'we can't change our wives but they *can* change *their* ways, at least in giving *their* victims greater variety in their victuals' (my emphases). 'Are you eating wisely?' was a familiar question that featured regularly in British propaganda and the

4 (above)
Your Baby's Food in War Time.
(PP/27/15A)

3 (opposite)
Wise Eating in Wartime (1943).
(PP/25/139A)

5
Doctor Carrot Guards Your Health.
(poster, Imperial War Museum)

pamphlet was intended to inform the public 'how we can make the most of our rations, and keep our bodies tuned up to concert pitch by eating sensible, balanced meals'. It began with an introduction which encouraged readers that 'a little of what you fancy' is perfectly compatible with a healthy diet. Interestingly, although the main focus was the British housewife, the pamphlet claimed that 'everyone, from the housewife catering for the family, to the bachelor eating alone, will profit from Dr Hill's cheerful and practical advice'.

Dr Hill's 'cheerful and practical' dietary advice also extended to the nation's newborn. In one of his BBC talks, the Radio Doctor said that 'Britain needs more babies', claiming that if current trends continued, 'the country was heading for a big reduction in our population'. In another broadcast he drew attention to the problem of predatory fathers who took more than their fair share of family food: 'If he does have a little more meat, he should have less cheese and fewer eggs.' The nation responded and some 4.6 million children were born in the war years, reaching a peak of 880,000 in 1944. To encourage and accommodate the rise in the birth rate, the welfare food scheme was introduced in December 1941. This proved a significant incentive to families since it gave extra rations to expectant mothers, including another pint of milk per day, an extra egg per allocation, and an extra half-ration of meat. Orange juice, cod liver oil, and vitamin tablets were also available.

The pamphlet *Your Baby's Food in War Time* (Fig. 4) is again taken from the *Kitchen Front* broadcasts and contains advice for expectant mothers ('food for one and a bit') and information on what constituted a healthy diet for older children from one year onwards. The advice was largely common sense. The diet for older children should satisfy three needs: for warmth and energy; for building new tissues and replacing old ones; and for protection against disease. A healthy diet should include food from each group. Under each of the three categories, the pamphlet provides examples of various foodstuffs. Mothers were advised that 'where a food is not available because of wartime shortages, try to use another *in the same group*'.

Dr Hill was renowned for his frankness and down-to-earth advice, but equally he was never afraid to state the blindingly obvious and there is something faintly patronising (certainly to a contemporary audience) in much of the advice given. Moreover, citizens had to pay for these pamphlets, although they were available to read in public libraries and community organisations such as the Women's Institute. As they were mainly MOI publications, they were subsidised and were, on the whole, considered good value for money. They tended to avoid jingoistic language or slogans, had very few illustrations, and were not viewed as overt propaganda.

Food, and in particular the lack of it, was central to the experience of World War II. The 'Dig for Victory' campaign was run for most of the war by Professor John Raeburn, an agricultural economist, who joined the Ministry of Food in 1939 as a statistician and two years later was appointed to lead the Agricultural Plans Branch.

Carrots were one vegetable in plentiful supply, and as a result were widely substituted for the scarcer commodities and used in several 'mock' recipes. To improve their blandness, people were encouraged to 'enjoy' the healthy carrot in different ways by the introduction of such characters as 'Doctor Carrot'. The Ministry of Agriculture suggested such culinary delights as curried carrot, carrot jam, and a homemade drink called Carrolade (made from the juices of carrots and swede). Carrots were also a major ingredient of the 'Dig for Victory' campaign, with songs and posters featuring Doctor Carrot and his chum, Potato Pete.

Carrots were a relatively cheap foodstuff and not rationed. There was a free market for carrots until the end of October 1941. After that time the government took over the sole purchase of 'all sound marketable carrots fit for human consumption, grown on holdings of one acre and above'. The price was fixed, nationwide, excluding the cost of bags.[7] In 1941 they cost an average of 2 (old) pence per pound (0.5 kg), retail. The selling prices, however, were strictly controlled by government orders. For example, in

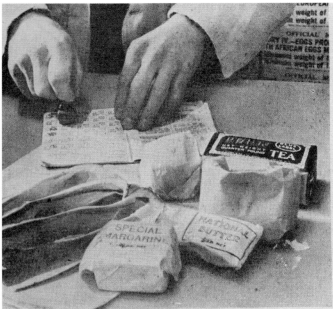

Rations are obtained only on presentation of the customer's ration book.

Many British fishermen are fighting; fish supplies are small and irregular.

The Clothing Ration Book has cut the British people's clothing purchases by half.

CIVILIAN CONSUMPTION

74 The average consumption of butter, fresh meat, sugar and fresh fruit, taken together, per head of the population has been almost halved.

75 The average consumption of margarine, canned meat, potatoes and flour, taken together, per head of the population is about one-third higher than before the war.

76 The average number of shell eggs eaten before the war was three and a quarter per head per week. In 1943 the amount available to adult civilians was just over half of one egg per week—less than one-sixth of what it was in 1939.

77 For every 10 pieces of clothing bought in 1938 only 5.5 were bought in 1943.

78 For every 10 pairs of boots and shoes bought in 1938 only 7.3 were bought in 1943.

79 For every 10 pieces of furniture and furnishings bought in 1938 only 2.3 were bought in 1943.

80 For every 10 items of hardware bought in 1938 only 3.3 were bought in 1943.

37

6
The People at War -100 Facts About the United Kingdom's War Effort (1943).
This is a section on 'Civilian Consumption' – or rather a list of 'reductions' in consumption.
(PP/11/25A)

1942 the Ministry issued the 'Emergency Powers Defence (Food) Carrots Order', which dictated that retailers of any description had to display the maximum selling price at all times. The maximum price was then 3½ pence per pound (half kilogram); it was 2 pence a pound by 1943. The maximum price at which a grower could sell to a retailer was 9 shillings and 3 pence per hundredweight (about 51 kg, or 112 lbs).

The Doctor Carrot character carried a bag labelled 'Vit. A', because the Ministry of Food recognised the value of the carrot in providing high levels of this vital vitamin, via beta-carotene. Doctor Carrot was referred to in the propaganda campaigns as either 'the children's best friend' or as someone who 'guards your health' (Fig. 5). People were encouraged to 'take the doctor's advice' and eat more carrots to be fit for the ensuing winter. It was reported that the shortage of batteries would no longer be a concern as people would 'develop cats' eyes' and see better in the dark. (One poster of a mother and child carrying a basket full of carrots in the blackout proclaimed: 'Carrots keep you healthy and help you see in the dark.') Famously, the government responded to a temporary wartime oversupply of carrots (there were 100,000 tons to shift!) by suggesting that the Royal Air Force's exceptional night-flying success was due to consuming more carotene, via carrots. The ruse worked: because people thought carrots might help them see in the blackout, consumption of carrots increased sharply, thus taking the pressure off other food supplies.[8] Carrots were considered to be the most important of vegetables from a health point of view and it was hoped that Doctor Carrot would carry out his mission as successfully as Potato Pete did for the potato. 'I'm always getting in hot water' says Potato Pete 'and there are plenty of other ways of cooking me.'[9]

The food propaganda campaign was successful. As mentioned, it was estimated that over 1,400,000 people acquired mini-allotments by turning lawns and flower-beds into vegetable gardens. By 1943 more than a million tons of vegetables were being grown in gardens and allotments. People were encouraged to keep chickens, and some kept rabbits and goats. Pigs were especially popular because they could be fed on kitchen waste. As the Minister of Food during this period, Lord Woolton was responsible for explaining the benefits of rationing to the British public and educating people into better eating habits. Later in the war, with plentiful vegetables being produced as a result of the success of the 'Dig for Victory' campaign, the legendary Woolton Pie was introduced, the ingredients for which were potatoes, parsnips, and herbs. Perhaps unsurprisingly, it was a dish that never really took off with the British public.

Official rationing began on 8 January 1940. There were three different ration books: most adults had a buff-coloured ration book; children aged between 5 and 16 had a blue ration book; and pregnant women, nursing mothers, and children under 5 had a green ration book – they had first choice of fruit, a daily pint of milk, and a double supply of eggs. Butter, meat, and fresh eggs were among the first foods to be rationed. In their place, people were encouraged to use margarine, corned beef, and substitutes such as dried egg powder. One person's typical weekly allowance would be one fresh egg, 4 ounces (about 110 g) margarine, 4 ounces bacon (about four rashers), 2 ounces butter, 2 ounces tea, 1 ounce cheese, and 8 ounces sugar. Meat was allocated by price, so cheaper cuts became popular. Points could be pooled or saved to buy pulses, cereals, tinned goods, dried fruit, biscuits, and jam. Fish was not rationed during the war, but was often scarce and by 1941 prices were 17 per cent higher than in 1939. The introduction of substitutes did not alleviate the situation, as most people hated them. This particularly applied to the replacement of the beloved British white loaf with its detested substitute – dark bread! In 1941 the National Wheatmeal Loaf of 85 per cent extraction (and with added calcium and vitamins) was introduced to save shipping space by reducing grain imports. A Ministry of Food publicity campaign to launch the new loaf referred to it as 'a *plus* bread! Not as dark as brown bread, not as white as white bread, but a creamy oatmeal colour. What a welcome change it is in wartime, when there are bound to be substitute articles of diet, to find one thing better than it was before – better and no dearer!'[10]

In 1943 a Mass-Observation survey found approval ratings of this new loaf a mere 14 per cent.[11] The MOI attempted to make light of these shortages and in *100 Facts About the United Kingdom's War Effort* all forms of rationing are set out in a very matter-of-fact fashion (Fig. 6). Fact 76 graphically illustrates the dramatic fall in the consumption of fresh eggs since the start of the war.

One of the problems of the 'fair shares for all' policy was that it failed to take account of differing needs. Supposedly 'fair' averages did not, in reality, make sense. For example, in arriving at the figure that the average man required 3,000 calories a day, the government had made no concessions to men working in heavy industry who needed 4,500 calories a day. As a result, miners, dockers, shipyard workers, and iron and steel workers were less well nourished than clerks or workers in light industry undertaking far less arduous work. Another pressing concern was the perceived inequality in the distribution of food. People had welcomed the government's proposal to set a ceiling on the price of restaurant meals, but Home Intelligence was reporting in 1942 that some sections of the public were complaining 'that everything is not fair and equal and that therefore our sacrifices are not worth while' – particularly as the rich are 'less affected by rationing than ordinary people'.[12] The issue of the fairness of food rationing undoubtedly reflected underlying tensions between the classes in wartime Britain, but generally the

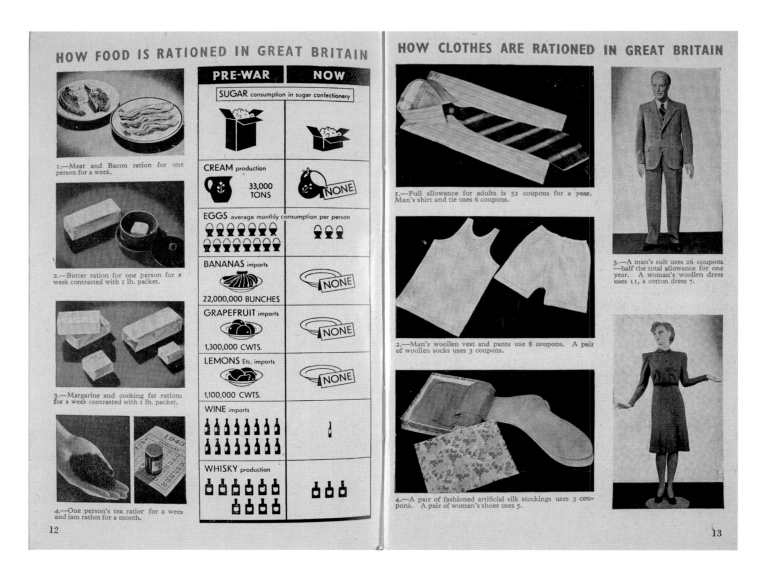

HOW FOOD IS RATIONED IN GREAT BRITAIN

1.—Meat and Bacon ration for one person for a week.

2.—Butter ration for one person for a week contrasted with 1 lb. packet.

3.—Margarine and cooking fat rations for a week contrasted with 1 lb. packet.

4.—One person's tea ration for a week and jam ration for a month.

	PRE-WAR	NOW
SUGAR consumption in sugar confectionery		
CREAM production	33,000 TONS	NONE
EGGS average monthly consumption per person		
BANANAS imports	22,000,000 BUNCHES	NONE
GRAPEFRUIT imports	1,300,000 CWTS.	NONE
LEMONS Etc. imports	1,100,000 CWTS.	NONE
WINE imports		
WHISKY production		

12

HOW CLOTHES ARE RATIONED IN GREAT BRITAIN

1.—Full allowance for adults is 52 coupons for a year. Man's shirt and tie uses 6 coupons.

2.—Man's woollen vest and pants use 8 coupons. A pair of woollen socks uses 3 coupons.

3.—A man's suit uses 26 coupons —half the total allowance for one year. A woman's woollen dress uses 11, a cotton dress 7.

4.—A pair of fashioned artificial silk stockings uses 3 coupons. A pair of woman's shoes uses 5.

13

7
Rationing of Food and Clothing.
The visual material sets out in stark terms Government restrictions on food and clothing by means of the coupon system, while the text remains 'upbeat'.

7
Rationing of Food and Clothing.
The visual material sets out in stark terms Government restrictions on food and clothing by means of the coupon system, while the text remains 'upbeat'.

feeling was that people were willing to bear the sacrifices demanded of them provided they felt that 'the burden is fairly borne by all'.[13]

Food rationing loomed large in most people's lives and was, at times, understandably a source of irritation – although by and large it was accepted as a necessary sacrifice.[14] Ration books effectively tied people to one butcher and one grocer, with whom it paid to stay on good terms. Queues were inevitable, imposing an extra time burden, particularly on working women with household responsibilities. Queues formed quickly outside shops when rumours spread that they had supplies of a hard-to-obtain food. Some people even joined queues without knowing what was at the end of them.[15]

In an attempt to offset potential unrest, the MOI produced a series of posters and pamphlets explaining the necessity of rationing and the concomitant sacrifices. In 1943 the government published a particularly interesting sixty-nine-page document entitled *The People at War*, which showed the determination and courage of the British people after more than three years of war. The notion of a united fighting front was a key feature of British propaganda (indeed, it was for all the belligerents). The introduction, written by the MOI, is especially revealing and I have included it in full:

> For over three years the British people have been at war. Through all that time – and it has been many days that none living through it will ever forget – the courage, the determination and the cheerfulness of the people has burned like a steady flame. Millions are still enduring severe hardships, much actual danger and many irksome

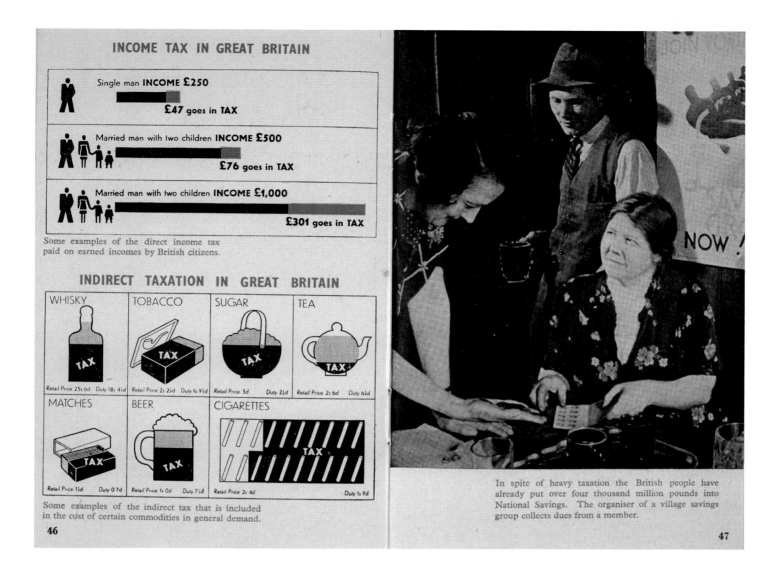

INCOME TAX IN GREAT BRITAIN

Single man **INCOME £250**

£47 goes in TAX

Married man with two children **INCOME £500**

£76 goes in TAX

Married man with two children **INCOME £1,000**

£301 goes in TAX

Some examples of the direct income tax paid on earned incomes by British citizens.

INDIRECT TAXATION IN GREAT BRITAIN

WHISKY	TOBACCO	SUGAR	TEA
TAX	TAX	TAX	TAX
Retail Price 25s 6d Duty 18s 4½d	Retail Price 2s 2½d Duty 1s 9½d	Retail Price 3d Duty 2¼d	Retail Price 2s 6d Duty 6¼d

MATCHES	BEER	CIGARETTES	
TAX	TAX	TAX	
Retail Price 1½d Duty 0 7d	Retail Price 1s 0d Duty 7¼d	Retail Price 2s 4d	Duty 1s 9d

Some examples of the indirect tax that is included in the cost of certain commodities in general demand.

46

In spite of heavy taxation the British people have already put over four thousand million pounds into National Savings. The organiser of a village savings group collects dues from a member.

47

restrictions. But the restrictions have not been imposed on them. The people have clamoured for them in the Press and at public meetings. Public opinion has forced the resignations of Ministers who seemed fearful of asking for recurring sacrifice. And now working hours are long; leisure time is short; and wartime duties have been shouldered by every class – these are a few glimpses of the ways in which total war has come into the home and changed the life of every citizen of Great Britain.

There was a substantial section devoted exclusively to 'rationing'. Although food restrictions were the immediate concern for most families, clothing was also rationed and in one section of the document (Fig. 7), restrictions on both food and clothes are set out in very simple terms. The pamphlet is at great pains to demonstrate that all sections of society were making sacrifices and that rationing 'sets the standard of living for everyone'.

What is striking about this document is that, although the pamphlet was distributed widely in Britain, it was primarily intended for the British Empire and overseas and was translated into a number of languages. The pamphlet proudly proclaimed that British citizens were the highest-taxed wage earners in the world ('a single man earning £500 a year pays nearly one third of his income in tax') – and yet, so the pamphlet claimed, 'he pays for it all with a smile!' And in spite of heavy taxation the British people have already 'put £4 million into National Savings'. So even under such demanding exigencies, it was possible to save and contribute to the war effort. One page provides a breakdown of

RATIONING OF FOOD IN GREAT BRITAIN

direct and indirect taxation with, opposite, a cheerful organiser of a village savings group collecting dues from a member.

Home Intelligence reported that, while people were prepared to put up with rationing, there was a rising tide of agitation against those thought to be avoiding the structure and the spirit of the rationing system.[16] Lord Woolton was forced to act. The government imposed draconian punishments for sharp practice by shopkeepers and profiteers of the black market. By 1944 over 900 inspectors were employed, ensuring compliance with the regulations. This was a signal of intent on the part of the government to ensure credibility and confidence in the fairness of the rationing system. It was

The first Ministry of Food communal feeding centre in South London, where a good meal could be obtained for 6d.

imperative that the government could demonstrate that it was doing its best to impose the burdens of war equally upon all sections of the community.

As late as 1945, with ultimate victory within sight, the government was still publishing information explaining the need to maintain rationing. (In fact, rationing would continue until 1954.)[17] *Rationing of Food in Great Britain*, published in 1945 (Figs. 8a and b), provided a summary of the achievements of rationing and how it must still be imposed. The front and back covers show a young child drinking milk supplied under the food welfare programme and happy mothers and children eagerly studying a 'rationed' menu in a local community kitchen.

Clothing: Make Do and Mend

The need to impose restrictions on clothing was equally important in wartime Britain. In June 1941 clothes rationing was introduced (although it was operating unofficially in 1940). It was a measure prefaced by a broadcast from Oliver Lyttelton, the President of the Board of Trade:

> *I know all the women will look smart, but we men may look shabby. If we do we must not be ashamed. In war the term ' battle stained' is an honourable one. We must learn as civilians to be seen in clothes that are not so smart. ... When you feel tired of your old clothes remember that by making them do you are contributing some part of an aeroplane, a gun or a tank.*

Adults were rationed to a fixed number of clothing coupons per year, each item of clothing having a coupon value, plus the price fixed by law. Adults were issued as few as 36 coupons a year to spend on clothes. A man's suit could cost 22 coupons, a coat 16 and a woman's dress 11, so the need to recycle and be inventive with other materials became more and more pressing. If you had the money, but no coupons, you could not buy, although an illegal black market grew up of traders willing to supply the unobtainable (at a price). Thus a 'make do and mend' ethos grew up, with people recycling old clothes, and unpicking the wool from old pullovers to darn socks, for example.

In 1942, Hugh Dalton, who had just left the Ministry of Economic Warfare to become the new President of the Board of Trade, asked the MOI to help produce pamphlets and posters that provided the public with information on how the people could 'make do and mend': a campaign intended to 'help you get the last possible ounce of wear out of all your clothes and household things' in an attempt to offset the restrictions imposed on clothing. The MOI prepared a booklet, *Make Do and Mend*, for the Board of Trade in 1943 (Fig. 9). Detailed instructions were given on how to make clothes last longer and readers were informed that 'a stitch in time now saves not only extra work in the end, but precious coupons'. Dalton wrote the preface, in which he

9
Make Do and Mend (1943). The five objectives are set out on the back cover. (PP/14/27L)

stressed the vital importance of taking resources away from clothing manufacturing to free up resources for the wider war effort.[18] But it was not just a question of 'making do': there was also the more creative aspect of 'mending' what already existed, and it is interesting that Dalton chose to compare the process of considering what can be done to existing clothing to that of thinking more imaginatively about preparing and cooking potatoes. So just as you could 'cook' yourself to victory, so, according to the 'make do and mend' campaign, you also could 'mend' your way to victory:

> *First, I would like to thank you all for the way in which you have accepted clothes rationing. You know how it has saved much needed shipping space, manpower and materials, and so assisted our war effort. … No doubt there are as many ways of patching or darning as there are of cooking potatoes.*

Aided by twenty-nine illustrations, the booklet (it refers to itself as a 'book' and consisted of thirty-three pages) specifically outlined five objectives that can be found on the back cover:

> *To keep clothes looking trim for as long as they have to last.*
> *To renovate children's outgrown clothes so cleverly that nothing is ever wasted.*
> *To turn every scrap of good material you possess to advantage.*
> *To keep your household linen in good repair.*
> *To make do with things you already have instead of buying new.*[19]

To achieve these objectives housewives were provided with useful tips on how to be both frugal and stylish in times of harsh rationing. With its thrifty design ideas and advice on reusing old clothing, the pamphlet was an indispensable guide for households. Readers were advised to create pretty 'decorative patches' to cover holes in worn garments; to unpick old jumpers to re-knit chic alternatives; to turn men's clothes into women's, as well as to darn, alter, and protect against the 'moth menace'. Mothers were informed that 'babies don't need nearly as many clothes as people used to think'. As for cots, 'a laundry basket or even a deep drawer, suitably lined, can be adapted to make a very useful cot for the first few months'. Mrs Sew-and-Sew (a doll-like figure who is herself stitched together – '"Make-Do and Mend" says Mrs Sew-and-Sew') was the ultimate exponent of 'make do and mend' and set the example for all housewives on how they could get that 'last ounce of wear out of all clothing and household things'.[20]

Keep the Nation Fighting Fit!

The exigencies of war forced the government to think more proactively about the nation's health. Fighting total war meant that the Home Front as well as the fighting front had to be physically fit in order to fight and work effectively, cope with air raids, and endure discomforts and food shortages. In 1943 the MOI prepared a booklet for the Ministry of Health entitled *How to Keep Well in Wartime* (Fig. 10). The cover drawing shows a typical family: father with his helmet and gas mask and mother carrying healthy provisions in her basket, accompanied on either side by their two happy, healthy children. There is a kind of upright determination about them as they stride home. The introduction was written by Ernest Brown, the Minister of Health. Brown started with praise: 'During the three years of total war the nation's stubborn good health has been invaluable to our war effort', but warned; 'as a nation we are still losing 22 million weeks' work each year through common and often preventable illnesses'. Brown calculated that this was equivalent to the loss of 24,000 tanks, 6,750 bombers and 6,750,000 rifles a year. The Minister of Health observed that the country was at a turning point of the war and called on the nation to maintain vigorous health by keeping fit – 'fit to hasten victory'.

The pamphlet offered common-sense advice on health issues ranging from proper exercise, excessive smoking and drinking (unusual for the time), and the importance of a balanced diet. People were urged to continue eating wheatmeal or brown bread, noting: 'Russians eat black bread, and they're a tough lot.' One health problem singled out was the need to combat venereal disease by avoiding casual sexual intercourse: 'A hospital full of cases of gonorrhoea means loss of tanks, loss of aeroplanes, loss of guns. It also means loss of happiness, loss of health, loss of efficiency.'

During this same period the MOI, together with Pilot Press, produced a series of booklets in the 'British Achievement' series. One of these was *The Art of Healing*, which attempted to demonstrate that all the 'blood sweat and tears involved in defeating Nazism'

10
How to Keep Well in Wartime.
(PP/10/11L)

and the 'knowledge gained in helping wounded soldiers and keeping the whole nation fit for total war will be available to banish pain and disease in a happier post-war world'. The booklet provides a comprehensive survey of medical achievements during the war and there are hints here of a post-war Jerusalem. It even refers to the need, once Nazism has been defeated, 'to win the peace'. The illustrations from the pamphlet (Figs. 11 a and b) provide examples of preventative measures introduced since the start of the conflict and, on the following page, the benefits in times of war and peace of positive health. The booklet claims that as a result of these medical advances people were undergoing a sustained period of healthy living 'such as has not been experienced since the Industrial Revolution'.

Much attention was given to the health of children, and this applied particularly to preventative care, as the illustrations in *The Art of Healing* demonstrate. As so much of this work took place in schools, the MOI were concerned to show how schools were making their own contribution to the war effort by nurturing a healthy and well-

11
The Art of Healing.
(PP/5/11A)

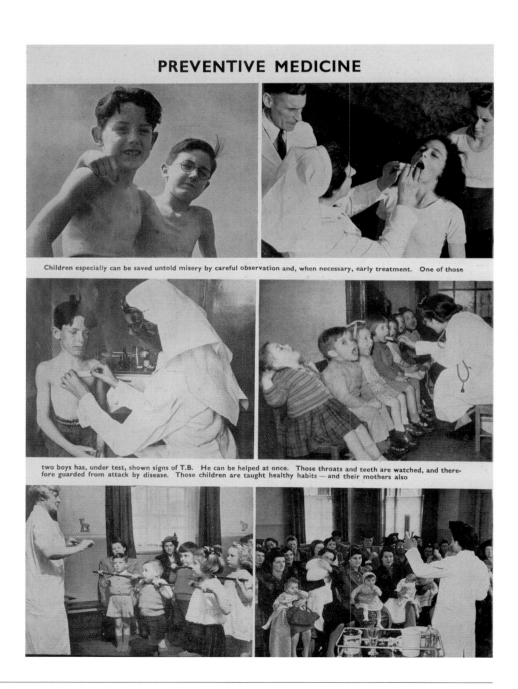

PREVENTIVE MEDICINE

Children especially can be saved untold misery by careful observation and, when necessary, early treatment. One of those

two boys has, under test, shown signs of T.B. He can be helped at once. Those throats and teeth are watched, and therefore guarded from attack by disease. Those children are taught healthy habits — and their mothers also

educated population for the future. No doubt the MOI felt that if it could demonstrate that children were well provided for, then adults would be more willing to undertake the sacrifices demanded of them. A booklet produced in 1943, *The Schools in Wartime* (Fig. 12), provided examples of this. It contained a foreword by Herwald Ramsbottom, the President of the Board of Education. The cover showed images of happy and healthy children, both in the classroom and in the open air. Over 4 million schoolchildren were receiving 'the essential food' each day at school by 1943, and the entitlement to free milk continued until Margaret Thatcher's time as Education Secretary in the 1970s. In a series of what Ramsbottom refers to as 'sketches' – ranging from the evacuation of schoolchildren to the countryside to schools 'under fire' – the booklet provided both an account of educational achievement and a tribute to 'the devotion of our teachers, and above all to youth's courage and resolution … in helping maintain the steadiness of our national life'.[21]

16. POSITIVE HEALTH

These examples will be sufficient to show that the achievements of medicine in war-time have not been one-sided, but that they have led to a general advance along the whole of our front against pain and disease. But that is not all. Medical science does not stop at disease, it concerns itself with health also, and this brief survey may be brought to a close with a consideration of what, in spite of our pre-occupation with the Nazi plague, has been done to bring a positive attitude into medical practice.

Total war has meant that the welfare of every citizen must be safeguarded in the interests of defeating Hitler. We began the war with much new knowledge that could be put into effect directly the concept of a totally healthy nation was accepted as a government objective.

By 1939, thanks to Drummond and Mellanby and others we knew enough about diet to use food to forestall ill-health and weakened resistance to disease. Lord Woolton's very successful control of the nation's larder was in itself an achievement of which Britain can be proud. No country, not even America, has come through the war with so overwhelming a proportion of its population getting a fair share of whatever food was going. One result is that five years of war has brought no epidemics and, that although we began the war with one-third of the community undernourished, we may hope to end it with a higher standard of health than we have ever enjoyed as a nation.

Although we have been helped in this achievement by our accumulation of new and accurate knowledge, we have learned that the future raising of the general standard of health depends chiefly on improved organisation. It is true to say that never before 1939 was it a definite social objective to secure good health for the whole population. It is nothing to be proud of that we were finally forced to accept this objective by the manpower demands of total war. Yet once we did accept it we were able to organise to achieve it. Will this be so in the future? If total peace is to follow total war it must be so.

It is a hopeful thing that we see rising on all sides a demand that medical services shall be used before the individual is sick in order to keep him well. Whatever the final arrangements with the medical profession on the subject of the White Paper proposals recently issued, there must be a Health Service capable of accepting this task. For the whole meaning of Tom Jones' fractured leg is lost if the world is to be no saner than it was before his generation faced and destroyed Nazism.

In the past the State has chiefly concerned itself with helping the least healthy members of the community. If a poor couple produce a congenital idiot, the State supplies hundreds of pounds to keep it alive, but if a poor couple produces a splendidly healthy child, the State, until recently, did nothing in its health services to make certain that the child remained healthy.

This attitude has already begun to change. Even before the war free milk and baby clinics and child guidance centres were beginning to minister to the healthy, but the distance we have to go can be measured by a few statistics.

Until the war put a stop to it, the Pioneer Health Centre at Peckham was doing excellent educational work. This centre did not treat or cure sick persons; it was attended by what the world calls well people. The Centre doctors examined these 'well' people and found that out of 3,911 individuals of both sexes and all ages only 358—less than 1 in 10—had no easily discoverable physical disorder.

Yet most of these people thought that they were 'well'; that is to say that instead of using their vital energy, their creative spirit, to live a full life of usefulness, good temper, contentment, they were using a large proportion of it to *cover up* from their minds their physical disabilities. In other words, a huge proportion of the community even when it imagines itself 'well' is fighting disease. It is impossible to tell how great an improvement in individual and social well-being would come if this exhausting fight could be ended.

It is this growing realisation that the Art of Healing should aim at discovering higher levels of positive health than most of us ever experience that will transform the future. We have seen it grow even out of the destructive experience of war: the knowledge that the cure of an injured leg must be continued till the whole man feels able to become once more a useful and therefore happy member of society at once transforms the doctor from the level of bone-setter to social physician: the limb, the whole man, the community, the healing of one leads on to and depends on the healing of the next—healthy limbs, healthy men, healthy communities lead on finally to a healthy world and there is no other path that leads to that goal, and away from the war-wounds and the world-wounds inflicted by Nazism.

THE Schools IN WARTIME

Conclusion

Despite the stresses of wartime, the health of the nation improved – especially that of the poor. Goods essential to health were distributed more fairly; prices for food and other essential items were pegged at a standard rate, so the poor could afford to buy them. They were eating a more balanced diet and drinking less. People were encouraged to eat protein, carbohydrates, pulses, and fruit and vegetables. Babies, pregnant women, and the sick were allocated additional nutrients such as milk, orange juice, and cod liver oil. Luxuries, including fish, alcohol, and cigarettes, were not officially rationed but were limited and expensive, as factories focused on the war effort. Therefore rich and poor people were eating almost the same diet. The ability of the rich to eat well at top hotels during the early period of the war led to such resentment that, from 1942, the government prevented restaurants charging more than 5 shillings per meal.

The rationing system was arguably one of the great achievements of wartime Britain. Although everyone complained about it, it meant that no one starved and that food was shared fairly across the Home Front. It is generally accepted that food rationing improved the nation's health, resulting in a better, more balanced diet with more essential vitamins, while people drank less alcohol. The Ministry of Food reported that people had lost weight, but were generally healthier for it. As a result, the population of Britain remained healthy throughout the war – in many ways, healthier than it has been before or since.[22]

Crucial to winning the 'battle for health' was the role played by propaganda. One of the MOI's key propaganda tasks was to inform people in general, and women in particular, of various issues regarding food during wartime. The information covered food creation, distribution, purchase, preparation, and rationing, at home, at work, and even when eating out. There were food advice centres, and, in conjunction with other relevant ministries, the MOI distributed hundreds of different posters, leaflets, and postcards, together with radio broadcasts and 'Food Flash' films and documentaries; speakers were also sent to women's groups and workplaces to provide specialist advice. All the time such propaganda was carefully monitored by various feedback agencies such as the Home Intelligence Reports and Mass-Observation. These multifarious activities – pursuing 'official' aims and objectives – provide excellent examples of how propaganda invaded the 'everyday' experiences of ordinary citizens fighting total war on the Home Front.

NOTES

1   Quoted in P. Addison, *Churchill on the Home Front 1900–1955* (London, 1992), 19.

2   *The Outbreak of War 22 August–3 September*, No. 1 (HMSO, Ministry of Information, 1939).

3   British Library (hereafter, BL), Central Office of Information Archive (hereafter PP), 17/25A.

4   In fact the pamphlet was nearly abandoned in October 1939 when W.H. Smith's warned that 'nobody would want to buy it' after it had been decided not to include photographic illustrations.

5   R. Overy, 'Saving Civilisation: British Public Opinion and the Coming of War in 1939' in D. Welch and J. Fox (eds), *Justifying War. Propaganda, Politics and the Modern Age* (Basingstoke, 2012), 179–99.

6   Gert and Daisy also made a number of broadcasts and film shorts on healthy eating in times of rationing which proved particularly popular. These propaganda shorts are rather mundane, but they captured the resigned mood of the period and their scripts contained all the propaganda messages that the government wished to be disseminated.

7   The National Archives (hereafter TNA), Ministry of Agriculture, March, 1941.

8   One of the stories disseminated perpetuates the myth involving the famous British night-fighter ace John 'Cat's Eyes' Cunningham, who was a very successful combat pilot, shooting down at least twenty enemy aircraft. Rather than admit to the existence of certain technological advances such as radar, propaganda suggested that eating carrots gave him the ability to see the enemy in the pitch black. The government hoped that young people in particular would be eager to emulate their heroes and in this case it would increase consumption of cheap, healthy, home-grown vegetables on the rationed home front – thus boosting Britain's carrot crusade.

9   Potato Pete was another character introduced to encourage the population to eat home-grown vegetables. As with the 'Dig for Victory' theme, Potato Pete also had his own song amplifying the message. With vocals by Betty Driver (later Betty Williams in the television soap opera *Coronation Street*), the recording was a great success and did a tremendous amount of good in getting the message across. For images of Pete and the lyrics to the song, see D. Welch, *Propaganda, Power and Persuasion* (London, 2013), 123–6.

10 Food Facts No. 35, 'Wheatmeal – the *plus* Bread!' (Ministry of Food, 1941).

11 Quoted in P. Lewis, *A People's War* (London, 1986), 154–5. For an authoritative account of the British diet in World War II see D. J. Oddy, *From Plain Fare to Fusion Food: British Diet from the 1890s to the 1990s*, especially chapter 'The Second World War: the Myth of a Planned Diet, 1939-1950' (Woodbridge, 2003).

12 TNA, INF 1/292, H.I. Weekly Intelligence Reports, 16–23 March 1942.

13 TNA, INF 1/292, H.I. Weekly Intelligence Reports, 2–9 March 1942.

14 Rationing features regularly in the Home Intelligence Reports. On 9 July, for example, tea was rationed. Following Lord Woolton's radio broadcast on 8 July 1940 announcing this new rationing restriction, the Home Intelligence Reports found that the public welcomed the measure as a sign 'of official determination and direction' and that it 'was in a mood to respond to any call for sacrifice'. TNA, INF 1/292, H.I. Weekly Intelligence Reports, 8–3 July 1940. The Wartime Social Survey of 1942 recorded that only one person in seven was dissatisfied with rationing and nine out of ten housewives approved of it. Cited in A. Calder, *The People's War* (London, 1997; orig. 1969), 405.

15 Queuing loomed large in most peoples' lives and was an unwelcome aspect of wartime life constantly featuring in the Home Intelligence Reports. The experience of queuing was also magnificently captured by a number of artists; notably Grace Golden in her wartime painting *The Emergency Food Office* (1941), showing a patient queue waiting for new ration books in St Pancras Town Hall, London and Evelyn Dunbar's *The Queue at the Fish Shop* (1944).

16 TNA, INF 1/292, H.I. Weekly Intelligence Reports, 2–9 March 1942.

17 The Wartime Social Survey monitored public attitudes to food and rationing in some depth between February 1942 and October 1943, presenting the results in the report 'Food During the War' by Gertrude Wagner. It found that in the main people had accepted rationing, would not object if it continued after the war, and welcomed price control in this context. TNA, RG 23/9a.

18 Unsurprisingly the rationing of raw materials on clothes caused particular concern within the clothing industry. This was picked up by Home Intelligence as early August 1940. A report from the North Midlands noted that: 'The rationing of raw materials for manufacture is a matter of serious concern for those engaged in hosiery, boot and shoe manufacture; it will almost certainly cause short time and employers are already apprehensive about continued employment in the late autumn'. TNA, INF 1/292, H.I. Weekly Report, 12–17 August 1940. Report from Nottingham, 16 August 1940.

19 An updated version of the book was recently released to coincide with the economic recession, offering similar frugal advice for twenty-first-century families.

20 One young mother remembered the austere
    wartime atmosphere of her Wiltshire village:
    'The Women's Institute was the focal point of
    the village; you could always get ideas there
    about what to make out of what. Most of the
    women were walking about without stockings
    on, you just couldn't get them. But we also used
    to get together in each other's houses. I
    remember one Christmas time we made the
    children quite a lot of toys out of knitting wool
    – most of my youngest child's toys were knitted
    clowns, policemen and soldiers that the ladies
    of the village had knitted. I was quite an expert
    myself on making do and mend.' Quoted in
    Jonathan Croall, *Don't You Know There's A War
    On? The People's Voice 1939–45. Voices from the
    Home Front* (Stroud, 2006).

21 One of the objectives of *The Schools in Wartime*
    (HMSO) was to offset what the MOI perceived
    to be a misplaced perception that 'the schools
    and the teaching profession stand a little apart
    and aloof from the main stream of ordinary life'.
    The publication concluded: 'When the nation as
    a whole is "on service", teachers would not
    wish to claim that they are doing more than
    others: but one thing is for certain – the
    schools and the teachers are in no sense
    outside the nation's war effort; they are right in
    it!' (p. 26).

22 Nevertheless, the diet did tend to be high in
    carbohydrates and low in vitamin D, which
    caused an increase in rickets in some areas.

'Methinks I see in my mind a noble and puissant nation, rousing herself like a strong man after sleep, and shaking her invincible locks.'

JOHN MILTON
AREOPAGITICA (1644)

CHAPTER THREE
The People's War

The Front Line: The Battle for Production

The experience of World War I had demonstrated the importance of mobilising Britain's industrial and labour resources. At the outbreak of World War II, the nation's labour was once again mobilised, and to an even greater extent. Soon after becoming Prime Minister, Winston Churchill recognised the importance of this mobilisation by appointing Ernest Bevin Minister of Labour and National Service. Bevin had served as General Secretary of the powerful Transport and General Workers' Union from 1922 to 1940. In March 1941 the Emergency Powers (Defence) Act gave Bevin complete control over the labour force and the allocation of manpower. It required all men over the age of 41 and women over the age of 20 to register for employment in war work. The Minister of Labour was given authority to schedule a factory as engaged on essential national work, which meant that workers could not leave or be dismissed without the consent of the Ministry. Employers for their part had to pay a guaranteed weekly wage and make provision for training and welfare.[1]

Following the seemingly miraculous evacuation of British forces from Dunkirk in June 1940, it became clear that a huge deficit of weapons and munitions had to be made up. The question was, how would industry respond and how would the morale of those working and suffering deprivation be sustained? It had been agreed as early as May 1939 that the Ministry of Information (MOI) would stress three basic propaganda themes: the justice of Britain's cause (see Fig. 1); Britain's strength (discussed in Chapter 5; and the commitment of the whole community to the war effort.[2]

Nowhere was this third theme more important than in the 'battle for production'. Bevin preferred to act by persuasion, in order to carry the people with him, rather than resort to his new formal powers by using coercion; one of his first tasks was to gain the co-operation of the employers and the trades unions. To this end, he set up a joint body to advise him on issues that would inevitably arise from the emergency wartime legislation. Bevin obtained agreement from the unions that they would abandon traditional demarcations between workers and allow large numbers of semi-skilled and unskilled workers into the armaments factories.

Women at War

One of the most controversial measures taken by Bevin was to conscript women for war work, because of the shortage of labour. World War II was the first war in which British women took part as enfranchised citizens. Facing a significant shortage of labour, Britain went further than any other combatant nation by gradually conscripting and enlisting nearly all women. Arguably one of the most important tests of citizenship in modern times has been service to the state in time of war. In December 1941 legislation was passed providing for the conscription of women into the women's armed forces and into areas such as civil defence and industry. They could, however, choose which service to enter. The new law applied to those between 20 and 30, but at first excluded married women. Until this time, the government's attitude towards the wartime role of women was ill-defined and the MOI initially had no propaganda directed specifically at women.[3] By 1942, with the Employment of Women Order, all women between 18 and 40 could be conscripted by the government. This had a significant effect on the type of women in employment; by 1943, 47 per cent of the female industrial force was married, and one-third had children.[4] Women who had decided to work in factories produced all manner

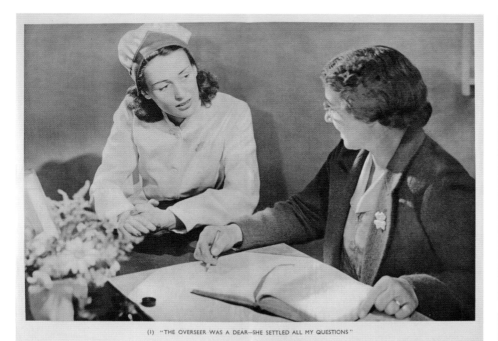

(1) "THE OVERSEER WAS A DEAR—SHE SETTLED ALL MY QUESTIONS"

(4) "FRESH AND CLEAN AGAIN. IT'S WORTH DIRTY HANDS TO MAKE THE STUFF THAT WILL BEAT HITLER"

(2) "BERYL TAUGHT ME HER JOB IN A FEW DAYS"

(3) "CANTEEN MEALS ARE FUN—EXTRA RATIONS, WITH MUSIC!"

(6) "WHAT A THRILL—MY FIRST PAY PACKET"

13
A selection of photographs taken from
an information booklet designed to
encourage women to 'enlist' for factory work.
The process is shown to be painless: from the
interview stage (the 'overseer was a dear'),
to being taught in a few days by Beryl, extra
rations of food in the canteen — with music,
to the washing facilities (fresh and clean
again to beat Hitler) — and the thrill of
the first pay packet!
(PP/BS51/29)

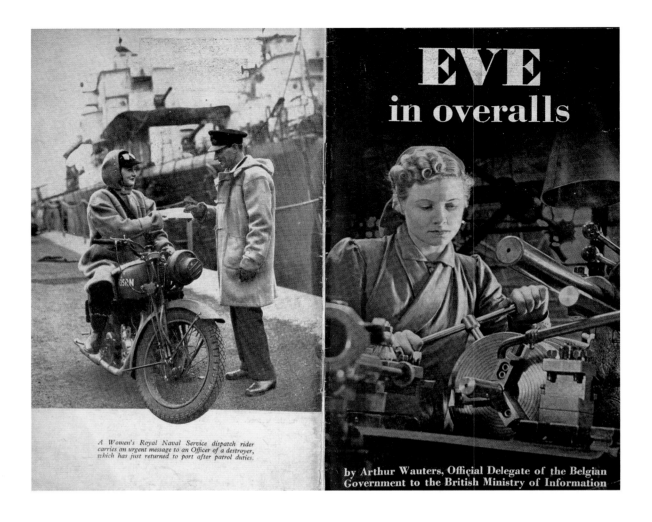

EVE
in overalls

A Women's Royal Naval Service dispatch rider carries an urgent message to an Officer of a destroyer, which has just returned to port after patrol duties.

by Arthur Wauters, Official Delegate of the Belgian Government to the British Ministry of Information

of goods, including ammunition, uniforms, tanks, and aeroplanes. The hours they worked were long, and some women had to move to where the factories were. Those who moved away were paid more. The picture that propaganda liked to depict was of an operationally smooth assimilation of contented women working happily in the workplace. While this is partly true, there were undeniably a number of tensions to be overcome. There was the initial reluctance of men (and trades unions) to accept women into skilled professions, and absenteeism among the women was high (which can only partially be explained by domestic duties and problems from the male workforce, poor pay or lack of appropriate facilities).

In 1943 the MOI co-operated with the film industry to produce *Millions Like Us*, a commercial feature with a strong propaganda message. Frank Launder and Sidney Gilliat were commissioned to write the script, which was intended to show the role of women in the British war effort and in particular to address the anxieties which many women felt about being conscripted for factory labour. Industry was not the most attractive option for women called up for National Service, and therefore conscription alone would not necessarily solve the problem of productivity – a better solution would be to make women feel more enthusiastic about such work. *Millions Like Us* does this by personalising the general experience ('the millions like us') into the story of Celia Crowson (Patricia Roe), an ordinary young woman who is sent to work in an aircraft factory. When she is called for an interview at the Ministry of Labour, she sees a poster for the WAAFs (Women's Auxiliary Air Force) on the wall and fantasises about joining one of the women's services. At the interview she is told by the civil servant Miss Wells (Beatrice Verley):

EVE

in khaki

LITTLE MORE than forty years ago the occupations open to women could be counted on the fingers. For centuries women have been housekeepers, dressmakers, milliners, governesses, secretaries, nurses, shop assistants, mill-girls and waitresses. The first woman lawyer, however, caused a great sensation; the first woman doctor and the first policewoman almost started a riot.

But nowadays women are playing a part in many other spheres of life, and war-time exigencies have brought many women into jobs which were previously only performed by men. This phenomenon has provoked a veritable psychological and social revolution. Technical developments and improvements, by removing or considerably reducing all physical effort, have made it possible for

2

A.T.S. are in the front line in Britain to-day, operating searchlights and gun-sights. This identification telescope picks up hostile aircraft, giving bearing and angle of sight.

3

There is nothing to be afraid of in a factory. Mr Bevin needs another million women, and I don't think we should disappoint him at a time like this. The men at the front need tanks, guns and planes. You can help your country just as much in an overall as you can in uniform these days.

This is the film's propaganda message and it was reinforced by numerous posters and pamphlets distributed by the MOI.[5]

Eve in Overalls (Fig. 14) is a forty-page booklet produced by the MOI that documents the different roles played by women in wartime, in both the armed ('Eve in khaki') and civil services.[6] The booklet illustrates the types of skilled and semi-skilled work on which women were successfully employed (working in shipbuilding and road construction, as postwomen, bus drivers, and dispatch riders) and it draws attention to the possibilities of employing them in a wider range of occupations than was hitherto thought suitable: 'More and more in the future of Great Britain, women will play the role which they deserve, and they will play it well. Britain, defending her freedom, has contracted an immense debt of gratitude to the women.' The document referred to this phenomenon as a 'veritable psychological and social revolution'.

In another publication, *50 Facts about the Women of Britain at War* (Fig. 15), Ernest Bevin paid tribute to women by writing that: 'Our women tipped the scales of war.' Fact 44 is typical of the accumulated information that is packed into this booklet. Housewives (it states) made over 4,500 tons of jam, 120 tons of bottled fruit, 340 tons of canned fruit and 150 tons of pickles, which were sold to the public under the rationing scheme. Moreover, during the period 1941–2 women picked 200 tons of rose hips, which were made into vitamin-rich syrup for babies.

When Ernest Bevin took office as Minister of Labour and National Service there were still

16
Laura Knight, *Ruby Loftus Screwing a Breech Ring*
(1943).
Imperial War Museum

Women painting a ship in a big dockyard.

50 FACTS ABOUT THE WOMEN OF BRITAIN AT WAR

15
50 Facts About the Women of Britain at War.
(PP/27/52L)

700,000 out of work. Towards the end of 1942 more than 8.5 million women were registered for National Service. By mid-1943 women constituted 40 per cent of all employees in the aircraft industry, 35 per cent in the engineering industry and 52 per cent in factories making explosives and chemicals. By 1944, 7 million women were employed in essential industries or in the services. A typical propaganda poster of the time urged reluctant women: 'Come on, Women – man the Factories ... We're playing one "man" short – and that's YOU!' Probably the most powerful image of women's war work was that produced by the artist Dame Laura Knight. In 1943 she was commissioned by the War Advisory Committee to paint the heroine of the factories. Ruby Loftus was the first woman to be employed on the highly skilled work of screwing the breech ring of the Bofors gun, which was considered to be the prerogative of a man with a nine-year apprenticeship behind him. Loftus, who worked in the Royal Ordnance factory in Newport, had gained the skill by the age of 21 after two years' training. Knight painted Loftus at her lathe and produced a masterpiece of heroic realism (Fig. 16).

Women's contribution to solving the manpower shortage was even celebrated in the 'For Victory' postcards series (see chapter Chapter 4 for the 'V for Victory Campaign'). Fig. 17 shows 'Britain's newest ordnance factory' where '80 per cent of the workers are women'. Rather patronisingly, it claims that 'two or three years ago many of them had never been inside a factory!'. Even the frequently cited provision of state day nurseries for working mothers, which was undoubtedly an historic initiative, was in itself the locus of intense ideological debate between realists such as Bevin in the Ministry of Labour and the traditionalists of the Ministry of Health. Although 1,345 nurseries had been established by 1943 (compared with 14 existing in 1940), this did not represent a real victory for women workers as it was merely a temporary wartime expedient and,

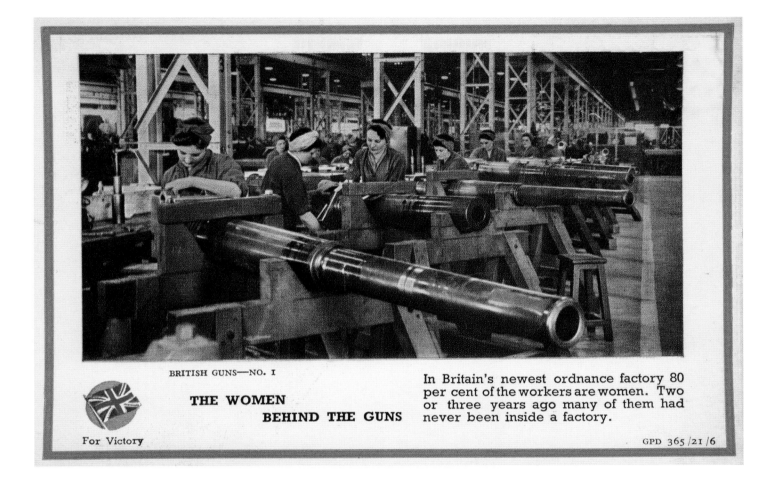

BRITISH GUNS—NO. I

THE WOMEN

BEHIND THE GUNS

In Britain's newest ordnance factory 80 per cent of the workers are women. Two or three years ago many of them had never been inside a factory.

For Victory

GPD 365/21/6

17
From the 'For Victory' series:
The women behind the guns.
(PP/20/18A, 24L)

moreover, failed to provide childcare for the duration of the mothers' working day. The transition that was taking place in British society was not as seamless as the official propaganda would lead us to believe; nonetheless, the response of women was quite remarkable and represented a major contribution to the British war effort. Most women continued to play domestic roles, caring for children and running the household. As men on the Home Front rarely readjusted their role to accommodate women, this often involved queuing for hours, mending clothes long after they would normally have been discarded, and organising childcare during working hours. In the aftermath of victory – and with men returning from service overseas – women retreated with rapidity, thus leaving very little evidence of their contribution to final victory.

Calling All Workers

In spite of all its problems, British industry rose to the challenge of war and achieved remarkable successes built largely on the principle of consent. In the vital struggle for finished war materials Britain outstripped its allegedly better-organised Nazi enemy with some ease. Aircraft (particularly bombers), tanks, guns, radar, and so on poured off British production lines. In contrast, Germany did not move into total war production until 1942.[7] Unsurprisingly, the MOI celebrated these achievements and a wide range of propaganda material was disseminated to the Home Front, the British Empire and its allies, and also to the civilian populations of Britain's enemies via leaflet drops. One example is a detailed sixty-page booklet produced by the MOI in 1944 (Fig. 18; shown

MAN POWER

PUBLICATION DATE
MAY 18TH 1944

THE STORY OF BRITAIN'S MOBILISATION FOR WAR

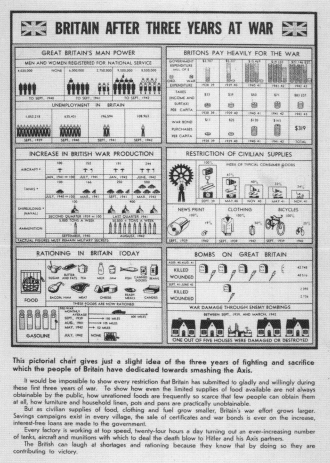

18

*Man Power: The Story
of Britain's Mobilisa-
tion for War* (Spanish
and English versions).

(PP/14/29L)

19

*Britain After
Three Years at War*
— a densely
factual leaflet laden
with statistical data.

(PP/3/26)

here in both English and Spanish versions) telling the story of how Britain is winning
the 'battle of production'. It was intended to raise morale and sustain civilian populations
– both at home and abroad – during the final push for victory. Significantly, British
'manpower' is symbolically represented as both an ordinary civilian and as a warrior
figure. The photograph captures a tranquil moment in which a civilian lights a cigarette
after a working shift, while bearing all the trappings of war: his rifle, gas mask, and
helmet. He is juxtaposed against the background figure of a soldier standing to attention
on duty, the implication being that both are fighting the same war and both are
contributing to ultimate victory.

In 1943 the MOI distributed a leaflet, *Britain After Three Years at War* (Fig. 19),
which pulled no punches but rather set out concisely the magnitude of Britain's industrial
and manpower achievements, as well as the price that all citizens were paying for this – in
terms of higher taxation and food prices, fuel and clothing restrictions, and even death.
There are even figures for civilian deaths caused by enemy bombing and the number of
homes destroyed ('one out of five houses damaged or destroyed'). But the leaflet makes
it clear – as if to stress the scale of the nation's achievements – that Britain has 'submitted
gladly and willingly … and as the supplies of food, clothing and fuels grow smaller,
Britain's war effort grows larger'. Diagrams reveal the impressive increases in the
production of aircraft, tanks, naval ships, and ammunition. Savings campaigns exist in

every village and every factory is working at top speed 24 hours a day turning out weapons of war 'with which to deal the death blow to Hitler and his Axis partners'.

Paeans to the British worker can be found in a number of film documentaries, notably Humphrey Jennings' work with the Crown Film Unit. *The Heart of Britain* (1941) examined the effects of war on the provinces and the diversity of British society. *Words for Battle* (1941) matched inspired images of the nation at war to inspirational texts from literature (Milton, Blake, Kipling) and from history (Lincoln and Churchill), spoken by Laurence Olivier. *Listen to Britain* (1942) dispensed with commentary altogether and created a symphony of sound, evocatively blending Big Ben, the BBC, and *Music while You Work*, with popular double-act Flanagan and Allen singing 'Underneath the Arches' in a factory canteen. The film culminates in a rousing choral rendition of 'Rule Britannia' – a fitting ending to a film intended to document the special community spirit of the Home Front in wartime Britain.

An important aspect of 'the people's war' theme was the projection of a united Home Front. The publications *All on the Job* and *The Men Behind the Job* were produced to reinforce this message. *All on the Job* (Fig. 20) was a small fold–out sheet that illustrated how 'Men and Women in Britain are mobilised for Victory'. One of the problems facing the government was residual absenteeism. A campaign was started to persuade workers not to become 'slackers' by taking days off. *The Men Behind the Job* is a very simple, pocket-size publication, in which workers stress the importance of a full weekly shift: 'If

20
All on the Job.
(PP/1/1)

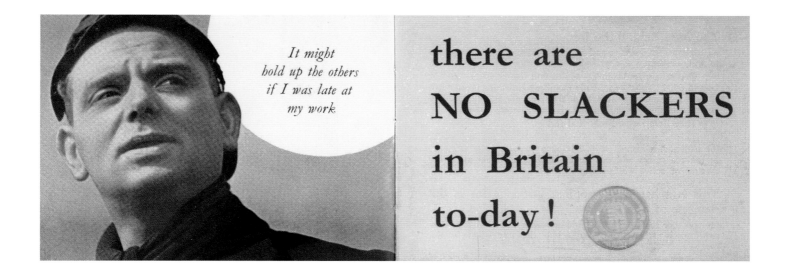

I slacked on my job it would let down the boys at the front'; 'There's a soldier needing every tank I help to make. That's why I am never absent'; and in Fig. 21: 'There are NO SLACKERS in Britain today!'.

Although Ernest Bevin was given sweeping powers he always claimed that he preferred to use them only as a last resort, and to act by persuasion and consent. Much was made in British propaganda of the idea that 'the people's war' represented all sections of society and was a spontaneous, consensual phenomenon. *Factories of Freedom* (Fig. 22)[8] was published shortly after the fall of France when Britain felt alone in Europe. The MOI attempted to contrast the oppression of life under the Nazis with the value placed on freedom in Britain. The booklet begins by outlining that for seven years Germany had been re-arming on an unprecedented scale: 'Remember Göring's famous slogan: "Guns or Butter"? There, symbolised in three short words, was the spirit of war slavery.' In contrast, by means of photographs and a pithy narrative, *Factories of Freedom* constructs the British Home Front as the bastion of freedom – the last, defiant bulwark, opposing tyranny: 'This long-accumulated mountain of arms forced the capitulation of peace-loving France, and the mighty hordes of Hitler lined the French Channel coast, facing the white cliffs of England.' While for some it may have appeared a contradiction to associate weapons of destruction with 'freedom', by presenting the conflict as Good vs Evil (I shall return to this later when looking at propaganda directed at the enemy), British propaganda could retain the moral high ground by suggesting that the ends justified the means.

Factories of Freedom, like much of the literature produced by the MOI during this period, stressed the solidarity and cheerfulness of factory workers. The BBC played an important role here by broadcasting live *Workers' Playtime* from a war factory. The programme was launched with the active support of Ernest Bevin and was aired every Saturday lunchtime from 31 May 1941 and three times a week from 28 October 1941. The show was normally broadcast from a factory canteen, and by its second anniversary had been performed in front of 270,000 workers and had a regular audience of 7 million. Equally popular with factory employees was *Music While You Work*, which played repetitive, light background music to provide a background rhythm to their work. Eric Coates composed the programme's signature tune, 'Calling All Workers'. Though some factory owners believed that it hindered production, the government and the workers thought that it helped greatly with the monotony and fatigue of factory work, and by 1943 almost 7,000 factories with 4 million workers in total were listening regularly. By 1945 the programme reached over 9,000 factories and 30,000–40,000 small plants.[9]

21
The Men Behind the Job.
(PP/14/43L)

PP/9/13L

22
Factories of Freedom.
(PP/9/13L)

Ernest Bevin devoted a special message to the value of these two programmes: 'The BBC is a factory for entertainment and education, and must be regarded as one of the vital services. It represents a necessary link and contribution to production.'[10]

The other pressing issue facing Bevin was the question of the trades unions and industrial unrest. The demands of total war placed the labour force in a powerful bargaining position. Though Bevin endeavoured to minimise strikes and industrial unrest by imposing arbitration mechanisms on industry, even his trades union credentials could not stop tension from boiling over in certain sectors. Coal miners, for example, took the opportunity to press for redress of longstanding grievances. Working in one of the most vital of war resources, coal miners were outraged that mine owners continued to accrue personal profits while their workers' sacrifices were granted scant reward. Bevin responded by diverting nearly 48,000 military conscripts (known as the Bevin Boys) to work in the coal industry – although this measure would not resolve the structural problems of the mining industry that the war had exposed.[11] It was imperative, nonetheless, to keep the trades unions united behind the war drive and not to allow production to falter. The Emergency Powers Act and Defence Regulations provided the government with all the power it needed to direct and control labour. Strikes and lockouts were banned under Order 1305 and the 1941 Essential Work (General Provisions) Order allowed for the dilution of labour and the direction of skilled workers to wherever they were most needed. Bevin established a Joint Consultative Committee of seven employers' representatives and seven trades unionists to advise on the conduct of the war effort on the Home Front. Until 1941, when the Soviet Union entered the war, Communists in Britain, having little commitment to the war effort, refused to be bound by the national unity consensus and in particular by the ban on strike action.

GREAT BRITAIN'S WAR EFFORT

MEN AND WOMEN FACTORY WORKERS

On essential war work

On work for essential civilian needs

Forty out of every fifty factory workers on
essential war work

O.P.D. 365/71/11

During the first few months of the war, there were over 900 strikes, almost all of them
very short, but illegal nonetheless. Despite the provisions of Order 1305 there were very
few prosecutions until 1941 since Bevin, anxious to avoid the labour unrest of World
War I, sought to promote conciliation rather than conflict. The number of strikes
increased each year until 1944. In 1943, 1,800,000 working days were lost in 1,785
strikes and 1944 saw the loss of 3,700,00 days. Coal and engineering were particularly
affected.[12] After Hitler launched his invasion of the Soviet Union in June 1941, the MOI
adopted an ambivalent position. On the one hand it welcomed Russia as a new ally,

John Bull has his coat off !

HOW BRITAIN'S WAR PRODUCTION IS INCREASING

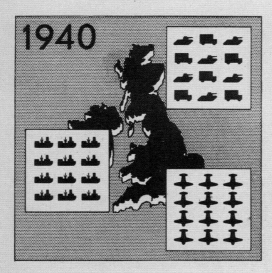

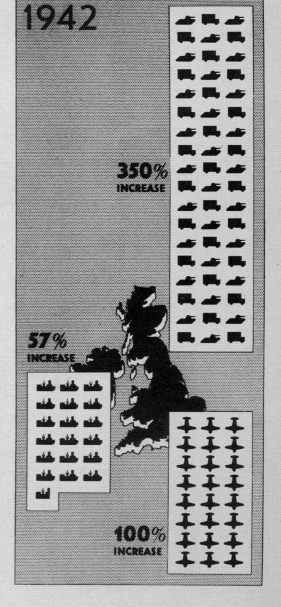

"We are producing tanks, jeeps and other mechanical vehicles at the rate of 257,000 a year . . . We have increased our production of aircraft 100% . . . We have increased our production of merchant ships 57%"

BRITAIN'S MINISTER OF PRODUCTION. June 10, 1942

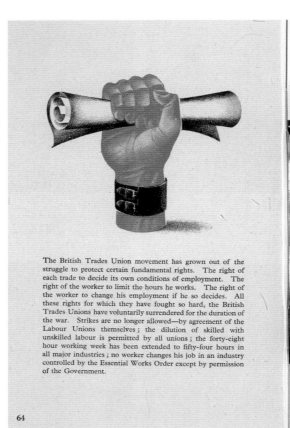

The British Trades Union movement has grown out of the struggle to protect certain fundamental rights. The right of each trade to decide its own conditions of employment. The right of the worker to limit the hours he works. The right of the worker to change his employment if he so decides. All these rights for which they have fought so hard, the British Trades Unions have voluntarily surrendered for the duration of the war. Strikes are no longer allowed—by agreement of the Labour Unions themselves; the dilution of skilled with unskilled labour is permitted by all unions; the forty-eight hour working week has been extended to fifty-four hours in all major industries; no worker changes his job in an industry controlled by the Essential Works Order except by permission of the Government.

64

BRITAIN'S WORKERS
voluntarily surrender their historic rights and customs

The Trades Union Congress meet in 1940 and pledge full support to the Government in the prosecution of the war against Nazi tyranny.

65

while on the other hand it was intent on dissuading the British working public from viewing Communism as a political and economic system that might best serve their interests after the war. As a result, the MOI enthusiastically promoted Anglo–Soviet co-operation in pursuit of victory, while cold-shouldering the British Communist Party.[13]

In 1944, a sort of 'unofficial' celebratory history, *The Trade Unionist and the War* (Fig. 24), was published. It was written by Herbert Tracey, the Publication Officer to the British Trades Union Congress, and contained fulsome praise from Oliver Lyttelton, the Minister of Production, of the role played by trades unionists. No mention was made of the number of working days lost. Instead, the publication chose to stress trades union acceptance of all the industrial restrictions demanded of them and their role in mobilising manpower: 'From the beginning of the war the millions of men and women organised in the British Trades Union have been resolute and united in their support of the nation's cause.' Lyttelton referred to their achievements in the area of production as 'remarkable' and Herbert Tracey declared that: 'The first objective of the Trades Unions in Great Britain today is to … WIN THE WAR!'

In *A People at War* (Fig. 25) a whole section is devoted to the concessions made by the trades union movement to suspend 'their historic rights and customs … in the prosecution of the war against Nazism'.

The statistics behind Britain's industrial effort make impressive reading (50,000 tons of munitions produced every minute; 275,000 fighting vehicles manufactured every year, and so on), and the trades unions played an important, consensual role. The war certainly had a positive effect on trades union membership, which increased by almost 3 million – from approximately 4.5 million in 1938 to around 7.5 million in 1946. Moreover, this was accompanied by the spread of recognition agreements to industries in which unions had previously had little import. In a conciliatory move, the coalition government even denied war contracts to firms (under the Essential Works Order) who failed to conform to minimum standards demanded by the unions.

THE TRADE UNIONIST AND THE WAR

BY HERBERT TRACEY
PUBLICITY OFFICER TO THE
BRITISH TRADES UNION
CONGRESS

Land at War: Agriculture

Food production was a priority (see Chapter 2), in large part to open up shipping for munitions. Domestically, the 'Dig for Victory' campaign captured the imagination of the people and proved a great success. But farmers also had a vitally important role to play and made a massive contribution to feeding the nation. One slogan signified their importance to the war effort: 'Ploughing on FARMS is as vital as ARMS'. Farmers increased the number of acres under cultivation from 12,000,000 to 18,000,000, and the farm labour force was expanded by a fifth, thanks especially to the Women's Land Army (WLA). This had been re-formed in 1939 to attract female volunteers for agricultural work, replacing men called up to the military. The WLA was organised entirely by women and at first it asked for volunteers (in fact only 7,000 women had joined by August 1940 at a time when German U-boats were crippling British food imports from America), but this was supplemented by conscription and by 1944 the WLA had over 80,000 members. Women who worked for the WLA were commonly known as 'Land Girls'.

An official document issued by the MOI in early 1945, *Land at War*, set out to provide an 'official' record of the achievements of British farming during the war (Fig. 26). It tells of a remarkable increase in land production as well as the crucial role played by the Land Girls. By 1944, cultivated arable land had increased by 50 per cent and pasture land by 66 per cent. Moreover, output of wheat nearly doubled and the potato yield soared by over 100 per cent. *Land at War* was published at a time when victory appeared near. It is more than simply a record of the farming industry's contribution to victory; rather, it is a celebration of a 'way of life' that was etched in the nation's memory and was being threatened. But this was not in the dark sense of *Blut und Boden* (blood and soil) that defined the strength of the *Herrenvolk* (German Master race) by emphasising the superior virtues of rural life. Instead, the British vision was of a gentler, more romantic scene of thatched country pubs, Morris dancing, and afternoon teas. This rural idyll had been deeply ingrained in the British imagination since Victorian times and was still deemed worth fighting for.

Civil Defence: the Civilian Soldiers

The land proved an important factor in maintaining the nation's food supplies, and food was recognised as a key factor in the maintenance of morale, but the urban conurbations were the hub for industry. From the very beginning of the war, the question of the impact of German air raids on British cities was a priority for the government. Of particular concern was the devastating impact air raids could have on civilian morale.

In May 1939 the government were concerned about the likely scale and consequences of enemy air attacks on British cities. In 1937 the Basque city of Guernica had been destroyed by German bombers supporting Franco in the Spanish Civil War. The reality of the destruction of Guernica, which was captured by the newsreels and shown to British cinema audiences (and later commemorated by the Spanish artist Pablo Picasso), provided a frightening glimpse of the horror of *Blitzkrieg* and a sobering reminder that cities like London were equally vulnerable to squadrons of bombers. There was a widespread acceptance, partly fuelled by films and literature such as H.G. Wells' *The War of the Worlds*, that the 'bomber would always prevail'.

The government had reacted to this fear as early as 1924 by establishing a Committee of Imperial Defence to look into Air Raid Precautions (ARP) and in 1938 Sir Samuel Hoare, the Home Secretary, broadcast to the nation appealing for volunteers

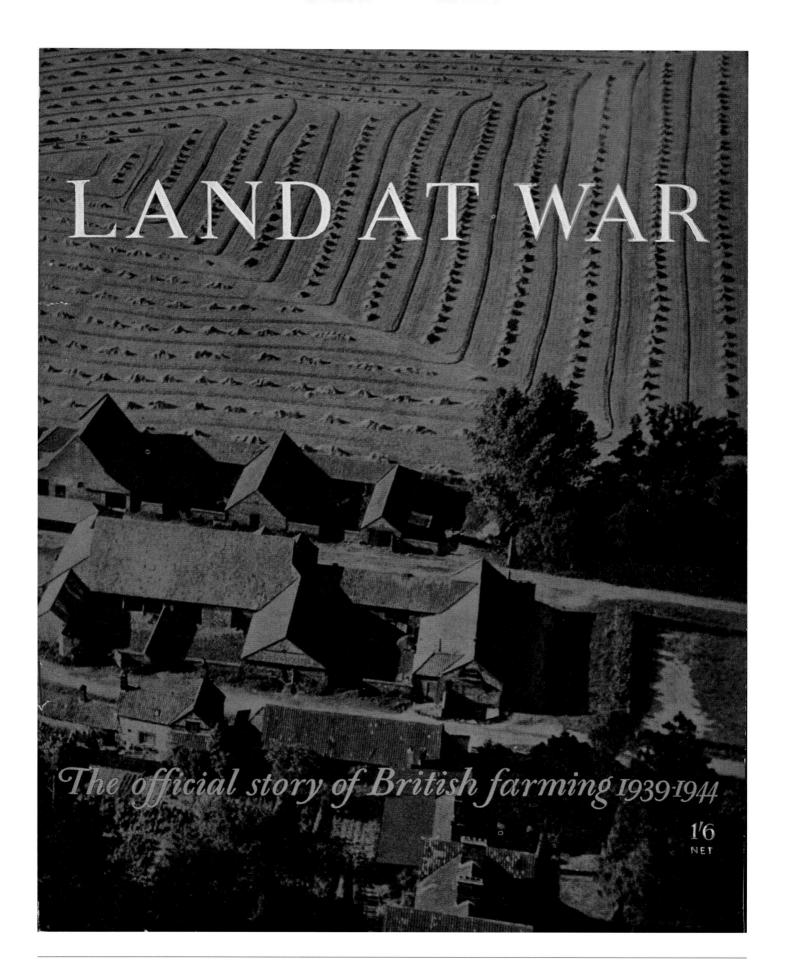

LAND AT WAR

The official story of British farming 1939-1944

1'6
NET

for recruitment to the ARP and other services such as the Auxiliary Fire Service. One of the first measures to help protect people from air attacks was the blackout, which was enforced as soon as war broke out. Guidance was provided in terms of leaflets distributed (such as *Public Information Leaflet No. 2*). The other major concern was gas attacks. Some 38 million gas masks had been distributed by September 1939 to protect civilians from gas bombs, which could be dropped during air raids. The MOI launched an intense propaganda campaign reminding people to carry their gas masks at all times: 'Hitler will give no warning – So always carry your gas mask.' Civilians were fined if they were caught without their masks.

The carrying of gas masks steadily declined and by late 1940 anxiety about gas attacks was replaced by fear of high-explosive bombs falling (it was a well-founded fear, as it has been estimated that between September 1940 and July 1941, 43,000 civilians were killed). The MOI launched advertisements warning citizens not to panic and encouraging rational behaviour: 'Keep a Cool Head'. An educational campaign was also started to advise on how best to provide air raid shelter within homes and in gardens. Citizens were encouraged to form a 'refuge room' in the house and to purchase a Morrison steel table shelter (because, it was claimed, such tables could bear the weight of a falling floor), and by September 1940 over 2 million corrugated steel Anderson shelters had been built – mainly half-buried in back gardens.

On 14 May 1940, Anthony Eden, Secretary of State for War, encouraged men aged from 17 to 65 and unable to serve in the forces to join the Local Defence Volunteers. Within twenty-four hours, 250,000 men had registered and, by the end of June 1940, nearly 1.5 million had volunteered. Weapons were in short supply, owing in part to the equipment losses at Dunkirk, so many initially improvised with brooms, umbrellas, and golf clubs. In July 1940 Winston Churchill changed the name to 'Home Guard' and the MOI distributed throughout the country a leaflet, *Beating the Enemy*, intended to counter prevailing fears of a German invasion. The people were urged to 'STAND FIRM' and Churchill wrote the preface, which attempted to reassure: 'The Home Guard, supported by strong mobile columns wherever the enemy's numbers require it, will immediately come to grips with the invaders, and there is little doubt will soon destroy them.'

27 (These pages and overleaf)
Two posters for London Transport,
in *The Proud City* series, showing
historic national buildings defiant
in the face of the Nazi Blitzkrieg.
(PP/BS51/29)

As men enlisted for the armed forces the emergency services began to appeal for volunteers, and both the Auxiliary Ambulance Service and the Auxiliary Fire Service (later the National Fire Service) were created. Their members were usually too old or too young for military service and most were unpaid part-timers. Initially perceived as 'service-dodgers', they became public heroes when the Blitz began. Of all the direct threats to the civilian way of life, bombing was the most extreme and ubiquitous during the war. The idea that civilians should volunteer in large numbers to organise home defences against the threat of bombing transformed the nature of popular commitment to the war effort and gave civilians a real sense that they were on a new and unpredictable front line.

However, the first days of the Blitz had a serious effect on morale and Home Intelligence and Mass-Observation both noted concerns about inadequate shelters, lack of facilities, insanitary conditions, and the danger to morale of rumours about air raid damage and casualties. Herbert Morrison, the Home Secretary, urged the Cabinet to introduce compulsory fire watching, but it was decided that the voluntary principle would be retained, though the government was given additional powers to compel participation should that be deemed necessary. ARP personnel were responsible for the issuing of gas masks and pre-fabricated air raid shelters, and for looking after public shelters. They were also responsible for maintaining the blackout, assisted in fighting incendiaries during air raids and undertook rescue work afterwards. There were around 1.4 million ARP wardens in Britain during the war, almost all unpaid, part-time volunteers who also held day-time jobs. The Fire Guard was formed in August 1941 (its main counter to fires being the stirrup pump) and Morrison set about improving conditions and facilities in the shelters so as to restore public morale. In London, for example, underground stations were fitted with bunks for 22,000 people, supplied with first aid facilities, and equipped with chemical toilets. Across the underground system, 124 canteens opened. Shelter marshals were appointed, whose function it was to keep order, give first aid, and assist in case of the flooding of the tunnels. An estimated 170,000 people sheltered in the tunnels and stations during World War II.

Underground stations were not entirely bomb-proof and there were disasters. At Balham 68 people lost their lives in October 1940, and in March 1943, 197 civilians were killed when a panic broke out at Bethnal Green station following a nearby explosion.[14] Air raids could also heighten social tensions. Following the incident at Bethnal Green, Home Intelligence reported that the crush was widely blamed on 'panicking Jews'.[15] Equally disturbing was a report from Coventry that the houses of pacifists had been stoned following a Luftwaffe raid.[16] Generally speaking, however, people stayed calm and morale remained high in spite of criticism that the 'siren policy' was confusing and inconsistent, and complaints about the condition of public air raid shelters. Home Intelligence recorded that 'the general feeling in raided areas is that "we can take it"'; what they wanted to know is 'what are we dishing out to the Germans!' (see Chapter 5).[17]

The courage and sacrifice of these 'civil defenders' was considered worthy of extensive attention by the MOI. Propaganda film documentaries such as *London Can Take It! / Britain Can Take It!* (1940) referred to 'the greatest civilian army ever assembled' and *Fires Were Started* (1943) showed the experience and courage of a crew of the Auxiliary Fire Service during a single night in the Luftwaffe's Blitz over London. The Blitz was already taking on mythic proportions – a shared experience in fortitude that provided proof of the distinct qualities of the island people.[18] *London Can Take It!*, for example, has a deadpan, matter-of-fact commentary by the London-based American journalist, Quentin Reynolds. He pays tribute to 'the people's army of volunteers', the civilians in the front line of the war, and emphasises their stoicism and courage: 'I can assure you that there is no panic, no fear, no despair in London town; there is nothing but determination, confidence and high courage among the people of Churchill's Island'.

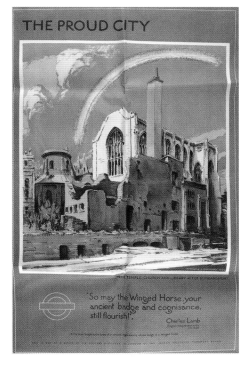

THE PROUD CITY

'So may the Winged Horse, your ancient badge and cognisance, still flourish!'

Charles Lamb

28
Mobile Canteen.
The pamphlet highlighted the
network of canteens that had been
set up in bomb-damaged towns
and cities and showed in graphic
detail how welcome a hot 'cuppa'
was to both wardens and victims
alike. (PP/14/40)

29
Transport goes to War.
(PP/23/23A)

In the final scene of the film, Reynolds concludes: 'It is hard to see five centuries of labour destroyed in five seconds. But a bomb has its limitations; it can only destroy buildings and kill people. It cannot kill the unconquerable spirit and courage of the people of London. London can take it!'[19] This closing statement is delivered over an image of Carlo Marochetti's statue of Richard the Lionheart, the sword held high but damaged by the bombing, and framed by the smashed windows of the Houses of Parliament in the background. Similarly, on 29 December 1940, the *Daily Mail's* front page carried a photograph of St Paul's Cathedral standing defiant while wreathed in smoke and flames. The headline proclaimed: 'War's Greatest Picture'. Similarly, London Transport produced a series of stunning colour posters entitled 'Proud City' that depicted

Transport goes to War

1/-
NET

1414

THE OFFICIAL STORY OF BRITISH TRANSPORT, 1939–1942

30
They Fight by Night.
(PP/23/36A)

32
*Aspectos De La Guerra
(Aspects of War).*
A lavishly illustrated booklet
intended to show allies and
neutrals all aspects of the 'people's
war' in action. This is a Spanish
version that shows how
Londoners have volunteered
to keep London's transport
running during the Blitz.
(PP/BS51/29)

31 (opposite)
Roof Over Britain.
(PP/20/7A)

ROOF OVER BRITAIN

THE OFFICIAL STORY OF THE A.A DEFENCES, 1939—1942

Then one night when BOO-BOO was almost tired of watching, there came a wonderful chance. He, BOO-BOO, caught an enemy aeroplane and sent it crashing to earth. Then BOO-BOO was indeed proud and happy that he had done his duty — and helped to save the land he loved.

33
The children's book *Boo-Boo the Barrage Balloon* (1943). Boo-Boo brings down an enemy aeroplane.
(Private Collection)

the heroic defiance of iconic buildings in London that had suffered bomb damage.

Together with films and radio broadcasts, the MOI lavishly produced pamphlets and books with some startlingly striking and artistic cover designs that captured all aspects of the 'people's war' on the front line, such as the voluntary spirit of urgently needed canteens set up in each civil defence region (Fig. 28; permanent canteen facilities were now provided for those in shelters). *Transport goes to War* and other booklets showed how, with the help of volunteers, transport in Britain kept moving in the face of prolonged air raids (Figs 29, 32). *They Fight by Night* paid homage to the unsung courage and determination of male and female air wardens (Fig. 30), and *Roof Over Britain* tells the 'official' story of Britain's courageous anti-aircraft defences on the Home Front (Fig. 31).

The notion of civil responsibility extended to children as well. As far as good health was concerned, the Ministry of Health targeted children with a series of posters that encouraged parents and children ('Milkman, Please leave extra milk for me') to order an extra pint of milk for their children – 'The Essential Food for Growing Children'. Moreover, a number of illustrated books for young children were produced that acknowledged the war and the manner in which the British community pulled together in the war effort (for example, *Wimpy the Wellington*, 1942).[20] The bulbous, protective shape of the barrage balloon proved particularly popular. In the 1943 book *Boo-Boo the Barrage Balloon* (Fig. 33), full-page coloured pictures have a simple narrative running beneath. Boo-Boo, a brave and patriotic barrage balloon (the invention of Professors Flip, Flop, and Pumblechook), married Belinda and they produced twin baby barrage balloons (Betty and Basil). Together, they guard the skies of Britain. Once they have caught an enemy aircraft and sent it crashing to earth, the text delivers the propaganda message of the importance of civil responsibility and pride: 'Then Boo-Boo was indeed proud and happy that he had done his duty – and helped to save the land he loved.' Boo-Boo was awarded a medal for his bravery, but interestingly, the book ends by emphasising the role to be played by the proud twins, Betty and Basil: 'Of course, nothing would satisfy the twins but that Boo-Boo should come down to earth and teach them to be good barrage balloons so that they could grow like Daddy, and perhaps some day win a medal. And splendid pupils they were, too!'

Official War Artists

Artists also had an important role to play in the people's war, and the integration of artists and intellectuals into the war effort was much more successful than in World War I. In the visual arts one of the most valuable wartime initiatives was the Official War Artists scheme (funded by the Pilgrim Trust) which ran from 1939 to 1943 and commissioned paintings (largely watercolours) of cherished buildings and landscapes perceived to be under threat. It prompted not only the famous bomb-damaged ruins captured by John Piper, but also evocative paintings by Eric Ravilious, evoking the alien world of submarines, and by Evelyn Dunbar depicting ordinary citizens queuing stoically for rationed food, and the rural heroism of Land Girls (Fig. 36).

Perhaps the most illustrative example of wartime initiatives involving the arts was the role played by Kenneth Clark, Director of the National Gallery, who established a War Artists Advisory Committee (WAAC) within the MOI that was ready to commission artists when war broke out in 1939. The scheme's intention was to create a historical and artistic record of Britain's involvement in war and to bolster morale through exhibitions and publications. Emphasis was placed on art that would embody a message of liberal cultural values; the antithesis of the controlled and centralised aesthetic of the Nazis (and the Soviets). Clark emphasised the unique role of art and the insight and vision that artists could bring to an understanding of war. The WAAC programme exploited a growing interest in the visual arts that can be traced back to World War I, and it served to transform British visual culture. By 1946, the programme had employed over 400 artists (2,000 had applied) and acquired over 6,000 works. Artists worked in a variety of

34
Paul Nash, *Battle of Britain* (1941). Nash's imaginative summary of RAF Fighter Command's successful struggle against the Luftwaffe in 1940. The scene is of the Thames estuary, with the Channel and France beyond. Against the approaching twilight new formations of Luftwaffe can be seen threatening. The painting went on display at the National Gallery in January 1942.
Imperial War Museum

Elsie Hewland,
*A Nursery School for War
Workers' Children* (1942).
A cloakroom at a nursery
school, with children putting on
their uniforms and exploring their
environment. The painting portrays
the 'everyday' experience of small
children while their mothers
were away producing weapons
of mass destruction.
Imperial War Museum

styles, from traditional to more modern, although it is probably fair to say that the majority of the compositions adhered to the representational. Works ranged from Stanley Spencer's teeming shipyards on the Clyde to Graham Sutherland's animated city and landscapes, and from Paul Nash's powerful imagery of British power and resistance to Edward Ardizzone's intimate scenes of daily life during the London Blitz.

In 1940, Paul Nash was made an Official War Artist to the Royal Air Force (RAF) and produced some of the finest paintings of the war. His 1941 *Battle of Britain* (Fig. 34) captured the RAF's great aerial victory over the advancing Luftwaffe. The coastline, as seen from a bomber, is evaporating in multi-coloured smoke. Against the approaching twilight threatening new formations of Luftwaffe can be seen. In Elsie Hewland's 1942

A Nursery School for War Workers' Children (Fig. 35) we see hints of the changes not just for the children but for their mothers, called into unfamiliar duties. Nursery schools were a new support for women conscripted into full-time employment.

Britain's World War II art programme went out of its way to encourage the painting of non-violent, sentimental, and rather parochial scenes of Britons 'doing their bit', intended to inspire people to protect their countryside and ways of life. As most artists supported the war aims, they tended to shy away from the confrontational. What we have in all these pictures is not a form of crude propaganda based on idealised images entirely dissociated from reality, but a far more subtle one, founded on implicit assumptions about the British national character.

36
Evelyn Dunbar,
Land Army Girls Going to Bed (1943).
Dunbar was one of the few female artists to be employed by the War Artists' Advisory Committee to record women's contributions to World War II on the Home Front.
Imperial War Museum

The arts, alongside social welfare and economic democracy, came to symbolise the antithesis of Hitlerism. Altogether the cultural gains of the war were very real ones: the founding of the Council for the Encouragement of Music and Drama (CEMA, renamed the Arts Council at the end of the war) as an agent of state patronage to the arts was an event of major significance. Writing in the Music Review in 1947, R.J. Manning declared that 'despite the blackout and general war-weariness, music has had in this country an extraordinary flowering'. The wartime National Gallery concerts performed by artists such as the tenor Peter Pears, contralto Kathleen Ferrier, and pianist Dame Myra Hess (and captured so memorably in Humphrey Jennings' documentary film, *Listen to Britain*) were intended to raise the morale of Londoners. Bomb damage had closed Sadler's Wells Opera in 1941, forcing the company to tour the provinces for four years. CEMA organised tours or exhibitions under the title 'Art for the People'. The reopening of the Sadler's Wells Theatre in the summer of 1945 was celebrated with the first performance of Benjamin Britten's *Peter Grimes* – one of the true operatic masterpieces of the twentieth century, symbolising the struggle of the individual against the masses. Britain's musical renaissance continued. By taking over the running of the Henry Wood Promenade Concerts, the BBC made them available to a much wider public. Under CEMA patronage, musicians toured the country, playing in villages and towns as well as cities and during lunch breaks at the war factories. CEMA also organised tours of exhibitions under the title 'Art for the People', with accompanying catalogues (Fig. 37).[21]

37
War Pictures by British Artists.
Two examples of catalogues produced by the Ministry of Information to accompany exhibitions of the work of official artists that toured the country.
(PP/27/9A, 10A)

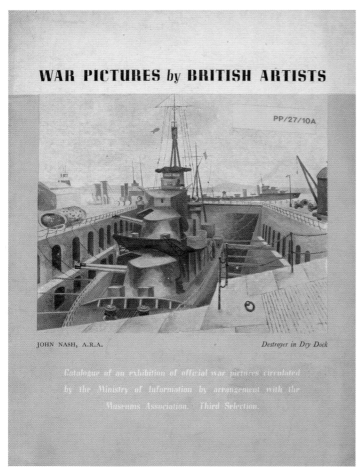

WAR PICTURES by BRITISH ARTISTS

PP/27/10A

JOHN NASH, A.R.A.   *Destroyer in Dry Dock*

Catalogue of an exhibition of official war pictures circulated by the Ministry of Information by arrangement with the Museums Association. Third Selection.

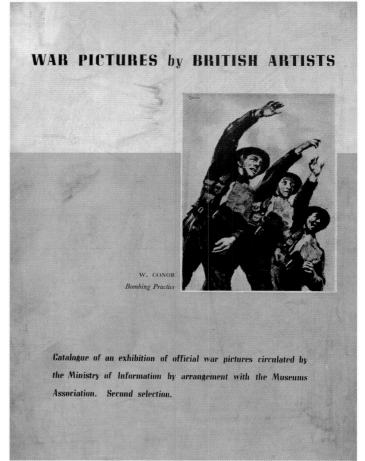

WAR PICTURES by BRITISH ARTISTS

W. CONOR
Bombing Practice

Catalogue of an exhibition of official war pictures circulated by the Ministry of Information by arrangement with the Museums Association. Second selection.

An Unconquerable People

The projection of 'the people's war' was one of the principal concerns of the MOI – not only to boost the morale of the Home Front, but also to show allies and nations overseas the unbreakable spirit of the British people. An intrinsic part of this narrative was the role played during the Blitz by the Royal Family. On 13 September 1940, a Luftwaffe attack on Buckingham Palace provided a public relations triumph for King George VI and Queen Elizabeth, who were in residence at the time. The intelligence reports suggested that this attack led to a fresh bond between the people and their monarch, because now they saw that the King and Queen 'were in the front line too'.[22] *The British Empire's King and Queen* (Fig. 38) was a fifteen-page pamphlet about the royal couple, intended primarily for the British Empire, but which also sold well in Britain.

Referring to the 'human record of Royalty', the pamphlet provided illustrated examples of intimate Royal Family life mixed with civic duties and described them as 'living symbols of the evolution of a mighty Democracy – that of the British Commonwealth of Nations'. *The British Empire's King and Queen* made much of the Royal Family's decision to remain in residence in London and their services to the war effort – many of which are illustrated.[23] Its summary is particularly revealing:

> *Ever since the war was wantonly inflicted on the peoples of the world, Their Majesties have gone about more than ever among their own folk, sharing too the experience of having their own home bombed and, like millions of their people, carrying on the work undaunted. Of all the lies which the enemy has uttered, none was more despicable than that which depicted the Royal Family as having fled overseas for safety! …[24] Through their ceaseless devotion to duty, and their simple humanity, the Empire's King and Queen have become living symbols of the British nation's unity, and an inspiring example of noble human attainment.*

There can be little doubt, from the evidence of all the reports that the MOI were receiving, that the presence of the King and Queen in London and their tours of bomb-

38
The British Empire's King and Queen.
(PP/12/8A)

39
A poster and leaflet in the 'For Freedom' series, showing the Royal Family solidly behind the war effort after leading their people in a National Day of Prayer.
(PP/BS51/29)

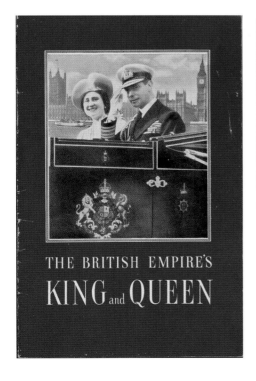

THEIR MAJESTIES THE KING AND QUEEN WITH PRINCESSES ELIZABETH AND MARGARET ROSE
leaving Crathie Church, near Balmoral, after attending Divine Service on a National Day of Prayer

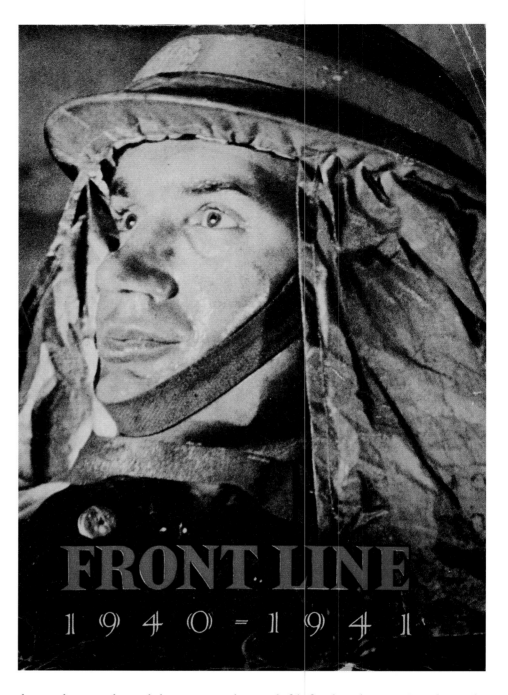

*Front Line 1940–1941:
The Official Story of the
Civil Defence of Britain.*
(Private collection)

damaged areas enhanced the respect and warmth felt for them by most British people.
In a radio broadcast on 23 September, King George VI announced a new honour, the
George Cross, specifically intended to mark the gallantry and heroism of civilians. It was
to rank with the Victoria Cross and to be supplemented by a more widely distributed
award, the George Medal.

In 1942 the MOI produced an illustrated booklet, *Front Line 1940–1941: The
Official Story of the Civil Defence of Britain*, intended to be a comprehensive account
(containing 159 pages) of the 'fall of bombs and what was done about them by the men
and women on the ground' (Fig. 40). The Blitz, according to this document, was aimed
at the people as the Luftwaffe sought a knock-out blow. Morale-boosting photographs
showed that, in spite of bomb damage, the milk continued to be delivered and the post
collected, and that life in the shelters had its compensations – namely a new
companionship. In a summary entitled 'The Achievement of the Many', *Front Line*

pulled no punches in summarising the price paid by Britain's civilians in defending their island:

> *During the air attack on Great Britain some 190,000 bombs were dropped up until the end of 1941; 43,667 civilians were killed – 20,178 men, 17,262 women, and 5,460 children under the age of 16 years. The seriously injured numbered 5,038; 4,061 of them children. The damage has been sufficiently indicated in the preceding pages. The failure to disturb civil morale or to reduce appreciably the flow of production was complete. The great German air offensive against the back kitchens and front parlours of Britain met with total defeat. … It was the conscious privilege of the British people to teach him (Hitler) two lessons – the earliest of all those which the free peoples of the world will yet enforce upon him. The first was the Battle of Britain, when the finest squadrons of his chief weapon of terror were brought low by lesser numbers of freer men. The second was the defeat of his air bombardment by a general and widespread power of thought, action and endurance, based upon the clear consciousness of a just cause.*[25]

Although *Front Line* was published in 1942, the very fact that the MOI felt confident enough to commission an 'official' history suggests that, following the Battle of Britain and the Blitz – and now with America's entry into the war – the worst appeared to be over and victory was in sight. On 12 April 1941, Winston Churchill, after inspecting the bomb damage inflicted during the Blitz, commented:

> *I see the damage done by the enemy attacks; but I also see, side by side with the devastation and amid the ruins, quiet, confident, bright and smiling eyes, beaming with consciousness of being associated with a cause far higher and wider than any human or personal issue. I see the spirit of an unconquerable people.*

It is fitting that this quotation is set large on the back cover of *Front Line*.

Conclusion

Official propaganda encouraged citizens to see themselves as 'soldiers in the front line'. As early as September 1940, Home Intelligence stressed 'that everything should be done to encourage this opinion of themselves' and suggested that: 'It might be a small but extremely telling point if, for instance, the dead were buried with Union Jacks on their coffins, or if the Services were represented at their funerals.'[26] Civil defence served many purposes beside preparing sections of the community for the work of rescue, and providing welfare in the wake of bombing raids. Mobilisation for civil defence was socially inclusive and it imposed social discipline through regular routines of air raid drills, and through the blackout. Civil defence training, which extended even to schoolchildren, mimicked the training practised by the regular forces, and encouraged civil defenders to identify themselves directly with the war effort.[27] Mobilisation of labour resources and essential supplies, in what amounted to industrial conscription in all but name, transformed the Home Front into a large war camp in which all citizens were supposed to share in the hardship and sacrifices that total war required of them. The national community became an exclusive zone, committed to the search for national victory. Propaganda proclaimed the will to fight to the end, defiance of the enemy, and a triumphant celebration of the ordinary people of Britain. The Home Secretary, Herbert Morrison, reflected in 1945 on the large civil defence forces for which he had been responsible; he described them as a 'citizen army' composed of 'rank-and-file warriors, men and women alike'.[28]

NOTES

1   For a detailed analysis of the machinery of compulsion and the introduction of industrial conscription in all but name, see N. Stammers, *Civil Liberties in Britain During the Second World War* (London, 1983), 163–94.

2   TNA, INF 1/725, Home Publicity Enquiry paper, May 1939, also quoted in I. McLaine, *Ministry of Morale. Home Front Morale and the Ministry of Information in World War II* (London, 1979), 30.

3   The MOI's attitude at this time was summed up by Sir Kenneth Clark in a policy paper of January 1941. TNA. INF 1/849: Policy Committee paper 'Propaganda Directed Exclusively to Women', 23 January 1941.

4   M. Connelly, *We Can Take It! Britain and the Memory of the Second World War* (Harlow, 2004), 173.

5   For a more detailed discussion of *Millions Like Us*, see J. Chapman, *The British at War. Cinema, State and Propaganda, 1939–1945* (London, 1998), 212–15.

6   The booklet was actually authored by Arthur Wauters, who had been Minister of Labour and Social Welfare and then Minister of Information in Hubert Pierlot's Belgian government until 5 January 1940. In June 1940 he was appointed Head of the Government Information Service of the Belgian government in exile, which operated through the British Ministry of Information. The MOI often commissioned 'foreign' observers to produce propaganda material in order to provide a wider perspective of 'how others see us' – suggesting by implication that this could not possibly be perceived as 'propaganda'.

7   J. Keegan, *The Second World War* (London, 1980), 170–8. For more recent works see R. Overy, *War and Economy in the Third Reich* (Oxford, 1994); A. Tooze, *The Wages of Destruction: The Making and Breaking of the Nazi Economy* (London, 2006); and G. Field, *Blood, Sweat, and Toil: Remaking the British Working Class, 1939–1945* (Oxford, 2011).

8   The weapon being constructed on the front cover of *Factories for Freedom* appears to be a howitzer 4.5 (a short-barrelled weapon which lobbed shells on to targets, instead of firing straight at them).

9   Much of this information comes from S. Nicholas, *The Echo of War: Home Front Propaganda and the Wartime BBC, 1939–45* (Manchester, 1996), 133–7.

10   Quoted in A. White, *BBC at War* (London, undated but probably 1942), 23–4.

11   During World War II conscripts who had signed up believing they would fight the Nazis were instead drafted to work in more than 1,800 coal pits nationwide, selected by an independent lottery. This did not always go down well with regular miners.

12   A. Calder, *The People's War* (London, 1997; orig. 1969), 395. For a more detailed analysis of the history of the trade unions in World War II, see M. Davis, *Comrade or Brother?: A History of the British Labour Movement* (London, 2nd edn, 2009).

13   It was not unusual for the MOI to turn down Communist Party offers to provide speakers for official campaigns to increase production. In September 1941, for example, the Ministry informed Harry Pollitt, the party leader: 'I am to inform you that, having regard to the Communist Party's previous attitude towards the national war effort, the Minister does not feel that it is open to him to invite speakers drawn from the Communist Party to participate in this proposed campaign for increased production.' Quoted in *Persuading the People* (HMSO, 1995), 29.

14   The official report into the Bethnal Green disaster was suppressed by Herbert Morrison at the time as being detrimental to morale.

15   TNA, INF 1/292, H.I. Weekly Intelligence Reports, 2–9 March 1943.

16   Home Intelligence reports for 31 July 1940 recorded that: 'houses of Pacifists were stoned in Coventry, where City Council had decided not to discharge conscientious objectors'. However, the Home Intelligence report of 29 August 1940, recorded 'some nervousness … but generally speaking, morale appears to be best in those places which have been heavily bombed', and this appears to be the overriding response across the country. TNA, INF 1/292, H.I. Weekly Intelligence Reports, 26–31 August 1940.

17   TNA, INF 1/292, H.I. Weekly Intelligence Reports, 17 August 1940.

18   For two interesting interpretations of the Blitz, see C. Ponting, *1940: Myth and Reality* (London, 1990) and M. Smith, *Britain and 1940* (London, 2000).

19   *London Can Take It!* was primarily produced by the MOI to influence opinion in the neutral United States. It was retitled *Britain Can Take It!* for its domestic release. It proved popular with both American and British film audiences. A Mass-Observation report noted that it was 'the most frequently commented-upon film, and received nothing but praise'. Quoted in Chapman, *The British at War*, 99.

20   'Wimpy' was a Wellington bomber that 'has been Right Round the World, AND has rescued a 'Very Famous American General, AND has a big Gold Bomb on his nose signed by the President of the United States of America'. The anthropomorphising of the bomber, complete with waistcoat button and eyes in the engine

nacelles, was undertaken by the political cartoonist of the *Daily Mirror*, Philip Zec. *Wimpy the Wellington* (London, 1942), 30. See K. Agnew and G. Fox, *Children at War* (London, 2001), 23–4.

21   See *Art from the Second World* War (Imperial War Museum, 2007). For a wider discussion of the role played by the arts as propaganda in World War II, see D. Welch, 'The Culture of War: Ideas, Arts, and Propaganda' in R. Overy (ed), *The Oxford Illustrated History of World War II* (Oxford, 2005), 373–401.

22   TNA, INF 1/292, H.I. Weekly Intelligence Reports, 9–14 September 1940.

23   Home Intelligence reported that recent newsreels showing the King and Queen visiting victims of air raids met with spontaneous 'warm applause'. TNA, INF 1/292, H.I. Weekly Intelligence Reports, 23 September 1940.

24   Rumours of the Royal Family leaving the country continued to be circulated. In June 1940, for example, Home Intelligence reported 'a recrudescence of the statement that the two Princesses are in Canada in spite of today's photographs!' TNA, INF 1/292, H.I. Weekly Intelligence Reports, 12 June 1940.

25   *Front Line 1940–41. The Official Story of the Civil Defence of Britain* (MOI/HMSO, 1942), 158–9.

26   TNA, INF 1/292, H.I. Weekly Intelligence Reports, 9–14 September 1940.

27   See R. Overy, 'Front Line II: Civilians at War' in R. Overy (ed), *The Oxford Illustrated History of World War II* (Oxford, 2005), 293–321.

28   For a wider discussion of the British Home Front in World War II see H. Jones, *British Civilians in the Front Line: Air Raids, Productivity and Wartime Culture, 1939–1945* (Manchester, 2006);

S. Grayzel, *At Home and Under Fire: Air Raids and Culture in Britain from the Great War to the Blitz* (Cambridge, 2012).

'Existing opinion is not to be contradicted,
but utilised. Each individual harbours a large
number of stereotypes and established
tendencies; from this arsenal the propagandist
must select those easiest to mobilise, those
which will give the greatest strength to
the action he wants to precipitate.'

JACQUES ELLUL
PROPAGANDA. THE FORMATION OF MEN'S ATTITUDES (1965)

CHAPTER FOUR

Know Your Enemy

Nazi Germany and Fascist Italy

No protracted war can be fought without attempting to rouse the people against the enemy. In 1939 there was less need than in 1914 to justify Britain's declaration of war against Hitler's Germany. Initially, the Ministry of Information(MOI) pointed out that Britain had done its utmost to avoid war and that the conflict was wholly the fault of aggression from Germany's Nazi rulers (see Fig. 1). At first the British approach was to make a distinction between National Socialism and its leaders, and the ordinary population.[1] As the war escalated in the spring of 1940, the MOI accepted that there should be no separation between the German people and Nazism, and launched its 'Anger Campaign' designed to draw public attention to the brutality of the Nazi regime. Literature detailing Nazi atrocities and human rights violations formed the staple content of MOI posters, leaflets, and pamphlets.

Germany's dramatic military successes in Europe, leading to the Dunkirk evacuation and the fall of France in 1940, had to be explained, and gave rise to the belief that a 'Fifth Column' had been operating as an advance guard for the German army. On 11 July the MOI launched a radio, press, and poster campaign urging the public to refrain from spreading rumours and to join Britain's 'Silent Column'. As a last resort they were asked to inform the police about indiscreet characters such as 'Mr Secrecy Hush-Hush', 'Miss Leaky Mouth', or 'Mr Pride in Prophecy'. The notion of the 'enemy from within' was behind the MOI's 'Careless Talk Costs Lives' campaign (Fig. 41) and it featured in numerous films, such as *Miss Grant Goes to the Door* (1940), *The Next of Kin* (1941), and *Went the Day Well* (1942). Films and posters about Nazi spies were ideal for propaganda purposes. They were also used to demonise the Germans as the 'same old Hun'.

Stereotypes invariably come ready-made, having evolved, whether consciously or subconsciously, over a considerable period of time. This was particularly the case with the anti-German motif in British propaganda. During World War I, stories of German treachery and atrocities predominated. In the years immediately following that war, various investigations, particularly in France and Britain, suggested that much of this atrocity propaganda was either false or exaggerated. As a result, atrocity propaganda was never used on the same scale in World War II (even when it would have been perfectly justified, as in the case of the Holocaust). The British took the view that Nazism itself was an atrocity. In fact, much of British propaganda in World War II was characterised by the use of humour to deflate the enemy.

In a series of broadcasts made on the BBC's overseas service in 1940, Sir Robert Vansittart, former Permanent Under Secretary at the Foreign Office, portrayed Germans as violent and aggressive, with Nazism being merely the latest manifestation of this national characteristic. The broadcast proved extremely popular, as did the pamphlet that followed, *Black Record: Germans Past and Present*. 'Vansittartism', as the phenomenon became known, suited well the MOI's Anger Campaign, in which it was pointed out that 'The Hun is at the gate. He will rage and destroy. He will slaughter women and children.'[2] In the face of a stream of pamphlets explaining the historical roots and antecedents of German barbarity – largely written by political refugees – some politicians expressed concern about the sheer vindictiveness of this propaganda, not least because it would make a settlement with Germany after the war all the more difficult. Noël Coward parodied those critics in his patriotic song 'Don't Let's be Beastly to the Germans'.

The MOI had initially decided that 'truth' should be the main weapon with which to attack the enemy in the minds of the public.[3] However, after the bitter and dramatic events in the summer and autumn of 1940, the MOI launched its Anger Campaign and British propaganda took a more drastic approach by emphasising the brutality of Nazi rule.[4] One publication in this vein published by the MOI was a pull-out pamphlet, *The*

41
Don't keep a diary. it might get into the enemy's hands. Part of the government's 'Careless Talk Cost Lives' campaign.
(PP/BS51/29)

Same Aggressor (Fig. 42), which drew a direct comparison between Imperial Germany under Kaiser Wilhelm II and Nazi Germany under Adolf Hitler. In 1914 the British stereotype of 'the Hun' provided a platform for British propaganda to launch a moral offensive against a culture portrayed as being founded on militaristic values. After 1940 the same stereotype was employed again to bring home to the population of Britain, and that of its allies, the unimaginable consequences of defeat:

> *Invasion, destruction, ruthlessness and hate, bursting over Europe in 1914 and again in 1939 on each occasion from the same sources, by the same people, with the same motives of greed, tyranny and conquest. … Murders in their own land by the thousand, and in other lands by the million, have attended the progress of the Nazis during the past eight years. They render it almost incredible that we should be living in the twentieth century. … It was the boast of Attila the Hun that no grass could grow where his hordes had trod. … As conducted by the Nazis, war is not fighting, but massacre.*

One detects within the MOI during this early period of the war an impatience and an implicit lack of confidence in the public – a belief that they were, according to Lord Macmillan, the Minister of Information, 'patient, long-suffering, slow to anger, slower still to hate'.[5] Although there was little evidence to support this view, it is true that there was nothing approaching the hysterically bellicose mood of the British in the early part of World War I. Nevertheless, the MOI deemed that there existed a dangerous complacency and that the working man in particular had little comprehension of the consequences of a Nazi victory and was, therefore, in need of a sharp dose of stiffening. Following the Dunkirk evacuation, an MOI pamphlet, *What Would Happen if Hitler Won*, posed the proposition that some people believed that Hitler would not 'bother with ordinary people like you and me: they think that everyday life here would carry on pretty much as usual'. On the contrary; the publication set out precisely what victory for Hitler would mean:

> *If Hitler won you couldn't make a joke in the pub without being afraid that a spy may not get you run in or beaten up; you could not talk freely in front of your children for fear that they might give you away (in Germany they are encouraged to); if you were a worker you would be at the mercy of your employer about hours and wages, for you would have no trade union.*

Another MOI publication, *NO!* (Fig. 43), drew an equally dramatic depiction of Nazi tyranny and reaffirmed that there could be no negotiation with Hitler. The dramatic front cover shows a red-hot swastika being burnt on the map of the world. This was a fight to the death:

> The despotic rule of a half-crazed Führer, the fantastic dreams of power with which he had in the past filled so many hysterical pages, became a horrible reality in Germany. … You cannot make terms with the tiger. It is YOU – or HE … you must kill him or cage him, before he kills you and yours after the manner of its kind.

During a five-month period from June to October 1940, the author J.B. Priestley made a series of ten-minute radio broadcasts on Sunday nights for the BBC General Overseas service, entitled *Postscripts*. He recorded his impressions of the developing conflict, while at the same describing the changing scenes around him. In the fourth of the *Postscripts*, aired on 23 June 1940, Priestley explored the two faces of Germany. He had always responded to what he called the 'bright face' of Germany: music, art, and beautiful landscapes. But 'after the Nazis came … the bright face had gone, and in its place was the vast dark face with its broken promises and endless deceit, its swaggering Storm Troopers and dreaded Gestapo, its bloodstained basements'. Priestley's language was robust and simple and an audience of 10 million listened weekly to his broadcasts. Priestly also wrote a wall poster for the MOI, printed in millions, on the frightening nature of the German enemy facing the people of Europe:[6]

> They are Europe's secret beasts, roused to senseless fury. It is all Europe's mission to cower them and cage them today, as all Europe has had to do before. … The Hun is at the gate. He will rage and destroy. He will slaughter the women and children. But in the end, he will run from the men as he has always run in the past. … Out then and kill … the extermination of the wild animal let loose on Europe is the plain business of Europe's citizens.

Such propaganda emphasised the brutality of Nazi rule in order to stir up anger, but it was important that it did not at the same time instil fear into the population and, as a consequence, destroy all hope of final victory. Accordingly, the MOI buttressed the fear factor by providing a more positive spin on events. For example in *The Same Aggressor*, the liturgy of German crimes is juxtaposed with a cartoon of Winston Churchill (taken from *Punch*) portraying him as St George 'The Dragon Slayer'. The text below the cartoon reads: 'But, no matter how the battle ebbs and flows, one thing is undeniable, and neither words nor deeds from Germany can change it: Britain is growing stronger everyday.' In a veiled reference to the French capitulation, it concluded: 'No longer is Germany faced only by the weak, who can be cowed into insensibility.' *NO!* juxtaposed the conflict as a fight between the free world versus the slave world: 'NO! The final victory of the forces of Freedom will ensure that the Nazi dream of a slave world shall never come to pass.' By the time of this publication, Britain could also draw comfort from the fact that it was not fighting Nazism alone. The back cover of the pamphlet reassuringly proclaimed:

> However long the road, however beset by pitfalls, defeats, delays, the peoples of the greatest Commonwealth and Empire the world has ever known fight on with great-hearted Allies and friends for the final liberation of mankind. All that they have … All that they know, all that they can, will be given, will be applied, will be done to that glorious end.

Literature about Nazi atrocities and human rights violations formed a staple diet of MOI leaflets and pamphlets. The Nazi educational system and the manipulation of young children came in for particular attention. *Children into Ruffians: The New Nazi Education* (Fig. 44) is a sixteen-page pamphlet, translated into several languages, which explained

43 (overleaf)
NO!
(PP/16/12L)

"However long the road, however beset by pitfalls, defeats, delays, the peoples of the greatest Commonwealth and Empire the world has ever known fight on with great-hearted Allies and friends for the final liberation of mankind. All that they have . . . all that they know, all that they can, will be given, will be applied, will be done to that glorious end."

how German youth were indoctrinated. The cover shows a jackboot crushing the paraphernalia of learning. The all-embracing nature of the new, radical, Nazi education system is outlined inside with a quote from Dr Ley, the Nazi Minister of Labour:

> *We start with the child when he is three years old. As soon as he begins to think, he gets a little flag put in his hand; then follows the school, Hitler Youth, the SA and military training. We do not let him go; when adolescence is past the Arbeitsfront takes him up again and does not release him till he dies* **whether he likes it or not**.

As for girls, 'the one absolute aim must be towards future motherhood'. The aim of the pamphlet is to demonstrate how innocent children are turned into ruffians and bullies who wish to dominate other cultures. Headings include: 'Each child is but a unit in the national stock-farm'; 'Nazi children have their own religion – Worship of the Führer'; 'Even school books dwell on death and destruction'; 'Shall this madness contaminate the whole earth?' The back cover includes a nihilistic children's marching song with the heading 'Learning and Culture in Utter Eclipse'.

While the MOI invoked the 'ideology' of National Socialism to discredit the regime, it also had to articulate specific British core values that represented both the antithesis of Nazism and something worth fighting for. In practice this generally meant focusing on long-standing values of decency and tolerance built on the platform of Christian humanism. The Religions Division within the MOI wished to avoid public criticism that the churches were being used as channels of official propaganda; but nevertheless it was determined to impart 'a real conviction of the Christian contribution to our civilization and of the essential anti-Christian character of Nazism'.[7] To this end, the MOI commissioned a number of simple but visually stunning images that employed stirring icons and symbols of Christianity's power to conquer the Nazis. In one famous poster ('I Believe …', Fig. 45) the symbol of the Cross is juxtaposed over the (black) swastika, and in another the Sword of Justice and the Cross is invoked in God's name to defeat the barbarian enemy ('O God Our Help …', Fig. 46).

The images to be found in these posters suggest that Britain and her allies were waging a religious crusade against anti-Christian forces of evil. In fact the MOI had asked Church leaders to issue a joint manifesto to this effect. When this manifesto was eventually published on December 1940, it proved to be a severe disappointment to the Ministry. Instead of casting Britain in the role of Christian warrior as the MOI had requested, it made no mention of Nazism but rather talked in general terms about inequality and the need to base a future peace on strong religious and spiritual foundations.[8] The MOI, in contrast, had few reservations about characterising the conflict as a 'religious war' and actively encouraged publishers to produce material that affirmed Britain's Christianity, which, in turn could be used to attack Nazism. As with the literature on Nazi education, the focus was on how Nazi Germany was undergoing an anti-Christian form of indoctrination. *They would destroy the Church of God* (Figs 47, 48) is typical of publications in this genre. It set visually powerful images against a text that accused the Nazis of paganism, Führer-worship, and the perversion of children's education. It begins with a catechism under the heading 'Hitler Speaks':

> *Thou shalt believe in me.*
> *Thou shalt believe that whatever helps the German race to world domination is right.*
> *Thou shalt believe that whatever I do, and say, or command, is right.*
> *Thou shalt have no other God.*

The pamphlet, probably published in late 1941, contains a veritable liturgy of quotations from Hitler and other Nazi leaders, chosen to demonstrate the manner in which Hitler was intent on destroying freedom of thought and worship: 'I take the little children – and make them mine'; 'The Cross must fall if Germany is to live'; 'One is either a German or a Christian. You cannot be both'; and 'Hitler is a new, a greater, a more

44
Children into Ruffians:
The New Nazi Education.
(PP/7/15A)

45
I Believe.
(PP/BS51/29)

46
O God Our Help …
(PP/BS51/29)

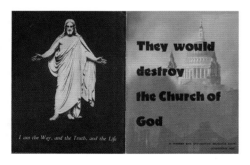

47 (middle left)
They would destroy the Church of God.
(PP/23/11L)

48 (left and detail opposite) 'I take the little children – and make them mine'. The Führer speaks in *They would destroy the Church of God.*
(PP/23/11L)

powerful Jesus Christ. Our God, our Pope is Adolf Hitler'. The final page reproduced the image of the poster of the Cross over the swastika (see Fig. 45) with the words; 'Arise in GOD's strength, to build a Christian future'.

The MOI was quick to expose the Nazi persecution of individual German clerics, such as Pastor Niemoller and Bishop Clemens August Graf von Galen, who had questioned Nazi rule. Fig. 49 is a reproduction in full of the sermon that Bishop Galen of Münster delivered on 13 July 1941, in which he denounced Gestapo lawlessness and the persecution of the Church. On 3 August 1941 he revealed how the Nazis' so-called euthanasia campaign killed the innocent sick, while their families were misled by false death notices. Bishop Galen's disclosures struck a responsive chord and copies of the sermons were distributed throughout the Reich. The BBC made propaganda capital out of it by means of numerous broadcasts, the RAF dropped copies of the sermon over Germany, and the story made the front cover of the *Daily Express.*[9] In the reproduction in Fig. 49, which the MOI framed as 'Gestapo v. Christianity', Galen ended his

49
'The Gestapo v.
Christianity'.
(PP/10/6A)

condemnation of the Gestapo's terror tactics on its own citizens by declaring: 'Therefore, as a German, as an honourable citizen, as a representative of the Christian religion and as a Catholic Bishop, I cry aloud: We demand justice!'

Much 'religious' propaganda targeted Christians, and many of the publications (including Galen's sermons) were reprinted in several languages and distributed to Protestant and Catholic Europe under occupation. But, of course, the British Empire had a large Muslim population and a number of Muslim nations remained neutral in the war. How British propaganda targeted Muslims and dealt with Islam is discussed in Chapter 6. Much more sensitive was the plight of European Jews. A Jewish section was set up in July 1941 as part of the Religions Division. However, its scope was circumscribed from the outset, confined almost exclusively to explaining Jewish religious life to Christian citizens and otherwise largely addressing itself to the Jewish community. Why, then, did propaganda place much greater emphasis on the persecution of the Christian churches in Europe than on the plight of European Jews under Nazi domination? Such questions are outside the scope of this work, but the MOI almost certainly drew back from revealing the full horror of the fate of Jews in Europe – even after December 1942 when the full facts were known[10] – because of the prejudice that was widely reported in the Home Intelligence Reports. Anti-Semitism was a regular feature of the weekly reports, in which Jews were accused of fleeing from Britain to the United States, controlling the black market, avoiding war work and military service, and exhibiting truculent behaviour in food queues.[11] The legacy of the dissemination of Hun atrocity stories during World War I is another factor. Such atrocity propaganda had been widely believed at the time, but in the interwar period many felt that they had been duped and came to associate propaganda with government lies. The negative impact of propaganda on political behaviour had such a profound effect that in World War II, when the British government attempted belatedly to educate the population about the existence of Nazi extermination camps, it was not immediately believed.

The notion of freedom of worship is closely associated with freedom of thought. British propaganda not surprisingly devoted much of its propaganda to highlighting how the Nazis had systematically destroyed the rule of law and free speech. On 14 August 1941, the Atlantic Charter was unveiled following a meeting in Newfoundland between Churchill and the US President Franklin D. Roosevelt. Signed four months before America entered the war, it was considered a pivotal policy statement consisting of eight articles that defined the Allied goals for the post-war world. Following this joint declaration, *Truth in Chains* (Fig. 50) was published to highlight the extent to which the 'free' press of nations occupied by the Nazis had now been shackled. Its striking cover consists of a man constructed out of newspaper cuttings from occupied states, dragging a ball and chain. Reprinted on the back cover is Article 6 from the Atlantic Charter – and the magnanimous implications for Germany 'after the final destruction of Nazi tyranny' – guaranteeing 'men in all lands' freedom from fear and want. The MOI was also keen to remind the British people and those in the occupied territories of the brave work undertaken by the resistance press. *Revolt in the Dark* (Fig. 51) sets out in detail 'the heroes behind Europe's underground press' who brought hope from 'the world outside their imprisoned frontiers'. The back cover consisted of a large 'V' for Victory symbol (see below) and an overlapping text that exhorted all citizens: 'Think always, work always for the defeat of the forces which would make of all free men a race of slaves.'

Major themes such as 'the Nazis versus civilisation' and 'the free world versus the slave world' continued in British propaganda throughout the war. On New Year's Day 1942, President Roosevelt, Prime Minister Churchill, Maxim Litvinov of the Soviet Union, and T.V. Soong of China signed a short document which later came to be known as the United Nations Declaration, and the next day the representatives of twenty-two other nations added their signatures. In a MOI leaflet (and poster) following the United Nations Declaration, World War I provided the template of the German beast destroying

ARTICLE 6 OF THE ATLANTIC CHARTER

"After the final destruction of Nazi tyranny, they hope to see established a peace which will afford to all nations the means of dwelling in safety within their own boundaries, and which will afford assurance that all the men in all the lands may live out their lives in freedom from fear and want."

Franklin D. Roosevelt

Winston S. Churchill

PP/23/40A

TRUTH IN CHAINS

50
Truth in Chains.
(PP/23/40A)

51
Revolt in the Dark.
(PP/22/31A)

THE HEROES behind Europe's underground press spread words of hope to the oppressed of the imprisoned continent

99   **KNOW YOUR ENEMY**

civilised values, ready to be revived and applied to the Nazi regime (Fig. 52). *Blitzkrieg* warfare delivered a suitable accompaniment of a war machine trampling over Europe. The final page of the leaflet warned: 'The Battle of France was lost. The Battle of Britain was won. We are now engaged in the last and most vital battle of all – the Battle of the World'.

British propaganda also contrasted the regimentation of life under Nazi rule with bucolic, peaceful Britain. The British way of life, imbued with values worth fighting for, figured prominently in all aspects of propaganda. Film documentaries were especially adept at constructing poetic images and sounds that conveyed a deep sense of nationhood and national identity. *The Heart of Britain* (1941) examined the effects of the war in the provinces and made imaginative use of words and music (including Handel's 'Hallelujah Chorus' performed by the Huddersfield Choral Society). *Word for Battle* (1941) matched inspired images of the nation at war to inspirational literature (Camden, Milton, Blake, Browning, Kipling) and historical speeches (Churchill and Lincoln), spoken by Laurence Olivier. *Listen to Britain* (1942) dispensed with commentary altogether and instead used music and natural sound to capture the spirit of Britain and its people. In the *NO!* pamphlet (Fig. 43, 53), symbols of 'Britain's ancient, progressive culture' are juxtaposed with a rallying text: 'ALL Britons will rally to the call – crying with a united voice IT SHALL NOT HAPPEN HERE!'

52
The Battle for Civilisation.
(PP/4/6A)

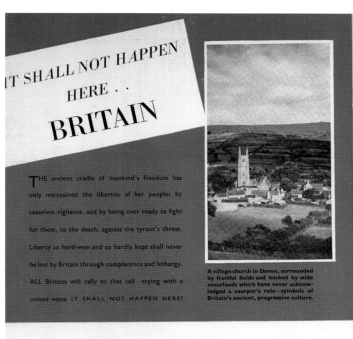

53
NO! 'A village church in Devon, surrounded by fruitful fields and backed by wide moorlands which have never acknowledged a usurper's rule – symbols of Britain's ancient, progressive culture.'
(PP/16/12L)

LIFE IN BRITAIN TO-DAY

A TYPICAL BRITISH VILLAGE

Painted by S. R. Badmin

Whoever thinks of Britain instinctively visualises the green British countryside, with its winding lanes, hedgerows of shrubs and wild flowers, its birds, gnarled and twisted trees, and its villages. Whoever wishes to find the best in Britain should seek the villages, for it is in them that the soul of Britain is to be found. The sturdy yeomen who for generations have wrested a living from the soil are specimens of British character at its best.

The picture above shows a typical village nestling in the shelter of surrounding hills, its soil, from the silent ruins of the moated castle on the distant hill, across the fields, to the village itself, steeped in history. The church, on which the village is centred, contains traces of historic events that go back for generations, while the tombstones in the church-

yard are silent witnesses, chronicles down the centuries of those who helped to plan and lay the foundations of village life.

Far from the cities and towns, the village is self-contained, but contact with the distant towns is made by the motor omnibus service. The small village shops cater for every need and there exists that personal and friendly feeling which is so typical of village life. Where there is such a small community with vast areas to plough and farm and so many cattle to tend it is surprising that the people can find time for leisure, yet an undying rivalry with other villages exists, that shows itself when the inter-village cricket matches are played on the green.

The local inn, built hundreds of years ago and once the hideout of highwaymen, is in the nature of a club where the men of the village meet

and discuss various topics. Although the modern tractor has revolutionised farming life, the old craftsmen remain. Each village, with its wheelwright, blacksmith, and thatcher, gives ample evidence of the undying skill that is handed down from generation to generation.

But life in the village has not lagged with the passing of the years. The village school-teaching covers a wide curriculum; radio has brought the village in close touch with world affairs ; the motor-car has shortened distances and opened up the countryside with all its beauties to millions. Even so the charm of village life is something that remains stable and dependable. Although the younger generations of village folk have travelled more and seen more of the world than their forefathers, these yeomen of Britain remain unspoiled by modern life and their feet remain planted firmly on Britain's soil.

O.P.D. 377/18/9/3.

54
*Life in Britain To-day:
A Typical British Village.*
(PP/BS51/29)

In fact a whole series of posters and handbills were produced to remind people of the ordinary scenes of British life that should not be taken for granted. 'Life in Britain To-day' was a series of highly romanticised and lavishly detailed productions full of national symbols and icons of everyday life, including *A Typical British Village* (Fig. 54) and *A Typical British Royal Pageant* (Fig. 55). Britain as a sunny arcadia was a recurring theme in much official propaganda. Core British values such as a love of the British countryside, a sense of history and culture, and a deep-rooted admiration for the common man were constantly juxtaposed throughout the war as the antithesis of Nazism.

Humour was widely used in World War II, because civilian morale needed tonics, such as the comedy radio programmes by Arthur Askey ('I theng-yew'), and Richard 'Stinker' Murdoch's *Band Wagon* or Tommy Handley's *It's That Man Again* (*ITMA*). Production posters in the factories often adopted a humorous approach, as did propaganda about careless talk, good hygiene, growing vegetables, and promoting salvage. Among the notable artists employed by the MOI for propaganda was Cyril Kenneth Bird (Fougasse), the cartoonist whose deflating, humorous, 'Careless Talk' posters were among the most popular of the war. One showed two garrulous housewives sitting in a bus, with Hitler and Göring seated behind them listening to their gossip.

LIFE IN BRITAIN TO-DAY

A TYPICAL BRITISH ROYAL PAGEANT

London is, on the whole, a somewhat matter-of-fact city. Normally it is essentially a city of work — full of the bustle and activity of millions of people going about their every-day business life. But on rare occasions the sober grey streets of London become a background for a brilliant procession, impressive and perhaps unique in its magnificence and traditional pomp. Above is an artist's impression of one of these parades. The procession is seen passing down Whitehall, the famous street in which are situated the British Foreign Office, the Admiralty and various other Ministries.
The King and Queen, dressed in their royal robes, ride in the golden Royal Coach, drawn by eight pure-bred horses. The postillions, in their ornamental liveries, walk beside the horses. The Yeoman of the Guard carrying halberds march at the side of the coach and behind it, followed by the officers of the

King's Household, a mounted escort of which also precedes the Royal Coach. These ceremonial processions are not intended as demonstrations of the power and authority of the sovereign. The splendour with which he is on special occasions surrounded is part of a symbolism which has served well the unity of the British Commonwealth of Nations.
It is not the majesty of rulership that is proclaimed by these processions. These spectacles, no matter what official occasion they celebrate, are impressive reminders of the existence and significance of British institutions, and what they imply in rights and privileges. Every British citizen has a share in the affairs of the State; he is not merely a subject, doing obediently what he is told to do. The historical character of these processions recalls to the mind the long growth of British institutions, and the long period of time — of which the

British are justly proud — during which those institutions have been functioning with efficiency. The Royal Coach still in use was built in 1761, when Britain was already a constitutional monarchy. The King, who occupies the central position in these displays, figures in them as a living symbol. He holds his office by life-tenure: he is the descendant of a venerable line of British sovereigns: he therefore symbolises stability of the British order. The British people enjoy these occasional processions with their music, colour and pageantry. They derive from them an enhanced pride in their country, their institutions and themselves, a more vivid appreciation of the reality and value of their free democratic institutions, and an increased reverence for those, who in the past, fought and worked to make Great Britain the trusted centre of a modern Commonwealth.

The most popular, and most outrageous, radio programme was *ITMA*, with Handley as the Minister for Aggravation and Mysteries, housed next to the Office of Twerps. The characters became larger than life and their catchphrases were etched into the fabric of everyday life: Funf the spy (Jack Train speaking into a glass tumbler), Ali Oop the saucy postcard vendor, Left the Gangster and his sidekick Sam Scam, the bibulous Colonel Chinstrap, the polite handymen Claude and Cecile ('After you, Claude … No, after *you* Cecile'), and the endearing Mrs Mopp ('Can I do you now, sir?') whose very name passed into the language as a synonym for 'cleaner'. The show was not afraid to mock the Nazis. Typical of the risqué language was Handley's opening line in the first wartime broadcast:

> Tommy: 'Heil folks, it's Mein Kampf *again. Sorry, I should* say Hello, folks, it's that MAN again! *That was a Goebbled version, a bit doctored. I usually go all goosey when I can't follow my proper-gander …'*

The show proved a great success; it became known that *ITMA* was the King's favourite programme and in 1942 a private performance was given at Windsor Castle for Princess Elizabeth's sixteenth birthday. The cast also toured factories and service bases. *ITMA*

55
Life in Britain To-day:
A Typical British Royal Pageant.
(PP/BS51/29)

found a place in people's hearts because it punctured pomposity.[12]

The commercial cinema was especially adept at using humour to get across messages on behalf of the government. The MOI sensibly recognised this – albeit after repeated promptings by Mass-Observation, born of its many surveys, which showed that humour was an important weapon in the propagandist's armoury in waging total war. Accordingly cinema stars such as Tommy Trinder comically savoured the delights of British restaurants in *Eating Out with Tommy Trinder* (1941), Arthur Askey warned of the number of working days lost through spreading 'coughs and sneezes' in *The Nose Has It* (1942), and Will Hay hilariously demonstrated the right and wrong ways to deal with incendiary bombs in *Go to Blazes* (1942). Humour was also employed to deflate the enemy. In 1941, film-maker Charles Ridley cleverly re-edited for the MOI real footage of goose-stepping Nazi soldiers at Nuremberg (taken from Leni Riefenstahl's film of the 1934 Nazi Party Congress, *Triumph of the Will*) to the popular tune of 'The Lambeth Walk'. At the beginning of the film, which was entitled *Germany Calling* (and also shown as a newsreel), the narrator exclaims: 'I'm going to show you a showman that we all hate … and it's going to be in the form of a ballet – a *Panzer* ballet. It's entitled "Retreat from Moscow" and it's going to be done to the Lambeth Walk.' Ridley chose this music because members of the Nazi Party had called the tune 'Jewish mischief and animalistic hopping'. By speeding up the film, the incipient threat of the SS was diluted and their formations – directed by a preposterous-looking Hitler – rendered comical, in a silent-film tradition. The reduction of a frightening enemy to the level of visibility and ridicule, as in this lampooning of Hitler and his forces, is, in psychological terms, a means of achieving power over him. The British used a similar technique to undermine and humiliate Mussolini; for example, Alberto Calvacanti's 1940 documentary film *Yellow Caesar* was a highly effective piece of propaganda, which reinforced the impression of Mussolini as a clown.

56
L'Art de Mentir
(The Art of Lying).
French edition.
(PP/1/15)

While the MOI was (eventually) prepared to allow the commercial film industry to get on with what it knew best, namely entertainment, the Ministry made a conscious effort to commission anti-German publications with a humorous slant. This would also apply to propaganda destined for occupied Europe. A key theme in British propaganda was Hitler's failure to keep his word. In the little pocket book, *The Art of Lying*, a series of Nazi speeches and pronouncements are exposed as hypocritical by satirical cartoons on the facing page. The example in Fig. 56 is taken from the French translation and, like the cartoons of Fougasse, mocks the level of surveillance that Belgian and French citizens have to endure on an everyday level.

The fold-out booklet *Adolf Hitler's Friendship* (Fig. 57) states how the countries that Germany had occupied since 1938 were all promised Hitler's 'Eternal Friendship'. The final page is a cartoon from Illingworth (*Daily Mail*) that shows Hitler stabbing Stalin – who is still clinging to the Russo-German Pact – in the back while grinning: 'Forgive me comrade but it seemed *such* a good opportunity!'

Growing belief in an Allied victory is reflected in more exuberantly satirical pamphlets that became more confident in tone. *10 German Blunders* (Fig 58) is a simple booklet that exposes key military mistakes, and *The German Military Lexicon* lampoons the vocabulary of Nazi military might in retreat. The version in Fig. 59 is in Spanish. Propagandists also mocked mercilessly the perceived hypocrisy of the Nazi version of the German language. In a small booklet, *Nazi German in 22 Lessons* (Fig. 60), cartoonists drew sketches that would prove useful 'for all Führers, Fifth Columnists, Gauleiters and Quislings'. For example, 'My patience is exhausted' is translated as: 'I cannot get what I want by lying and deception. I shall therefore take by force.' 'No further territorial ambition' is a conversational phrase meaning: 'I intend to invade tomorrow.' Lampooning the power of Hitler and his forces in such a way could only have a positive psychological impact on its target audience because there was now a confident belief in ultimate victory.

57
Adolf Hitler's Friendship.
(PP/1/22)

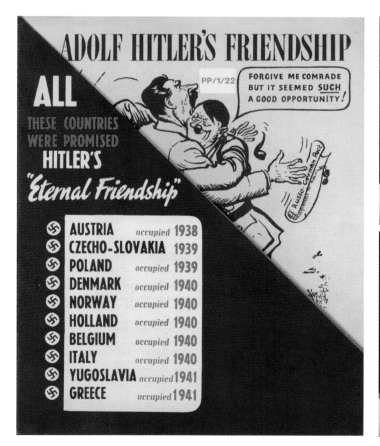

10th blunder

The belief in

German Victory in 1941 . . .

Hitler, Order of the Day
to the Army, 31/12/40

" Soldiers of the National Socialist
Army of the Great German Reich.
The year 1941 will bring the
consummation of the greatest victory
in our history."

" Frankfurter Zeitung." 6/4/41

" The Führer has recently done
something that he has never publicly
done before. He has mentioned a
date. And several others, Herr
Ribbentrop among them, have
emphatically stressed this date. By
the end of the year final victory will
be assured. This is no mere
consolation. It is a guarantee."

1st JANUARY 1942

—and the scene of the

victory Herr Hitler ?

In Russia ?

In Libya ?

Or perhaps Herr Ribbentrop

may be able to tell us ?

RETIRADA ESTRATÉGICA

Ingeniosa invención táctica alemana para obligar a
avanzar a sus enemigos. Cuando se ha conseguido esto,
es usualmente recomendable una segunda retirada
estratégica. De esta forma, astutamente, no se le deja
al enemigo otro recurso que el de avanzar todavía más.

18

STALINGRADO

El Führer ha dispuesto que el nombre de esta ciudad
sea suprimido de todos los mapas alemanes. ¡Ha
cesado, pues, de existir Stalingrado y puede con-
siderarse como una victoria alemana ! ¡Viva Hitler !

19

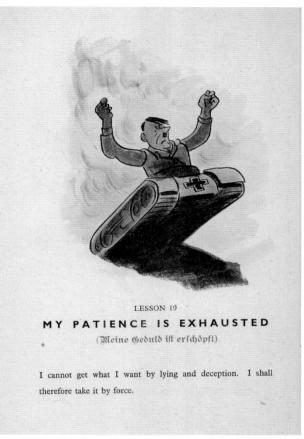

LESSON 19
MY PATIENCE IS EXHAUSTED
(Meine Geduld ift erfchöpft)

I cannot get what I want by lying and deception. I shall therefore take it by force.

58 (top opposite)
10 German Blunders.
(PP/10/16A)

59 (bottom opposite)
Lexico Militar Aleman
(The German Military Lexicon/Vocabulary).
Spanish edition.
(PP/10/34L)

60 (above and right)
Nazi German in 22 Lessons.
(PP/16/16A)

LESSON 20
NO FURTHER
TERRITORIAL AMBITION
(Keine weiteren territorialen Forderungen)

A conversational phrase meaning "I intend to invade to-morrow."

61
An extract from
It's A Long Way to London.
(PP/13/4A)

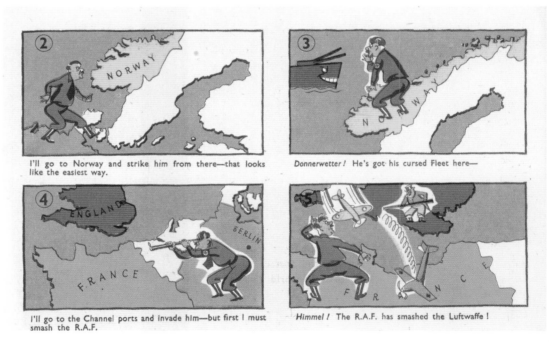

62 (opposite
and overleaf)
*Italy Stabs herself
in the BACK!*
'The Lesson'.
(PP/12/11L)

It's A Long Way to London (Fig. 61) is another pocket book containing seventeen episodes, which sketch various military engagements in the war. It starts with Hitler sitting on a volume of *Mein Kampf* dreaming of world domination. His only obstacle is a peace-loving John Bull in England, happily engaged with a spade and pipe; it ends, via the Battle of Britain, with Hitler being chased out of Egypt by John Bull, now brandishing a rifle, following the Nazi defeat in the North African campaign. The final sketch reveals a ragged Hitler looking back at the Channel separating Europe from Britain and lamenting: 'Funny! It didn't seem so far away on the map … when … I first … started!'

Humour was invariably used to pierce Italian bombastic claims. Mussolini and the Italian Fascists did not figure in British propaganda as much as the Nazis, probably because they were not so feared. Nevertheless, deeply held stereotypes of Italians (which

would be further reinforced by World War II), holding that they were cowardly, bombastic, and opportunist, surfaced from time to time. In the pamphlet *Italy Stabs herself in the BACK!* (Fig. 62), Mussolini is accused of taking his people to war against their will on the coat-tails of initial German military advances. His big mistake was to declare war on Britain. The lesson is graphically illustrated by the Italian cartoonist Garretto: in 1936 Italian 'gangster militarism' had set its sights on London, following Britain's ineffectual challenge to its illegal occupation of Abyssinia (parts of modern Ethiopia and Eritrea). By 1941 the British Lion had discovered its appetite and was now chasing Mussolini – depicted as a petrified sheep – all the way to Rome as the Allied Italian campaign was launched. The lesson is clear: 'History has shown that the disciples of brute force and the high priests of militarism must inevitably fail in a war against civilisation. The gangster always loses in the end.'[13] The lies and duplicity of the Axis powers was also satirised in a series of postcards entitled 'Words That Don't Ring True!' (Fig. 63) drawn by Nicholas Bentley. Like almost all of this material, the cards were translated into French, Dutch, Arabic, and Persian.

In July 1941 the BBC launched 'V for Victory', a propaganda campaign that encouraged listeners across Nazi-occupied Europe to show their support for the Allies by scrawling the letter V wherever they could. 'Splash the V from one end of Europe to

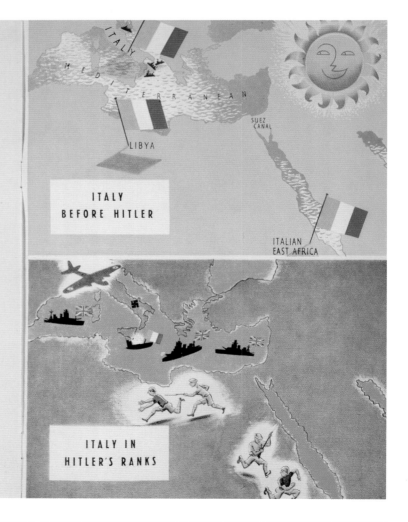

THE LESSON

THE Italian people did not want war. The idea of war was imposed on them by a man who gained control of Italy by unscrupulous and opportunistic methods, gathering around him a group of sycophants and careerists who were prepared to sell Italy for the price of their own advancement. Their foreign policy was a simple one—they wanted certain things which they proposed to get by threats, blackmail, or ultimately by force. To further their plans they formed an alliance with another State, inspired by the same cynical disregard for life and law. United by the creed of the sword, or the threat of the sword, as a solution to all problems, these two nations defied world opinion and renounced the respect of civilisation to pursue a war of unprincipled aggression.

At a later date they were joined by a third nation, Japan. Scared by the way the German war was going in Russia, flattered by Axis blandishments and frightened by Axis propaganda, seeing her last chance to strike already slipping away from her, Japan struck in the traditional Axis manner—the blow of treachery and cowardice. Her first blow has carried her far—as with Germany and Italy. The picture will be a different one in a year's time.

One of these countries—Italy—has already been brought to its knees. The gangster militarists who seized power now totter in their high places. Their bombastic threats have proved vain and empty, their wild military gambles have brought their people to ruin.

Their partner, Germany, is now floundering in a sea of bloody resistance and sullen opposition, as she plunges madly right and left in a desperate effort to free herself.

The lesson is plain. History has shown that the disciples of brute force and the high priests of militarism must inevitably fail in a war against civilisation. The gangster always loses in the end.

ITALY BEFORE HITLER

ITALIAN EAST AFRICA

LIBYA

SUEZ CANAL

ITALY IN HITLER'S RANKS

WORDS THAT DON'T RING TRUE!

"The relations between the Führer and the Duce are as cordial as those between two brothers."

"Asahi Shimbun" on Matsuoka's impression of his journey, quoted in a German broadcast to England, 23rd April, 1941.

WORDS THAT DON'T RING TRUE!

"Danger from British air attacks, according to experience so far, does not make any action necessary."

D.N.B. (German Official News Agency), 16th October, 1940.

WORDS THAT DON'T RING TRUE!

"Italy's main function consists in drawing the best British Imperial forces like a magnet."

Signor Gayda to the Press, 8th March, 1941.

63
Postcards from the series 'Words That Don't Ring True!'
(PP/25/72,73,90)

another', said the assured voice of the European service, Douglas Ritchie, who went by the on-air pseudonym of Colonel V. Britton. It was inspired by Victor de Laveleye, former Belgian Minister of Justice and director of the Belgian French-speaking broadcasts on the BBC, who urged his countrymen to use the letter V as a 'rallying emblem' since it is the first letter of the French word for victory (*victoire*), the Flemish and Dutch words for freedom (*vrijheid*) and, of course, the English word victory, making it a multi-national symbol of solidarity. Ritchie also realised that the three staccato notes and one long note at the start of Beethoven's 5th Symphony echoed the Morse code for the letter V (dot-dot-dot-dash). Ritchie made it the theme song for his radio programme and listeners began to replicate the sound any way they could as a symbol of resistance. Across occupied Europe, people daubed the V symbol and tapped out the sound to show their solidarity.

Although the 'V for Victory' campaign was aimed at the occupied nations, it took off in Britain. On 19 July 1941, Winston Churchill referred approvingly to the campaign in a speech, from which point he started using the V hand sign. Fig. 64 shows a fold-out booklet produced by the MOI as part of this campaign. The cartoons are so imaginatively conceived and crafted – playing on the 'V for Victory' theme – that no words were necessary. As with most of this material it was translated into many languages.

64
'V for Victory' —
fold-out booklet showing
there is no escape for Hitler.
(PP/25/127)

Imperial Japan

While Mussolini's Italy was viewed as morally bankrupt, the same level of barbarity as Nazi Germany was never attributed to it in British propaganda. The image of the Japanese was somewhat different. The Japanese enemy did not figure prominently in British propaganda – although the MOI would occasionally use Japanese anti-symbols in its overseas propaganda – examples of which can be found in Chapter 5. Anti-Japanese propaganda was a peripheral activity largely because the Pacific War was remote to a population preoccupied with the European conflict. Nevertheless, the government was concerned to educate the people on the nature of this specific enemy. In a pamphlet entitled *The Japanese People* (1943), Japan was characterised as follows:

> *Japan was ahead of Germany in the follow-my-führer dance macabre, but was also tremendously influenced by Germany. Amazing though the parallel between them is – in pseudo-religious, tribalism, aggression, brutality, false-swearing, density about other mentalities, contempt for women, contempt of freedom, contempt of the human spirit and negation of God …*[14]

65
Japanese Aggression.
The cover shows Chinese refugees fleeing from the terror of Japanese invasion.
(PP/13/23L)

This was once a prosperous harbour in China. The Japanese left it a scene of desolation and raging fires.

Millions of Chinese refugees have fled from the terror of Japanese invasion.

JAPANESE CO-PROSPERITY

66
Japanese Co-prosperity.
In this pamphlet the racial stereotype depicts the Japanese as a deadly spider and the Japanese flag as its ever-extending web of horror.
(PP/13/26L)

67 (overleaf)
Axis Criminals.
Japanese Tyrants in Korea.
(PP/1/14)

JAPANESE TYRANTS IN KOREA

1 There is, in the Pacific Ocean, a small country called Korea. It is drawn in red on the globe above.

2 Korea is very near to Japan as you can see here. The red part is Korea, the black part Japan.

3 The people of Korea are quite different from the people of Japan and wear a pretty national costume.

4 A long time ago artists from Korea were invited to Japan to teach painting and writing there.

5 The Japanese were always very polite to these wise men because they wished to learn their skill.

6 In 1904 Japan and Russia went to war. Japan won the war in the end.

7 So Japan signed a treaty with Korea promising that the country would still be free.

8 But the Japanese did not keep their promise and they forced the Emperor to give them his country.

9 And in 1910 Korea became a part of Japan in spite of the treaty that had been signed.

10 Soon Koreans were made to work for the Japanese and were turned into slaves.

11 The people of Korea were made to leave their farms by the Japanese and were paid no money for them.

12 Korean officials in government departments had their jobs taken away by Japanese officials.

13 The Koreans were forced by the Japanese to make roads but the Japanese settlers were not.

14 The Japanese had no respect for the Koreans' burial grounds and profaned their graves.

15 There were many examples of Koreans being murdered by the Japanese when they complained

16 Even women and children were quite often beaten in the streets by Japanese soldiers.

17 In a village called Chai-an all religious men were shot and bayonetted in their church.

18 Then the church was set on fire and all the houses except six in the village burned.

19 Ten thousand people were put in prison and the prisons were so crowded they could not sit down.

20 One thousand of these were later killed, 1,500 injured and the rest were beaten.

21 Admiral Saito, a Japanese Governor, was murdered by his own countrymen for being too kind

22 Japan cannot grow enough rice to feed her own people so she takes rice from Korea.

23 Korean gold is stolen by Japan to pay for the things Japan needs to buy from other countries.

24 There is a shortage of food and clothing in Korea, the Japanese have taken everything.

25 They even force the Koreans to change their own names to a Japanese name.

26 Only Japanese history is taught in Korean schools and the children must learn to speak Japanese.

27 Koreans are not allowed to worship their own gods any more. They must worship Japanese gods.

28 Co-prosperity means only poverty, hunger and unhappiness. Japan has murdered Korea.

Like much of American propaganda in the Pacific War, British propaganda was characterised by highly emotional appeals and crude stereotypes that demonised the Japanese. Often this reflected a pre-existing racism, which was reinforced by Japan's brutal behaviour in the Far East. An MOI pamphlet, *Japanese Aggression* (Fig. 65), charts a liturgy of crimes carried out by the Japanese in Formosa (modern Taiwan), China, Korea, and Manchuria. The front cover shows Chinese refugees fleeing in panic from the Japanese. The document is illustrated by means of a number of photographs that demonstrate Japanese oppression, but interestingly there are no racial stereotypes. Nevertheless, the opening paragraph sets the tone: 'The Japanese are a dangerous race. Japan considers itself superior to every other race … conquest by Japan means ruination, starvation and oppression.'

One of the claims made in Japanese propaganda was that its occupation of territories in the Far East brought 'co-prosperity'. The front cover of *Japanese Co-prosperity* (Fig. 66) depicts Japan as a buck-toothed spider wearing a military helmet and spreading its expanding web in the form of the national flag – one of the Japanese military's most powerful symbols – over a continent. The text refers to Japanese aggression as 'a horrible disease' and instead of the promised 'co-prosperity' claims that Japanese militarism has 'brought only poverty, slavery and evil in its wake'. *Axis Criminals. Japanese Tyrants in Korea* (Fig. 67) is in a double-sided comic-book format and graphically details Japanese atrocities and the subjugation of the Korean people.[15] It is similar to the 'yellow peril' approach of US propaganda in the Pacific War, which depicted the Japanese military as monkey-like, buck-toothed, and short-sighted.[16] At the top of the comic all three Axis tyrants are revealed, but the comic strip that follows singles out the brutality of the fanatical Japanese soldiers, who are depicted as animals. The image of a subhuman primate (compare the ape-man in anti-Nazi propaganda) was key to devaluing the humanity of the enemy. Many British and American saw the Japanese as racially inferior, scarcely to be regarded as a match for Allied forces, with *Punch* in January 1942 depicting Japanese troops swinging from trees in the jungle. A Special Report conducted by the British Institute of Public Opinion for Home Intelligence in July 1944 discovered that 'nearly 90 per cent of people consider we should stay in the war until Japan is beaten' and that hatred of the Japanese 'appears to be at least as strong as hatred of the Germans'.[17]

Conclusion

The image of the enemy was an important feature of propaganda for all the combatant nations during World War II. In British propaganda, Germans, Italians, and Japanese are represented as people inclined towards regimentation and willing to sacrifice their freedoms. Britain, on the other hand, could claim to have 'God on our side'; to be a nation that has proudly pioneered ideas of freedom and justice and is the staunch defender of Western civilisation. In depicting the 'slave' world of the totalitarian tyrants, Hitler, Mussolini, and Emperor Hirohito are presented as objects of fanatical worship by the masses, who were prepared to implement Utopian imperial visions in the name of their leaders. However, it is one thing to know your enemy and depict the evil of the foe you are fighting: for such propaganda to be effective it has also to demonstrate that it is possible to defeat him. This will be the theme of Chapter 5: how the MOI persuaded the British people and its allies abroad that the tide of the war was changing in their favour and that the Axis nations were in retreat.

1 This reflected a rather forlorn opinion held within some sections of the government at this time that the German people might overthrow their leader. TNA. INF 1/302, 'Aims of Home Publicity', 23 September 1939. Interestingly the new Minister of Information, Sir John Reith, had warned against such an approach: 'You are fighting the German people. ... The Germans have been taught to be ruthless and hate the British. They are merciless.' Reith suggested that 'the Ministry should now begin to stir up people's more primitive instincts.' TNA. CAB 67/4, Memorandum by Minister of Information, 26 January 1940.

2 The back cover of *Black Record* referred to Sir Robert Vansittart as Chief Diplomatic Adviser to the British Government. Vansittart not only portrayed Nazism as the latest manifestation of Germany's continuous record of aggression but also went further and claimed that after Germany was defeated, it must be stripped of all military capacity, including its heavy industries. Vansittart argued that the German people had enthusiastically supported Hitler's wars of aggression, just as they supported World War I, and so they must be thoroughly re-educated under strict Allied supervision for at least a generation. This is precisely what the British attempted to implement after 1945. See D. Welch, 'Priming the Pump of German Democracy: British "Re-Education" Policy in Germany after the Second World War', in I. Turner (ed), *Reconstruction in Post-War Germany. British Occupation Policy in the Western Zones 1945–1955* (Oxford, 1989), 215–38, and D. Welch, 'British Political Re-Education and its Impact on German Political Culture', in K. Rohe, G. Schmidt, H.-P. von Strandmann (eds), *Deutschland – Grossbrittannien – Europe. Politische Traditionen Partnerschaft und Rivalität* (Bochum, 1992), 239–52.

3 TNA. INF 1/302, 'Aims of Home Publicity', 23 September 1939.

4 The Policy Committee of the MOI took the decision not to distinguish the German people from Nazism in May, and in June the same

Committee agreed that: 'we should now pay more attention to stirring up people's anger ...' TNA. INF 1/848, Policy Committee minutes, 2 May 1940.

5 TNA. CAB 75/2, Memorandum by Lord Macmillan, 20 September 1939.

6 Quoted in I. McLaine, *Ministry of Morale. Home Front Morale and the Ministry of Information in World War II* (London, 1979), 147.

7 TNA. INF 1/396, Memorandum by Kenneth MacLennan, July 1940. A summary of the functions of the Religions Division can be found in TNA. INF 1/396, February 1940.

8 Lord Macmillan had made this request when he addressed a group of Church leaders in Lambeth Palace in September 1939. TNA. INF 1/403 Memorandum for meeting with Church leaders, 12 September 1939. The declaration was published by most of the press on 21 December 1940. In 1940 the MOI commissioned the Boulting Brothers' *Pastor Hall* (1940), based on the true story of Martin Niemoller, a German priest who spoke out against the Nazis. The film dramatised the conflict between Christianity and Nazism and between the individual and the state.

9 For a discussion of the impact on Bishop Galen's sermons on German society and the wider Nazi euthanasia campaign, see D. Welch, *The Third Reich. Politics and Propaganda* (London, 2002), 82–91.

10 In December 1942 the Inter-Allied Information Committee had produced a detailed report of Nazi extermination procedures, and these were reported in the British press. Following these accounts one Home Intelligence Report, while noting 'widespread indignation, anger and disgust', nevertheless came to the conclusion that as a result of such publicity, people are more conscious of the Jews they do not like here ...' TNA. INF 1/292, H.I. Weekly Intelligence Reports, 29 December–5 January 1943. In September 1944 the pamphlet *A Catalogue of*

Crime documented authoritative evidence of the Nazi extermination of Jews and other ethnic groups.

11 For examples of anti-Semitism see TNA. INF 1/264, H.I. Weekly Intelligence Reports, 29 July–3 August 1940; INF 1/292, 18–26 May 1943; INF 1/292, 29 December–5 January 1943. For a highly critical analysis of the rise of anti-Semitism following the outbreak of war, see A. Goldman, 'The Resurgence of Anti-Semitism in Britain during World War II', in *Jewish Social Studies*, Vol. 46, No. 1 (Winter, 1984), 37–50.

12 The phrase is taken from T. Hickman, *What Did You Do in the War, Auntie? The BBC at War* (London, 1995), 50. For a perceptive analysis of the show from the point of view of its producer, see also F. Worsley, *ITMA. 1939–1948* (London, 1949).

13 Home Intelligence reported that the public felt that Italy had not suffered enough. A report in October 1942 recorded that news of the recent bombing of Italy had been 'the really bright spot of the week'. The reports noted that the bombings had been greeted with widespread enthusiasm as there had been a feeling for some time 'that the Italians are getting off too lightly – possibly for political or religious reasons'. TNA. INF 1/292, H.I. Weekly Intelligence Reports, 20–27 October 1942.

14 Quoted in McLaine, *Ministry of Morale*, 159.

15 For a fascinating history of Japanese rule in Korea, see T. Henry, *Assimilating Seoul: Japanese Rule and the Politics of Public Space in Colonial Korea 1910–1945* (Berkeley, CA, 2014).

16 For a brief analysis of US anti-Japanese propaganda, see D. Welch, *Propaganda. Power and Persuasion* (London, 2013), 174–6.

17 TNA. INF 1/293, H.I. Special Report, 11 July 1944.

'Some of the damage in London is pretty heart-breaking but what an effect it has had on the people! What warmth – what courage! What determination! … Everybody absolutely determined: secretly delighted with the privilege of holding up Hitler.'

HUMPHREY JENNINGS
LETTER TO HIS WIFE IN AMERICA, OCTOBER 1940.

'Black day for me. Dad wrote to say we were not entitled to a free (Anderson) shelter, so after washing went to Town Hall to see if I could buy one. Nothing doing. Don't know where to turn for help. Cannot see the likelihood of getting one under £40. Dad said order one, but it isn't so easy, he did not say where the £40 was to come from. I have about £8. We have had about 12 bombs dropped today just around us. I feel thoroughly depressed having no shelter. What a life. Pipes are leaking in the bathroom again….'

MRS EMILY RIDDEL
DIARY ENTRY, OCTOBER 1940.

CHAPTER FIVE

We Happy Few...

Key narratives in the history of Britain's contribution to World War II involved the mobilisation of the Home Front for total war and the changing fortunes of the British armed forces. As for the propaganda war, a major task facing the Ministry of Information (MOI) was to construct a third narrative that would convince the people of the Empire and its allies that these two strands were inexorably linked and that Britain – even when standing alone – was a united fighting force to be reckoned with.

Conscription

The Emergency Powers (Defence) Act of August 1938 had empowered the British government to take certain measures in defence of the nation and to maintain public order. On 27 April 1939 the government responded to the growing threat of Hitler's aggression in Europe by introducing the Military Training Act. All British men aged 20 and 21 who were fit and able were required to take six months' military training. Other European countries had kept conscription between the wars and were able to raise much larger armies than Britain. When war broke out the British army could muster only 897,000 men, compared to France's 5 million. Another Act of Parliament was necessary to increase the numbers. The National Service (Armed Forces) Act of 1939 made all able men between the ages of 18 and 41 liable for conscription; as part of the legislation it was decided that single men would be called to war before married men. Conscription was by age, and in October 1939 men aged between 20 and 23 were required to register to serve in one of the armed forces. They were allowed to choose between the Army, the Navy and the Royal Air Force. This was the start of a long and drawn-out process which saw 40-year-olds registering only in June 1941, the same year that single women aged between 20 and 30 were also conscripted. As discussed in Chapter 3, women did not take part in the fighting but were required to work in reserved occupations – especially factories and farming – to enable men to be drafted into the services. By 1942 all male British subjects between 18 and 51 years old and all females of 20 to 30 years old resident in Britain were liable to be called up, with some exemptions.

The Myth of Dunkirk

Winston Churchill called it 'a miracle of deliverance'. Only eight months after World War II had begun, the British army faced annihilation. The British Expeditionary Force (BEF) had been fighting the Germans in France but was on the retreat, and Churchill faced the possibility that they would be trapped. ('Nothing but a miracle can save the BEF now,' wrote General Brooke in his diary.) On 19 May (when the advancing German army had severed the main lines of communication between the BEF and French headquarters) the Commander of the BEF, Lord John Gort, decided that evacuation was the only way to save the British army. Without informing his allies – the French – he ordered the BEF to withdraw to the French port of Dunkirk (Dunkerque) and asked the British government to evacuate it by sea.

In London, Churchill and the Admiralty had reached the same conclusion and began to plan for Operation Dynamo – the evacuation of the BEF from France. On the east coast of Britain, ships were being assembled in readiness for the evacuation order. In France the BEF was retreating further towards Dunkirk. On 24 May Boulogne fell to the Germans and Calais was only just holding out. German tanks were now just 15 kilometres (about 9 miles) from Dunkirk. At this crucial juncture, Hitler ordered his tanks to stop ('Halt order'), having apparently agreed with Field Marshall von Rundstedt

(Army Group A) that the armoured divisions should be husbanded for the second phase of the campaign (Operation Red), thus allowing the infantry and Luftwaffe to tackle the Allied troops. (The Luftwaffe Commander-in-Chief, Hermann Göring, had reputedly boasted that his air force could finish the task on its own.) When Calais fell on 26 May, Operation Dynamo was put into effect.

Owing to wartime censorship and the desire to keep up the morale of the nation, the full extent of the unfolding 'disaster' around Dunkirk was not publicised. However, the grave plight of the troops led King George VI to call for an unprecedented week of prayer. Throughout the country, people prayed on 26 May for a miraculous delivery. The Archbishop of Canterbury led prayers 'for our soldiers in dire peril in France'. On 26 May the British and the French had both decided to form a beachhead around Dunkirk, but for different reasons. While the British hoped to escape from the German trap, the French still hoped to fight on (this would later fuel the French belief that the British were ready to fight to the last Frenchman).

As the last of the BEF landed in England, a different kind of war was being waged. It was the propaganda battle, and in Britain it would be disseminated largely through the MOI and its new Minister, Duff Cooper (Lord Reith had just been replaced). Even though Britain had suffered a catastrophic defeat, 'Dunkirk' took on an immediate mythic resonance for the British people. It symbolised their brave and resourceful resistance to German military might. To that extent, Dunkirk had a profound inspirational effect, which helped Britain continue fighting even when her position seemed hopeless. Out of the feat of human salvage, the British forged a propaganda triumph.

Although Churchill had warned in the Commons that 'wars are not won by evacuations', his own radio broadcasts (largely repeated from speeches given in the House) did much to catch the defiant mood of the people and express the spirit of the hour. (This is interesting, because he had *not* previously been rated highly as a radio speaker. His resonant voice and rotund phrases were out of keeping with the fashionable radio undertones – to paraphrase A.J.P. Taylor.) The newspapers were the first to pick up on the propaganda significance of the evacuation. On 31 May, the *Daily Express* reported that tens of thousands of British troops were safely home already: 'tired, dirty, hungry – they came back unbeatable!' The report was one of the first to pay tribute to the crews of the civilian rescue ships: 'the old tramp steamers, ships of all sorts and sizes, even barges in tow … whose crews went into the blast and hell on the other side'. On 3 June, the *Daily Sketch* reported reassuringly, over a photograph headlined 'The Navy's here – with the Army' that four-fifths of the BEF had been saved. Interestingly it was not until 6 June (that is, after the evacuation had been completed) that the British newsreels began to trumpet the extraordinary achievements of the evacuation from Dunkirk.

Myth is part of the national memory of World War II. It can be broken down into various 'sub-myths' including those of the evacuation of Dunkirk, the Battle of Britain, and the Blitz. The myth of Dunkirk was created by people's active acceptance of an interpretation of events, often inspired by the media, which in turn provided a model that shaped actions in other times of crisis. Following Dunkirk, Britain stood alone and in desperate trouble (another slogan taken up by the media when France was forced to sign an Armistice). When France collapsed, King George VI famously wrote to his mother: 'Personally, I feel happier now that we have no allies to be polite to and pamper.'[1]

So Dunkirk allowed us to fight another day – but essentially alone. Mass-Observation detected a sense of relief that Britain could now concentrate all effort on the *defence* of the home country, and 'standing alone' reflected a genuine patriotism, founded upon centuries of belief in the apartness of Britain (home of an island race). J.B. Priestley had alluded to this in his *Postscripts* radio broadcast of 5 June: 'Now that it is all over, and we can look back on it, doesn't it seem to you to have an inevitable air about it – as if we can turn a page in the history of Britain and see a chapter headed

"Dunkirk"?' David Low captured this spirit in one of his most famous cartoons of World War II. In 'Very Well, Alone' (*Evening Standard*, 18 June 1940), Low summed up a common feeling of stoic resolution (Fig. 68). Unlike many of Low's cartoons, there is no humour in the message. He sketches, instead, an angry-looking English soldier standing on the white cliffs of Dover, his arm outstretched towards France (which had just fallen) and his fist clenched at the oncoming Luftwaffe emerging from a looming black cloud. Low's cartoon captured the image of dogged resilience, the apotheosis of the bulldog spirit the British liked to project in times of adversity.

Winston Churchill also appealed to this mixture of patriotism, insularity, and xenophobia in his 'We shall fight on the beaches ... We shall never surrender' speech to the House of Commons on 4 June (extracts of which were later that evening broadcast on the BBC):

I have, myself, full confidence that if all do their duty, if nothing is neglected, and if the best arrangements are made, as they are being made, we shall prove ourselves once again able to defend our island homes, to ride out the storm of war, and to outlive the menace of tyranny, if necessary for years, if necessary **alone**.

The heroism of the Dunkirk campaign and of the BEF had set a benchmark for the British people; the 'Dunkirk spirit' or in this case the 'Dunkirk mood' had become a shorthand for heroism and resilience. Noel Coward's filmic portrait of the Royal Navy *In Which We Serve* (1942) – the most popular film in Britain in 1942 – includes a Dunkirk sequence. HMS *Torrin*'s crew (with Coward at the helm) pick up survivors and take them to Dover where they disembark. Gradually a bedraggled company are called

68
'Very Well, Alone',
David Low,
Evening Standard, 18 June 1940.
(Associated Newspapers)

" VERY WELL , ALONE "

to order, their spirit restored as they march off in perfect time to the sound of a band. Leading seaman 'Shorty' Blake (John Mills) makes the only comment: 'If I wasn't so tired, I'd give 'em a cheer and no mistake.' It is an extraordinarily poignant scene that somehow freezes the national myth of Dunkirk and echoes the headline of the *Daily Mirror* on 3 June, which proclaimed: 'And still they come back – Gort's unbreakables!'

The Battle of Britain: 'We Happy Few'

In the summer of 1940 – after Hitler swept through France and drove the British army out of the European mainland – the people of Britain made ready for a Nazi invasion. Before Hitler could conquer the country, however, he needed to gain air superiority. The Luftwaffe launched a large-scale attack, intent on wiping out Britain's air defences. The Battle of Britain was one of the most pivotal moments in the country's history. The battle for air supremacy lasted officially from August until the end of October 1940 and overlapped with the Blitz, the period of sustained night bombing attacks, which continued until May 1941. By preventing Germany from gaining air superiority, the British forced Hitler to postpone and eventually cancel Operation Sea Lion, the planned amphibious and airborne invasion of Britain. Prime Minister Winston Churchill had set the tone for the forthcoming battle in his famous speech in the House of Commons on 18 June:

> The battle of France is over. The battle of Britain is about to begin. Upon this battle depends the survival of Christian civilisation. Upon it depends our own British life and the long continuity of our institutions and our Empire. The whole fury and might of the enemy must very soon be turned on us. Hitler knows that he will have to break us in this island or lose the war. If we can stand up to him, all Europe may be free and the life of the world may move forward into broad, sunlit uplands. But if we fail, then the whole world, including the United States, including all that we have known and cared for, will sink into the abyss of a new Dark Age made more sinister, and perhaps more protracted, by the lights of a perverted science. Let us therefore brace ourselves to our duties, and so bear ourselves that, if the British Empire and its Commonwealth last for a thousand years, men will still say, 'This was their finest hour.'

Although RAF Fighter Command was outnumbered by the Luftwaffe in July 1940, Britain ramped up factory production and by October Fighter Command had more fighter planes than Germany. Presented at the time as David against the Goliath of Nazi Germany, the image of Britain as the plucky underdog has also spread to our wider perception of the war. In fact, Britain was in far better condition than that image suggests, and won the Battle of Britain because it was ready and prepared to fight such a battle. It had the world's first and only fully co-ordinated air defence system, aircraft production that was out-producing Germany at a ratio of 2:1, and it had the mechanisms to fight a protracted war.[2] Yet that is not how it was depicted in official propaganda.

An official publication that came out towards the end of the war summarised reaction on the Home Front to the Battle of Britain in rather understated terms. *Ourselves in Wartime* focused not on the heroism of the fighter pilots but on the stoicism of the civilians:

> One memory of the civilian aspect of the battle of Britain stands out above all else. It is not of the aerodromes in Kent and the docks in London being set on fire; or of a bomb falling on a warehouse above a large shelter in London and driving bricks and dust down upon thousands of the poorest of the population, but the fact that no panic was caused by the bombs. Quietly people moved in and out of their offices and

HOW BRITAIN WON THE GREATEST AIR BATTLE OF HISTORY

...FOR FREEDOM...
THE BRITISH ROYAL AIR FORCE GROWS STRONGER EVERY DAY!

THE BATTLE OF BRITAIN
AUGUST-OCTOBER 1940

How the German air-invasion of Britain was hurled back and defeated by the Royal Air Force

DURING August, September and October 1940, the entire weight of the German air force was hurled against Britain. After the fall of France, the Germans advanced their bases for air-attack and made all ready for the invasion and destruction of the one supreme foe.

The onslaught was planned with the utmost care. It was to be in four parts. It was to make fullest possible use of the total first-line force of the Nazi air-arm—at that time by far the strongest in the world.

The four stages of attack were aimed at the destruction of convoys and ports along the Channel coast—the destruction of inland airfields all over south England—the destruction of the "inner ring" of airfields protecting London—and, finally, the mass attack upon London itself—when London should be lying open, unguarded by fighter aircraft—as the prelude to invasion and conquest.

The first stage began. The British "Spitfires" and "Hurricanes" which had already met and beaten the German air force over Dunkirk, inflicted heavy losses on the Nazi dive-bombers attacking Channel shipping. To their surprise, the Germans found that their big forces of aircraft were suffering heavy losses. It is not yet known whether they realised that the attacks were entirely failing to achieve their object—the closing of ports, and the isolation of southern England from supplies

and reinforcements brought by sea against the time when later attacks should have cut off communication by land with the rest of Britain. It seems that German thoroughness was once again its own victim. The plan had to go on : the Nazis, unable to improvise because of their reliance on organisation of every detail, were forced to assume that the plan was in fact doing all it was intended to do.

The second stage began. A very large number of attacks were directed against the inland airfields on which defending British fighter-aircraft might be expected to be based. The German losses mounted—the airfields continued to function—but the Nazi machine rolled on, and intensive bombing-attacks upon London's airfields heralded the third stage.

Nazi losses became heavier and heavier. The Germans, throughout the entire period of the Battle of Britain, tried every device at their disposal in order to reduce the crippling losses which were gradually reducing their first-line strength to a dangerously low point. They used different formations—they increased the numbers of both bombers and protecting fighters. But the losses still grew. Yet, true to the German principles of organised, total war, they continued to fling in their aircraft in hundreds. Heedless of the fact that not one of their planned objectives had, in fact, been achieved, they opened the final stage of their onslaught—the mass attack on London.

It failed more abjectly, and with heavier losses, both in numbers and as a proportion of the attacking aircraft sent, than ever before. No air force, however strong, could continue in the face of such devastating casualties. The Germans gave in : they abandoned their attacks ; they retired from the Battle of Britain to lick their wounds and take stock of the truly fearful reduction of their air-strength that had occurred between the 8th August and the 31st October.

IN THOSE 84 DAYS THE GERMANS LOST 2,471 AIRCRAFT AND OVER 6,000 TRAINED AIRMEN.

The Fighter Command of the Royal Air Force, by comparison, lost 733 fighter aircraft and 375 pilots, many pilots being rescued.

It would be long before the great German air force was in a position again to throw in hundreds of machines regardless of the consequences. The day of its total numerical superiority was gone for ever. The cream of German air-personnel lay dead on the English fields, or languished in British prison-camps—thousands of German aircraft littered the English landscape, food for the scrap-heaps. British air-strength was higher at the end of the Battle of Britain than it had ever been before and it has grown steadily since.

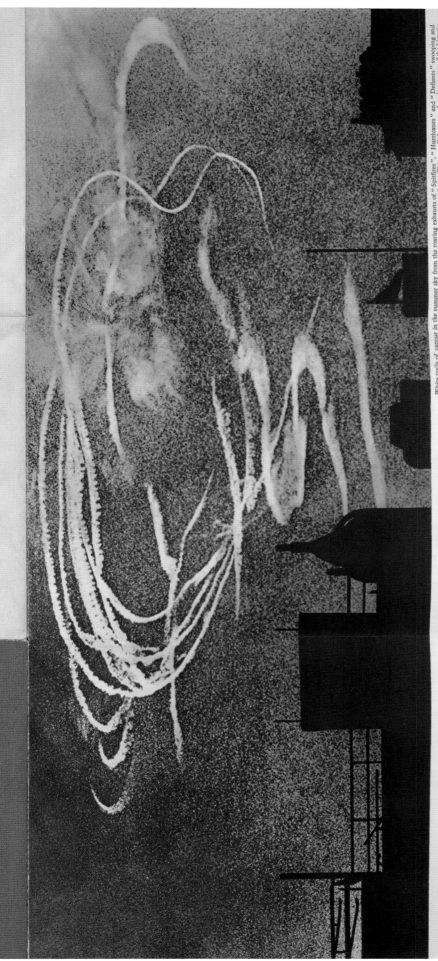

ONE OF THE WORLD'S DECISIVE BATTLES

White trails of vapour in the summer sky from the roaring exhausts of "Spitfires," "Hurricanes" and "Defiants" swooping and turning as they wrought destruction on an invader vastly superior in numbers. This was all that many Londoners saw of the historic air battle that raged above their rooftops in September 1940 when the vaunted Luftwaffe launched its full-scale day-after-day attack and was crushingly defeated by the British R.A.F. and ground defences.

69
The Battle of Britain
– a fold-out leaflet.
(PP/49/7L)

homes all through the days of the battle, going about their normal business, and pausing only momentarily to look up at the phenomenon of the white vapour trails in the sky caused by the twistings and turnings of the aircraft engaged in mortal combat several miles above their heads.[3]

This account is very much at odds with the excited reactions recorded by Mass-Observation and Home Intelligence. Home Intelligence reported that the spectacle of the great air battles, fought out in full view of the civilians on the ground, was generating not indifferent curiosity but a sense of euphoria, many expressing a sense of exhilaration 'by the feeling that they are now in the front line'. The BBC reported miners on the slag heaps cheering as they watched the air battle, and reports from Edinburgh suggested that the Scots were now waiting impatiently 'for their turn to come, in the first glimpse of a Spitfire chasing a Dornier!' In the East End of London, streamers were even being made privately to celebrate victory, with people remarking that 'it would only be a matter now of a few months'.[4]

The Battle of Britain was won by the Few in the skies over the rolling countryside of southern England. At the height of the battle on 20 August Winston Churchill set the seal on their fame in a speech in the House of Commons:

The gratitude of every home in our Island, in our Empire, and indeed throughout the world, except in the abodes of the guilty, goes out to the British airmen who, undaunted by odds, unwearied in their constant challenge and mortal danger, are turning the tide of the World War by their prowess and by their devotion. Never in the field of human conflict was so much owed by so many to so few.

These famous words from Churchill became the text of one of the most famous propaganda posters of the war. Newsreels captured the immediacy of the dogfights, which cinema audiences all over the country were keen to witness, and the press eulogised the pilots' character and their deeds. Referring to the exploits of Fighter Command, the *Daily Express* wrote 'these fine young men of ours continue to write without halt or interpretation, the most exciting story of the whole history of the world wars'.[5] The nature and immediacy of the aerial combat not only made heroes of the pilots and their chivalrous code, but also made them medieval knights of the sky in the public imagination. The *Daily Mirror* carried a front page photograph under the headline, 'These Noble Knights'.[6] Even the BBC's Charles Gardner cast the Battle of Britain as some sporting jousting match. On 14 July he was sent to Dover to cover the Luftwaffe attacks on convoy shipping:

… Ah! Here's one coming down now! There's one coming down in flames!… somebody's hit a German, and he's coming down … Oh, we have just hit a Messerschmitt! Oh, that was beautiful! He's coming down…. He's finished. … Yes, they're being chased home, and how they're being chased home! There are three Spitfires chasing three Messerschmitts now. Oh, boy! Look at them going! …And there's a Spitfire just behind the first two – he'll get them! Ah, yes! Oh boy! I've never seen anything so good as this! The RAF fighters have really got these boys taped![7]

The drama unfolding over the skies of England was quickly seized upon by Lord Beaverbrook, the Minister of Aircraft Production, to encourage 'patriotic' housewives to hand in aluminium household items to the Women's Voluntary Service. 'We will turn your pots and pans into Spitfires and Hurricanes, Blenheims, and Wellingtons'.[8] The Battle of Britain marked the first major defeat of Hitler's military forces, with air superiority seen as the key to victory. Not surprisingly, the MOI swiftly took advantage of the exploits of Fighter Command for propaganda purposes. The date of 15 September was to be celebrated as 'Battle of Britain Day' and numerous publications were produced to commemorate the victory. A fold-out brochure explained, by means of a sequence of photographs, 'How Britain Won the Greatest Air Battle of History' (Fig. 69). This was

70
The Battle of Britain. August – October 1940.
The Ministry edition boasted an illustrated cover, eye-catching diagrams and action photographs. It sold 4.8 million copies in Britain in the six months following its release.
(PP/49/5A)

THE BATTLE OF BRITAIN

OF BRITAIN

AUGUST–OCTOBER 1940

1940 · THE BATTLE OF BRITAIN · AUGUST-OCTOBER 1940 · 1942

In the Autumn of 1940, Hitler launched the air attack on Great Britain that was going to finish the War in the West. But his "invincible" Luftwaffe was utterly defeated by the dauntless heroism and superb skill of Britain's fighter pilots. This Battle of Britain was fought when the British Empire stood alone against the massed might of the Axis. The tide of war turned when it was won. And now in 1942 four-fifths of the human race are ranged against the Axis tyranny. Salute to the heroes of the R.A.F. who, in 84 days of desperate air fighting, saved the cause of freedom for the world!

IN DAYLIGHT 2,375 GERMAN PLANES WERE SHOT DOWN
This mass of tangled wreckage is one of the graveyards of Hitler's Luftwaffe

followed in 1941 by the Air Ministry's official thirty-four-page account of *The Battle of Britain: the Great Days from 8 August–31 October 1940* (Fig. 70). Priced at 6 pence, the booklet's inside cover juxtaposes Churchill's 'Never in the field of human conflict was so much owed by so many to so few' speech with a photograph of nine young pilots striding purposefully away from an iconic Spitfire. Their carefree, smiling faces recall Sir William Rothenstein's portraits, which were reproduced in *Picture Post* in September 1940. The battles are carefully reconstructed so as to maintain the David versus Goliath myth. Indeed, historical parallels with previous invasion threats are maintained by constant reference to the Luftwaffe as 'an armada'. Victory of course came with a price. The final page refers to 375 RAF pilots killed and 358 wounded. 'Of those who died let it be said that: *All the soul of man is resolution which expires Never from valiant men till their last breath.* Such was the Battle of Britain in 1940. Future historians may compare it with Marathon, Trafalgar and the Marne'. In its first (unillustrated) edition, *The Battle of Britain* sold 2 million copies and the second (illustrated) edition sold 900,000 copies in ten days. *The Battle of Britain* became the first in a series of large-format paperbacks or pamphlets referred to as 'Official War Books'. Titles such as *Coastal Command*, *His Majesty's Minesweepers*, *Roof Over Britain* and *Transport Goes to War* aimed to 'tell the British war story' by providing insight into particular parts of the war effort. This focus was consciously designed to 'stimulate the effort of all other groups through psychological force of example and the evocation of team spirit'. With each book based upon at least one of the main themes of MOI propaganda (the most popular being 'the projection of Britain as a progressive, efficient, equalitarian democracy'), they were also regarded as a good way of influencing opinion abroad.

In the following year, with British forces close to defeat almost everywhere, the MOI issued a commemorative poster, which was produced in many languages (Fig. 71). It was intended to inspire at a time when Britain was desperate for a major military victory. At this stage of the war, 'holding out' was the catchphrase of a nation that saw itself alone. The circular icon of the casual, young, smiling fighter pilot in his flying helmet became a lasting symbol of British indomitable will. Remember that the Battle of Britain came only a few months after the 'miracle' of Dunkirk. Both were inspirational for different reasons. The poster sets both the context ('The Battle of Britain was fought when the British Empire stood alone') and the significance of the Battle of Britain ('Salute the heroes of the RAF who, in 84 days of desperate air fighting saved the cause of freedom for the world!'). Shortly after the poster was distributed the war was to take on a new direction in Britain's favour. But that came later.

The Battle of Britain also captured the imagination of the younger generation, which had been brought up on Biggles stories. Puffin Books brought out a five-page colour booklet for young children (Fig. 72). Setting out the history of the battle, it produced a number of exciting lithographs that captured the intensity of the aerial dogfights, described as 'One Against Twelve'. The Luftwaffe were referred to as 'Göring's armada of death … but that battle overhead, fought by so few, saved us from being enslaved like the French and the Poles.'

One should not underestimate the importance of a British victory (of sorts) in the summer of 1940. Although RAF Fighter Command was outnumbered in July 1940, Britain increased factory production and, as already mentioned, by October Britain had more fighter planes than the Luftwaffe. The fighter pilots' exploits, and the propaganda images, helped to fix the image of these young men – the Few – in a heroic mould. Of course the pilots were not alone; they depended on the dedication of the ground crews, the radar operators, anti-aircraft command, and workers toiling with tireless dedication in aircraft factories. Nevertheless, the country needed a victory of sorts and heroes to believe in, and it was the young pilots that captured the public's imagination. Immediately they joined the highest ranks of the participants in the people's war.[9]

72
The front and back
cover, and pp. 14–15, of
the Puffin children's book,
The Battle of Britain.
(PP/49/19A)

The Battle of Britain

BY DAVID GARNETT & JAMES GARDNER

*Based by permission on The Air Ministry
Official Account of Great Days of 1940*

A PUFFIN PICTURE BOOK

THE SECOND ACT

FIGHTER AERODROMES
ATTACKED

The attacks on Portsmouth went on. One
afternoon three or four hundred German aircraft
came over to bomb it. But the Germans were
learning that our Fighters were better than they
had known. Their losses were too great so they
tried to get rid of our Fighters by bombing our
aerodromes. They hoped to destroy our Fighters
on the ground. It seemed easier than fighting
them in the air. But the aerodromes were well
guarded with guns and the British Fighters were
not in their sheds but were cunningly hidden under
trees and haystacks in fields near by. So they did
not do much damage after all.

Hundreds of German bombers and Fighters
were shot down. On the fifteenth of August
one hundred and eighty enemy aircraft were
shot down. Next day five or six hundred German
aircraft came and two days later the same number
came again. In those two days they lost two
hundred and forty-five Bombers and Fighters.
One Heinkel bomber was brought down by a
Sergeant Pilot in one of the Anson trainers in
which R.A.F. pilots learn to fly. The Anson
had no guns to shoot with. But the British

Page 14

Death Dive

The Battle of Britain

A PUFFIN PICTURE BOOK

GERMAN FIGHTERS COME ALSO

Sergeant rammed the Heinkel and both aircraft fell together to destruction. In the evening the Germans came to raid the mouth of the Thames. A squadron of thirteen Hurricanes swooped on them and shot down thirteen of the enemy. They did not lose a single machine or man. The German Air Force had lost nearly seven hundred Bombers and Fighters in ten days.

The Germans had lost so many bombers that they sent more and more Fighters with them to protect them after this. High up they sent a screen of Fighters to try and stop our Spitfires from diving on them from above. In front and behind and on each side of the German bombers there were more Fighters weaving their way in and out among them. The Fighters could fly faster than the bombers so they could stray from side to side.

Sometimes the first squadrons of our Spitfires and Hurricanes would all be engaged by the German Fighters and so the German bombers were able to fly on without being attacked. But when the bombers got separated from their protectors, our last squadrons to be sent up would fall upon them. Many of them were shot down.

Bombers with Fighter Screen

Page 15

Bomber Command

73
Royal Air Force Raids Are Smashing German Industry.
(PP/BS51/29)

74
'They will go on falling!'
– a quote from Winston Churchill.
(PP/BS51/29)

Both Dunkirk and the Battle of Britain represented significant defensive, rearguard actions. In 1940, the MOI had to adapt quickly from the tedium of the 'phoney war' to a national emergency which threatened Britain's very survival. Reluctant to hand the enemy propaganda material, the press continued to stress cheerful courage and the determined endurance of civilians under fire. Typical is this headline from the *Daily Mirror* above a photograph showing victims of the Blitz recovering what they could from their homes following a Luftwaffe raid: 'They Took It, With Chins Up'. Revealingly, in smaller print the storyline hinted at not just stoicism but revenge: 'After the raid, these street residents rallied and helped each other as best they could. Their homes are wrecked, but not their morale. There's nothing of despair about them –only a fervent hope that we don't bring any more bombs back from Berlin'.[10]

While British civilians continued to 'take it' during the Blitz, what of our offensive strategy? How were we retaliating? This was down to Bomber Command. One of the problems confronting MOI was the government's insistence that British policy be restricted to knocking out enemy war production. In contrast, when the Luftwaffe raided, emphasis was laid on the bombs that hit schools, churches, hospitals, and homes. RAF sorties, on the other hand, were always said to have destroyed munitions factories and transport infrastructure. The Ministry was fully aware of the public's desire for retaliation, but a delicate path had to be navigated between its need to show that German civilians were also suffering and the obligation to repeatedly stress the essentially strategic nature of Bomber Command's operations.[11]

The situation changed after February 1942 when the decision was taken to direct the main weight of the RAF's attack against German civilians.[12] It is no coincidence that this decision coincided with the appointment of Air Chief Marshall Arthur T. Harris as the new Commander-in-Chief of Bomber Command. Harris was a single-minded advocate of both the strategic use of the RAF, and of the specific strategy of attacking large urban areas (and thereby German morale), rather than solely economic targets. In 1942 the MOI commissioned the prestigious feature-length documentary film *Target for Tonight*, directed by Harry Watt, which showed RAF attacks on German cities. It proved highly popular with British cinema audiences and the film, described by the documentary film-maker Paul Rotha as 'dramatised actuality', went on to win an honorary Academy Award in 1942 and was named 'Best Documentary' by the National Board of Review in 1942.[13] Coinciding with the release of the film a number of posters were produced on the theme of 'bigger and better bombs' (Figs. 73, 74).

In May 1942 Bomber Command attacked Cologne in the first of the 'thousand bomber' raids (Operation Millennium) and followed it up with extremely heavy attacks on other Ruhr cities. Churchill, too, was an enthusiast for the bomber – although not as the sole means of winning the war. The press lapped it up and presented the British people with aerial photographs showing vast swathes of destruction. Following the heavy raids on Cologne on 30 May 1942, the MOI published a pamphlet *As Hitler Sowed … so Shall Hitler Reap* (Fig. 75a), which was intended as much for overseas as it was for the British public: 'Ninety minutes bombing created devastation over an area eight times the size of London … Steadily the storm will increase in violence.' The pamphlet begins by setting Bomber Command's strategy in context. 'Ever since Hitler came to power the Nazis have thought they could subject the whole world to their will by force.' Refuting Göring's claim that 'We shall not expose the Ruhr to even one single bomb from enemy aircraft', it documents how, between 1941 and 1942, Britain's striking power had grown. Quoting Churchill's speech in the House of Commons on 8 September 1940 ('From June onwards … we have discharged nearly double the bombs upon Germany …') it warns the Nazis what they can expect: 'The heaviest bombs … the latest bombers … and

1940
1941
1942
KIEL
ROSTOC
LÜBECK
WILHELMSHAVEN
OSNABRÜCK
MÜNSTER
BREMEN
HAMBURG
DORTMUND
UISBURG
HANOVER
MAGDEBURG
ESSEN
KASSEL
LEIPZIG
ÜSSELDORF
BERLIN
COLOGNE
MAINZ
FRANKFURT-ON-MAIN

Ever since Hitler came to power the Nazis have thought they could subject the whole world to their will by force.

AS FAR BACK AS 1935 German armament factories began to work twenty-four hours a day, 168 hours a week. Furnaces glowed brightly and factory windows spread their light throughout the night. Germany's air power was to be built up to hold a hapless world in trembling respect. The Nazi air force was preparing for destruction. What could not be obtained by threats was to be obtained by aerial bombardment.

This has been made clear time and again by high officials of the Nazi party.

ADOLF HITLER : "Germany will be a world power or nothing." (Mein Kampf)

REICHSMINISTER FRANK : "It is necessary to think in terms not only of a national state but of a world empire." (22.11.40.)

MARSHAL GÖRING : "Remember that the German air force can do 100 to 1,000 times more damage than the British ever do us." (11.1.41.)

Do you remember September 1939?

Spring and Summer 1940?

ALL OVER EUROPE civilians were terrorised. There was the horror of Warsaw. Then Rotterdam, where 30,000 people were blown to bits or burned alive, "improved" the Nazi record for ruthlessness. After the fall of France it was London's turn to "take it." London had to face the storm of bombers night after night, week after week. Despite the harrying enemy the United Kingdom factories continued to function. The spirit of resistance grew firmer still. The nation which had already won the Battle of Britain in the daylight summer sky faced the future with unflinching courage. The Germans could not destroy a war industry that became ever more decentralised. With better searchlights, more anti-aircraft guns, night fighter planes, new methods of detecting the enemy's approach, defence against the bomber grew.

WARSAW

ROTTERDAM

LONDON

It looked so very easy . . .

1940

1940 The number of individual attacks by the R.A.F. had already mounted to the impressive total of 1,500. Many of the towns bombed received frequent visits by small numbers of aircraft dropping bombs weighing 500 lbs. Up to 100 bombers took part in the largest raids. At that time the maximum bomb-load that could be carried by a bombing plane was two tons.

1941 By the end of 1941 Bomber Command aircraft had flown over 28,000,000 miles. Forces up to 300 bombers took part in large-scale attacks. Many bombs weighed one ton—they were soon to be twice as heavy. Maximum bomb-load for a heavy bomber was three times as great as the previous year.

1942 Now, two-ton bombs are in general use, and bombs weighing nearly FOUR TONS are being dropped on vital targets. The heaviest bombers of 1942 can carry eight tons of bombs at a time. Germany has already felt the full weight of attacks by a thousand planes.

1941

"Our photographs show widespread destruction wherever our new heavy bombs fall — and they will go on falling, more and more, night after night, until the German people, shattered and disillusioned, decide for the second time that war is not worth while."

Sir Archibald Sinclair (3.9.41)

2 tons bomb-load

6 tons bomb-load

The scale of Britain's striking power GROWS

Each symbol equals 25 planes taking part in large-scale raids

1942

8 tons bomb-load

the greatest army of pilots the world has ever seen … there can only be one end. … As Hitler sowed … so shall Hitler reap!' The cover depicts a world in flames. Two terrifying black and white expressionistic landscapes reveal the changing fortunes of aerial warfare in 1942; the front (*As Hitler Sowed*) is of British civilians scurrying for an Anderson shelter and the back (… *so Shall Hitler Reap!*) shows Germany in flaming ruins below a burning swastika (Fig. 75b).

The public greeted news of the heavy attacks on Cologne and other cities with enthusiasm.[14] Although a semantic debate was unfolding behind the scenes between the Air Ministry and Sir Arthur 'Bomber' Harris, the Commander-in-Chief of Bomber Command, over directives regarding the bombing of German civilians, the government was now committed to the prosecution of a bomber war with more dedicated energy than any other combatant nation. The Battle of Britain had kept the nightmare of invasion at bay but it had not secured victory in the war. Attention now focused on the role of Bomber Command. The second part of Churchill's 20 August speech is often overlooked. Having immortalised the Few of Fighter Command, he went on to remind the nation of the crucial on-going role being carried out by Bomber Command over the skies of Germany:

> *All hearts go out to the fighter pilots, whose brilliant actions we see with our own eyes day after day, but we must never forget that all the time, night after night, month after month, our bomber squadrons travel far into Germany, find their targets in the darkness by the highest navigational skill, aim their attacks, often under the heaviest fire, often with serious loss, with deliberate, careful discrimination, and inflict shattering*

75a (opposite)
*As Hitler Sowed …
so Shall Hitler Reap!*
Bigger and better bombs.
(PP/1/5)

75b (below)
The front and back cover of
*As Hitler Sowed …
so Shall Hitler Reap.*
The Greek version.
(PP/1/5)

... ΕΤΣΙ ΘΑ ΘΕΡΙΣΗ !   ΟΠΩΣ ΕΣΠΕΙΡΕ Ο ΧΙΤΛΕΡ ...

WE HAPPY FEW...

blows upon the whole of the technical and war-making structure of the Nazi power. On no part of the Royal Air Force does the weight of the war fall more heavily than on the daylight bombers who will play an invaluable part in the case of invasion and whose unflinching zeal it has been necessary in the meanwhile on numerous occasions to restrain …

Responding to an increasing public interest, a number of publications appeared intended to raise the profile of Bomber Command. In the absence of any major military victories on land or sea to report, the exploits of Bomber Command were followed closely by a public eager for news of retaliatory British bombing strikes. Home Intelligence discovered that the public was less interested in hearing about attacks on specific industrial targets than in following the destruction of German cities. By August 1942 Home Intelligence was reporting that the public complained that these raids were neither regular enough nor sufficiently drastic: 'There is a renewal of hope that with longer nights, the RAF will blow a bloody big hole where Berlin is.'[15] In October 1943 the *Daily Telegraph* gleefully reported: 'Hamburg has had the equivalent of at least 60 "Coventrys", Cologne 17, Dusseldorf 12, and Essen 10!'[16] The MOI obliged with a further series of striking posters

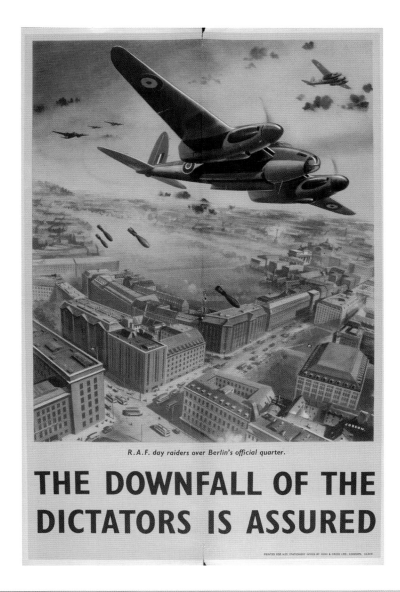

R.A.F. day raiders over Berlin's official quarter.

THE DOWNFALL OF THE DICTATORS IS ASSURED

76 (opposite)
Poster. Dramatically graphic details, in a comic-book format, of an RAF night raid over strategic targets in Germany – all very *Boys Own*.
(PP/BS51/29)

77 (left)
The Downfall of the Dictators Is Assured. Explicit details of bombs being dropped by a Mosquito over Berlin.
(PP/BS51/29)

PP/20/85A

AIR CHIEF MARSHAL SIR ARTHUR T. HARRIS, K.C.B., O.B.E., A.F.C.

FOR VICTORY
G.P.D./365/63

78
A postcard of a determined-looking Air Chief Marshal Sir Arthur 'Bomber' Harris in the 'For Victory' series.
(PP/20/85A)

that became increasingly lurid and colourful, concentrating less on the number of bombs dropped and more on the (melo)drama of the raids (Figs 76, 77). An earnest-looking Air Chief Marshal Arthur Harris (Fig. 78) appeared in the 'For Victory' series of postcards – one of the first British military leaders to do so – and the Air Ministry brought out their own 'official' account of Bomber Command's exploits over Germany in exactly the same format as its *The Battle of Britain* pamphlet (Fig. 79).

Bomber Command never received the adulation or hero status of Fighter Command pilots during the Battle of Britain. Partly this was due to the different nature of the two forms of aerial warfare; one was perceived as a heroic one-to-one dogfight, and the other a more furtive implementation of total war. There was also the question of the morality of the bombing campaign and a residual, underlying unease about celebrating large-scale civilian casualties. In the years following the war the British public turned their backs on the bomber boys and it proved extremely difficult to rehabilitate the reputation of Bomber Command in the light of the haunting images of Dresden and other German cities that suffered saturation bombing.[17] There can be little doubt, however, that at the time, following the Battle of Britain and the Blitz, the public were aware of the nature and intention of Bomber Command's raids, and fully endorsed them.

79

Bomber Command. The official record. This pamphlet was based on interviews with returning aircrews and promised to tell the story of a battle unlike any 'fought before in the history of mankind'. Published just after the release of the Ministry of Information's acclaimed documentary film *Target for Tonight*, it rapidly sold 1.25 million copies.

(PP/3/22)

Monty and El Alamein:
The End of the Beginning …

The Battle of Britain had prevented an invasion and Bomber Command had demonstrated that they possessed the capacity and courage to damage German infrastructure – but Britain had still not secured a victory in the war. Britain went on to suffer defeats in virtually every theatre of war until General Montgomery came along in late 1942 and won a decisive victory in the North African campaign. Earlier in the year Singapore had surrendered and Tobruk had fallen.[18] In July in the First Battle of Alamein the Eighth Army had brought Rommel to a standstill and allowed the British and Commonwealth forces to regroup. The *Daily Express* referred to the rearguard action as a resurrection of the Dunkirk spirit.[19] In August 1942, Lieutenant-General Bernard ('Monty') Montgomery was appointed commander of the Eighth Army, the British and Commonwealth forces fighting in the Western Desert. The Second Battle of El Alamein began on 23 October 1942, and ended twelve days later with the first large-scale, decisive Allied land victory of the war. On 4 November, the BBC news announced that the Axis powers were in full retreat. The victory at El Alamein was to turn the tide of the war.

The defeat of the Germans was the first they had experienced and within North Africa, they could only retreat; they quit North Africa in May 1943. The headline in the *Daily* Mirror proclaimed, 'Rommel Routed. Huns Fleeing in Disorder'.[20] After a series of defeats from Dunkirk to Singapore, Churchill could finally tell the House of Commons that 'we have a new experience. We have victory – a remarkable and definite victory'. It is difficult to overstate the importance of Montgomery's victory at El Alamein – from both the military and the propaganda points of view. Churchill ordered church bells to be sounded for the first time since 1940 and on 10 November the Prime Minister referred to what he called the 'Battle of Egypt' in his famous speech at Mansion House: I have never promised you anything but blood, tears, toil and sweat. Now, however, we have a new experience: we have a victory.... A bright gleam has caught the helmets of our soldiers. … This is not the end. It is not even the beginning of the end. But it is perhaps the end of the beginning.

From the propaganda perspective this was a cause for national celebration and henceforth the MOI could point to subsequent victories in different theatres of war to demonstrate that the direction of the war had irrevocably shifted. The *Daily Mirror* printed Montgomery's picture on its front page beneath the headline, 'He Dished it Out!'.[21] From this point on, the Montgomery legend started to take shape.[22] The newsreels provided extensive coverage of the campaign and the MOI commissioned a documentary film, *Desert Victory*, which was released in March 1943. Compiled mostly from actuality footage taken by the Army Film and Photographic Unit, the film proved a great critical and box-office success. In a Mass-Observation survey it emerged as the third most popular film of the year. Churchill personally was delighted with the film and sent prints of it to Roosevelt, Stalin, the prime ministers of the Dominions, and other Allied leaders.[23]

Accompanying the release of the film the MOI published a number of lavishly produced booklets. *African Victory with the British Forces* (Fig. 80) was directed specifically at a US audience and contained a photograph on the back cover of the 'historic meeting' between Montgomery and the American Commander-in-Chief North Africa, General Eisenhower. *The Battle of Egypt* (Fig. 81) was the 'official record in picture and maps' of the Alamein campaign and cost 7 pence. Produced in multiple languages, it is a high-quality illustrated history very much in the style of *Picture Post*. The prose is devoid of jingoism and focuses instead on the professionalism and efficiency of the Eighth Army. The 1939 image of the Army in constant retreat had been finally eclipsed.[24]

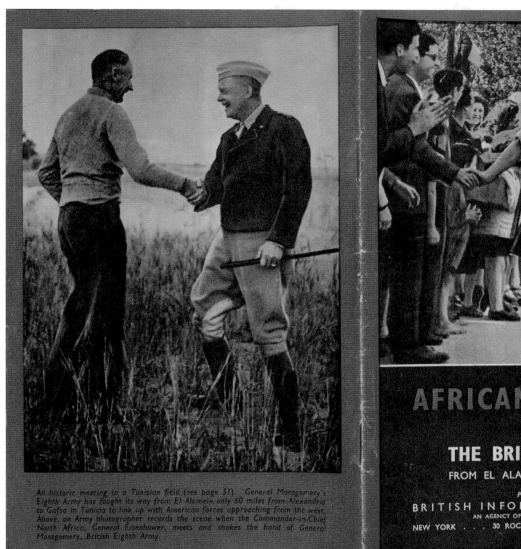

An historic meeting in a Tunisian field (see page 51). General Montgomery's Eighth Army has fought its way from El Alamein only 60 miles from Alexandria to Gafsa in Tunisia to link up with American forces approaching from the west. Above, an Army photographer records the scene when the Commander-in-Chief North Africa, General Eisenhower, meets and shakes the hand of General Montgomery, British Eighth Army.

GP. 39/557.

AFRICAN VICTORY
With
THE BRITISH FORCES
FROM EL ALAMEIN TO CAPE BON

Published by :
BRITISH INFORMATION SERVICES
AN AGENCY OF THE BRITISH GOVERNMENT
NEW YORK . . . 30 ROCKEFELLER PLAZA . . . CIRCLE 6-5100

80
*African Victory with the
British Forces* (1943).
(PP/49/13A)

"The bright gleam has caught the helmets of our soldiers and warmed and cheered all our hearts."
WINSTON CHURCHILL, November 10th, 1942.

THE BATTLE OF
EGYPT

Sherman Tank Driver

THE OFFICIAL RECORD IN PICTURES AND MAP   7D.

DIE SLAG OM
EGIPTE

Sherman-Tenkdrywer

DIE AMPTELIKE GESKIEDROL IN BEELD EN KAART   7D.

LA BATTAGLIA DI
ALAMEIN

Carrista di uno Sherman

CRONISTORIA UFFICIALE ILLUSTRATA

Following the victory of the Eighth Army at El Alamein, the Army, like the RAF before it, now became an esteemed fighting component of the people's war. The victory parade that was held in Tripoli received widespread coverage in all the media and formed the finale of *Desert Victory*. Victory had come none too soon and the parade of soldiers marching in perfect formation, accompanied by the skirl of the bagpipes, in front of a visibly moved Churchill, proved both stirring and inspiring. Henceforth the MOI celebrated subsequent campaigns, and the Army in particular became heroes with the younger generation. Even colouring books for young children publicised the exploits of the British Army. *The British Commandos* proved particularly popular and consisted of a brief, simplified history ('… the Commandos are the crack guerrilla fighters of the British Army … they are especially selected and trained') followed by sections that allowed children to colour in their daring exploits in Norway and St Nazaire (Figs 82, 83). The British in general – not just the younger generation – fell in love with the Commandos. In 1943, the MOI published *Combined Operations*, which showed how these modern warriors were in fact a continuation of an English tradition that stretched back as far as the Elizabethan sea dogs who knew 'how a combination of sea and land forces could inflict hurt on an enemy'.[25] The daring raids of these unorthodox, highly trained, buccaneering men were just what the British wanted. The Germans denounced them as war criminals.

The notion of a people's war implied that 'we were all in this together', and the MOI was unstinting in demonstrating how all the armed forces were playing their part. The posters and pamphlets collected on the following pages were produced for international distribution to show the role played by the Royal Navy during the Battle of the Atlantic and in keeping sea routes open, and also by the Merchant Navy – who were referred to in one pamphlet as the 'Lifeline of Democracy' (Figs 84, 85, 86, 87). A series of posters entitled 'Back Them Up!' was commissioned to remind the Home Front that all the armed services continued to require their backing (Fig. 88). These inspirational posters and publications were supplemented with the 'pocket facts' approach of handy stickers or postcards (Fig. 89).

Conclusion

Following the fall of France, Britain was alone yet morale remained high. Much of this was due to Churchill's leadership and his indomitable bulldog spirit. This was probably *his* finest hour. The Royal Navy and the 'little ships' had rescued British forces stranded at Dunkirk. The RAF had demonstrated how the sacrifices of the Few could inspire the many, and by the time of the Army's victory in the Desert War, official propaganda was expanding its narrative to embrace not just the possibility of a British triumph but a much wider Allied victory. Britain felt confident enough to present itself to the rest of the world as 'Freedom's Fortress' – with all guns blazing (Fig. 90).

81
The Battle of Egypt (1943)
– in three languages.
(PP/52/17A)

BRITISH COMMANDOS

Woodcraft and fieldcraft

COMMANDOS are the crack guerrilla fighters of the British Army and they come from every unit of the Army—cavalry, artillery, sappers, infantry.

They are all specially selected and must possess certain qualities which are necessary for the daring jobs they have to do.

2

First and foremost they must be strong and absolutely fit. Secondly, they must be quick-thinking, alert and resourceful.

All Commando troops undergo special training.

For months they live in tents without any ordinary issue of food. They must learn to find their own food from the land. Woodcraft and fieldcraft are taught them. They are expert with their knives and with all types of small arms.

Every Commando soldier is trained

Making a bivouac from branches of trees

3

COLOUR THESE PICTURES FOR YOURSELF . . .

8

9

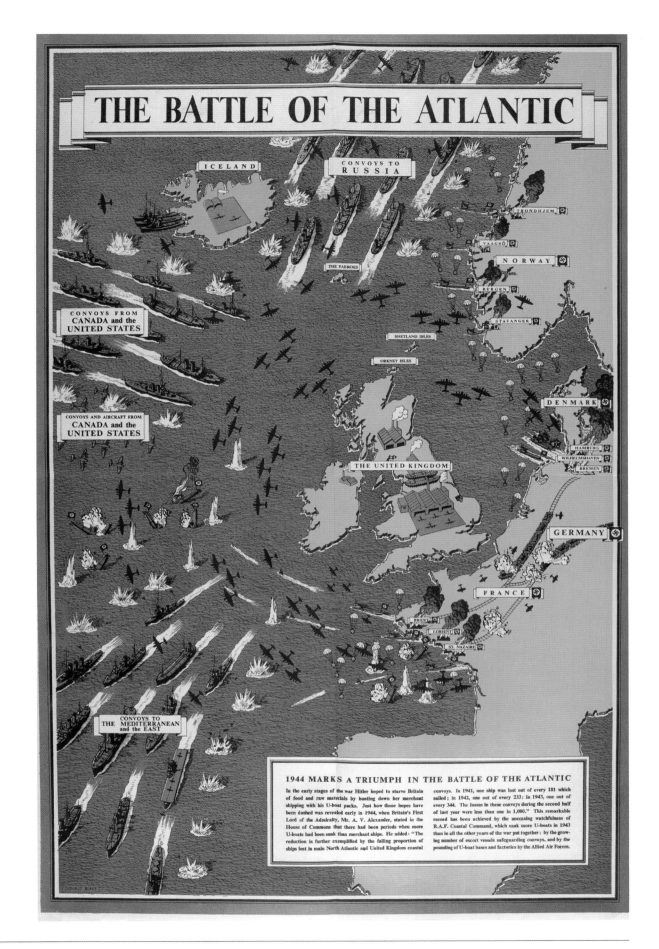

84
Poster.
The Battle of the Atlantic (1944).
(PP/BS51/29)

MERCHANT MARINE
The Lifeline of Democracy

85 (opposite)
Poster, created
to be dropped
into Europe.
*British Warships
Keep Open
80,000 miles
of Sea Routes.*
(PP/BS51/29)

86 (left)
Poster.
*To the Merchant
Navy. Thank You!*
(PP/BS51/29)

87 (top)
*Merchant Marine. The
Lifeline of Democracy.*
(P/14/1L)

WE HAPPY FEW...

The capture of the German submarine U 570 by a Lockheed "Hudson" of the British Coastal Command.

BACK THEM UP!

88
(these pages
and overleaf)
Back Them Up!
Four examples of
the poster campaign
linking the Home
Front to the military
exploits of all the
British armed forces.
(PP/BS51/29)

A British tank attack in the Western Desert

BACK THEM UP!

WE HAPPY FEW...

A British cruiser ramming an Italian submarine in the Mediterranean

BACK THEM UP!

A British "Commando" raid on a German-held port in Norway

BACK THEM UP!

PRINTED IN ENGLAND BY FOSH & CROSS LTD., LONDON. (51-2400)

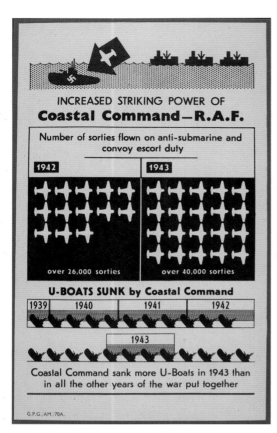

INCREASED STRIKING POWER OF
Coastal Command—R.A.F.

Number of sorties flown on anti-submarine and convoy escort duty

1942	1943
over 26,000 sorties	over 40,000 sorties

U-BOATS SUNK by Coastal Command

1939	1940	1941	1942

1943

Coastal Command sank more U-Boats in 1943 than in all the other years of the war put together

G.P.G./AM./70A.

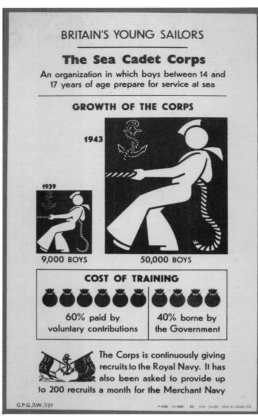

BRITAIN'S YOUNG SAILORS
The Sea Cadet Corps
An organization in which boys between 14 and 17 years of age prepare for service at sea

GROWTH OF THE CORPS

1943

1939

9,000 BOYS   50,000 BOYS

COST OF TRAINING

60% paid by voluntary contributions | 40% borne by the Government

The Corps is continuously giving recruits to the Royal Navy. It has also been asked to provide up to 200 recruits a month for the Merchant Navy

G.P.G./SW./73Y

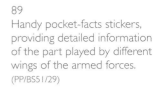

89
Handy pocket-facts stickers, providing detailed information of the part played by different wings of the armed forces.
(PP/BS51/29)

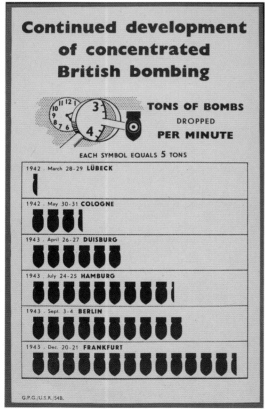

Continued development of concentrated British bombing

TONS OF BOMBS
DROPPED
PER MINUTE
EACH SYMBOL EQUALS 5 TONS

| 1942 . March 28-29 LÜBECK |
| 1942 . May 30-31 COLOGNE |
| 1943 . April 26-27 DUISBURG |
| 1943 . July 24-25 HAMBURG |
| 1943 . Sept. 3-4 BERLIN |
| 1943 . Dec. 20-21 FRANKFURT |

G.P.G./U.S.R./54B.

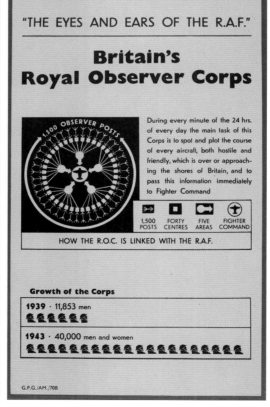

"THE EYES AND EARS OF THE R.A.F."
Britain's Royal Observer Corps

1,500 OBSERVER POSTS

During every minute of the 24 hrs. of every day the main task of this Corps is to spot and plot the course of every aircraft, both hostile and friendly, which is over or approaching the shores of Britain, and to pass this information immediately to Fighter Command

| 1,500 POSTS | FORTY CENTRES | FIVE AREAS | FIGHTER COMMAND |

HOW THE R.O.C. IS LINKED WITH THE R.A.F.

Growth of the Corps

| 1939 · 11,853 men |
| 1943 · 40,000 men and women |

G.P.G./AM./70B

90
Freedom's Fortress (English version). A fold-out brochure that could also be used as a poster, showing the changing fortunes of war. 'Britons today are fighting for the freedom of the world.' It was produced in many languages and dropped over occupied Europe and in the Middle East.
(PP/27/20L)

FREEDOM'S FORTRESS

YESTERDAY

TO-DAY

NOTES

1 Quoted in L. Thompson, *1940: Year of Legend, Year of History* (London, 1966), 132.

2 For revisionist interpretations of the Battle of Britain, see: S. Bungay, *The Most Dangerous Enemy: A History of the Battle of Britain* (London, 2000); R. Overy, *The Battle of Britain: The Myth and the Reality* (New York, 2001); J. Holland, *The Battle of Britain.* (London, 2011). Compare also Vol. 1 of Holland's latest work, *War in the West. A New History* (London, 2015).

3 *Ourselves in Wartime* (Odhams Press, undated), 65.

4 TNA, INF 1/292, H.I. Weekly Intelligence Reports, 12–17 August 1940.

5 *Daily Express*, 16 September 1940.

6 *Daily Mirror*, 28 June 1940. http://www.bbc.co.uk/archive/battleofbritain/11431.shtmlhttp://www.bbc.co.uk/archive/battleofbritain/11431.shtml (last accessed December 2015).

7 The full text of Charles Gardner's report can be found at: http://www.battleofbritain1940.net/document-23.html (last accessed December 2015). The full recording can be heard at: http://www.bbc.co.uk/archive/battleofbritain/11431.shtml. (last accessed December 2015). Charles Gardner actually got many of the details wrong in his report. The Ju87 Stuka that Gardner described was in fact a Hurricane and the pilot bailing out was actually Pilot Officer M. Mudie, who was later picked up by the Navy, but died the next day of his injuries. The style of the broadcast proved controversial, prompting the BBC to launch an 'urgent inquiry' by means of their own Listeners Research Reports. The Home Intelligence report concluded that 'a considerable majority spoke enthusiastically of the broadcast'. TNA, INF 1/292, H.I Weekly Intelligence Reports, 15 and 16 July 1940.

8 Beaverbrook's appeal was met by an eager response initially, but Home Intelligence discovered that enthusiasm waned when housewives noticed that aluminium kitchen utensils were still on sale in the shops. TNA, INF 1/292, H.I. Weekly Intelligence Reports, 8–13 July.

9 Interestingly, few feature films were made during the war about Fighter Command and the Battle of Britain (that would come after 1945). The one exception is *The First of the Few* (1942), which was a biopic of the designer of the Spitfire, R.J. Mitchell (played by Lesley Howard). It begins in September 1940 at the height of the battle. Wing-Commander Geoffrey Crisp (David Niven) tells his pilots the 'true' story of the Spitfire. Mitchell, suffering from deteriorating health, dies just after learning that the Air Ministry had commissioned the Spitfire. The film ends back in 1940: following a dogfight, Crisp opens his cockpit hood, looks to the sky and says, 'They can't take the Spitfire, Mitch, they can't take 'em!' It proved to be the most successful British film of 1942, second overall to *Mrs Miniver*.

10 *Daily Mirror*, 5 June 1940.

11 As early as August 1940, Home Intelligence noted the 'bombing of Berlin has caused great satisfaction'. TNA, INF 1/292, H.I. Weekly Intelligence Reports, 26–31 August 1940.

12 For a further discussion of how strategic policy shifted and the deceptions of the Ministry of Information over the question of the bombing of civilian targets, see I. McLaine, *Ministry of Morale. Home Front Morale and the Ministry of Information in World War II* (London, 1979), 159–66.

13 Although both the critics and the public enthused about the realism of the action, in fact the bomber mission itself was staged in the studio and the film claimed a degree of accuracy Bomber Command knew to be well beyond its capability. See K.R.M. Short, 'RAF Bomber Command's *Target for Tonight*', in *Historical Journal of Film, Radio and Television* 17, 2, (1987), 181–218.

14 Home Intelligence reported the following response '… nothing has given such a life to public confidence for many months as the raid on Cologne. The public's astonishment and awe appear to have been almost as marked as their elation and satisfaction … even the most soft hearted feel that it is the only way, however distasteful, to drive home to the German people what their airman have been doing in other countries'. TNA, INF 1/292, H.I. Weekly Intelligence Reports, 26 May–2 June 1942.

15 TNA, INF 1/292, H.I. Weekly Intelligence Reports, 4–11 August 1942. In 1940 there had been a War Weapons Week to replace armaments lost at Dunkirk, and in 1942 the Government launched a Warship Week and a Spitfire and a Tanks for Attack Week.

16 *Daily Telegraph*, 21 October 1943.

17 In fact a monument to Bomber Command was not inaugurated until 27 June 2012 when the Queen unveiled the sculpture in Green Park, London. Their average age was just 22 and out of 125,000 aircrew, more than 55,000 died – a fatality rate on a par with the infantry in the World War I trenches. A further 8,403 were wounded in action and 9,838 became prisoners of war.

18 The fall of Tobruk had a particularly devastating impact on public morale that lasted for about three weeks. Cf. TNA, INF 1/292, H.I. Weekly Intelligence Reports, 16–23 June 1942.

19 *Daily Express*, 22 July 1942.

20   *Daily Mirror*, 5 November 1942.

21   Ibid.

22   In 1944 Montgomery was sent around the war production factories to encourage the workers to maintain their efforts in support of the Second Front (D-Day landings). *Warwork News*, March 1944 ('Monty at the Factory Front') filmed one of these meetings in which 'Monty' addresses the workers, behaving like a patronising headmaster. It is farcically Monty-Pythonesque – but the workers appeared to love him.

23   For a detailed analysis of *Desert Victory* see J. Chapman, *The British at War. Cinema, State and Propaganda, 1939–1945* (London, 1998), 144–8.

24   An important point made by M. Connelly, *We Can Take It! Britain and the Memory of the Second World War* (Harlow, 2004), 212.

25   *Combined Operations, 1940–1942*, (London, 1943), 9. In 1942 Ealing Studios produced the feature film *Next of Kin* which presented a more sober view of combined forces operations. See A. Aldgate and J. Richards, *Britain Can Take It: The British Cinema in the Second World War* (Edinburgh, 1994), 96–114.

' "This is D-Day," came the announcement over the British radio and quite rightly, "This is the day." The invasion has begun! … Would the long-awaited liberation that has been talked of so much, but which still seems too wonderful, too much like a fairy tale, ever come true? … the best part of the invasion is that I have the feeling that our friends are approaching. We have been oppressed by those terrible Germans for so long, they have had their knives at our throats, that the thought of friends and delivery fill us with confidence!'

ANNE FRANK
DAIRY ENTRY, JUNE 1944.

CHAPTER SIX
On to Victory

Our Friends Abroad: Empire Crusade

In October 1940, the Ministry of Information (MOI) decided to inaugurate a new initiative to inspire the British people: its Empire Crusade. This was the brainchild of H.V. Hodson, an Oxford don and Director of the Empire Division. In a memorandum to the MOI in late September, Hodson had suggested that Britain's justification for war needed to be re-cast. Rather than focusing on the need to 'defeat Nazi Germany' – with all its negative connotations – propaganda should place greater emphasis on the more positive sentiment of preserving the Commonwealth. This new emphasis, which amounted to a form of 're-education', would reinforce the conviction in the moral superiority of Britain's way of ordering the world. Although it was agreed to trial this campaign for ten weeks, not all within the MOI were convinced, including the Minister, Duff Cooper. Equally opposed to the campaign was the MOI's Parliamentary Secretary, Harold Nicolson, who wrote in his diary: 'I do not think we should spend large sums on anything which is not essential. The public do not want at present to be told about New Zealand or the Lugard system'.[1]

91
Playing Their Part.
(PP/42/9A)

Planes—and the men behind them...

Top left : Flight Sergeant James J. Hyde, from San Juan, Trinidad, trained in England. He is a close friend of "Dingo," the squadron mascot.

Top right : The Wing Commander chats to Ceylon bomber crew. Men of the Ceylon Squadron have taken part in raids on Berlin, Essen and Kiel.

Left : Twenty-two-year-old Robert Ngbaronye reached Britain as a stowaway from Nigeria, set on studying medicine ; he joined the R.A.F. instead and is now learning to fly.

Right : A volunteer from the West Indies now serving with the R.A.F. West Indians are serving as pilots, technicians and ground crew.

Pictured with this "Hurricane" of the Mauritius Squadron are : Left, a French Flight-Sergeant, and a Maori Sergeant who played for the famous "All Blacks" rugby team.

Donations have come from every quarter of the Empire to buy planes to fight with the R.A.F. Pictured above is a "Hurricane" paid for by the people of British Honduras.

PP/42/9A

PLAYING THEIR PART
THIRD EDITION

Empire Day Message from H.M. THE KING to the Colonial Empire.

"My Colonial troops, side by side with their comrades from all parts of the Empire, have fought, and are fighting with their traditional bravery. Success crowned their arms in Africa as I know it will in other theatres of war. But fighting in battle is only one part of total war. The organisation of large and small communities and their resources on a war footing, the carrying out of urgent war measures and the planning and execution of programmes of war production have thrown a heavy burden upon my Colonial Governments and Legislatures. They have, I know, been helped in their task by the outstanding and loyal co-operation of the people."

The venture was only half-heartedly taken up by the MOI and eventually dropped. It consisted mainly of strategically placed positive statements in national newspapers on the values of the British Empire ('a family of free nations') and was intended to impart a 'dynamic faith' in the British people. The campaign failed in both its educative and morale-boosting objectives.[2]

Although this specific campaign, which was dubbed 'exhortation propaganda' within the MOI, was swiftly abandoned, propaganda directed to and about the British Empire proliferated. It developed organically and took on different forms and had different target audiences. Although Britain claimed she was alone after the fall of France, the reality was that the British Empire and Commonwealth remained staunch allies providing troops, food, and equipment. Recognising this, the MOI set about detailing the vital contribution made by these countries to the common cause. The BBC devoted radio programmes to the Empire and Commonwealth, providing opportunities for their leaders to address the nation with information about individual countries and their contribution to the war effort.

One major plank of MOI propaganda was to show the people of Britain what other countries were contributing *within* Britain. *Playing Their Part* was an annual publication that highlighted the significant contribution made by individuals, and also countries, from the British Empire. Fig. 91 shows the third edition, which focuses on 'Planes – and the men behind them'. The cover consists of the Union Jack with an extract taken from the King's annual Empire Day message:

> *My Colonial troops, side by side with their comrades from all parts of the Empire, have fought and are fighting with their traditional bravery. Success crowned their arms in Africa as I know it will in other theatres of war. But fighting in battle is one part of total war …*

The King went on to praise his colonial governments and legislatures for placing their countries on a war footing and for their contributions to war production, adding that they had been helped greatly in their tasks 'by the outstanding and loyal co-operation of the people'. Examples of individual and collective contributions to the Royal Air Force were cited, ranging from individual pilots from Trinidad, Ceylon, Nigeria, West Indies, and New Zealand, to the purchase of a Hurricane to fight with the RAF paid for by donations from the people of British Honduras. Other editions in this series highlighted the multifarious roles played by women and there was also a small section on children from the Empire. Under the heading 'Don't forget the children', brief biographical details and a photograph of Stephen Antia, a 5-year-old from Nigeria, are accompanied by the words: 'Stephen … knows the importance of helping the merchant Navy, in which his Daddy is serving, by eating up all his lunch.' The purpose behind this series of pamphlets was not only to educate the British people about the culture and geography of the countries that made up the British Empire and Commonwealth, but also to provide a human context within which individual contributions are framed. For example, in the third volume mention is made of 22-year-old Robert Ngbaronye, who can be seen smiling proudly in his RAF uniform (see Fig. 91). Readers are informed that 'he reached Britain as a stowaway from Nigeria, set on studying medicine; he joined the RAF instead and is now learning to fly'. Posters and postcards were also used. Fig. 92 shows a postcard on the theme of 'War Work in Britain' in the 'For Victory' series. Like so much of this type of propaganda it is very low-key and matter of fact, and shuns the use of hyperbole or jingoism. The postcard, in high-quality colour, shows an intent-looking Mr G. Mustaja, working on the frame of an aircraft, 'who came to Britain from the North-West Frontier under the Ministry of Labour's industrial training scheme. He is seen here at work in an English factory'.

Much of the MOI's propaganda was devoted to the contributions made by individual countries. Pocket-facts postcards proved an effective means of combining

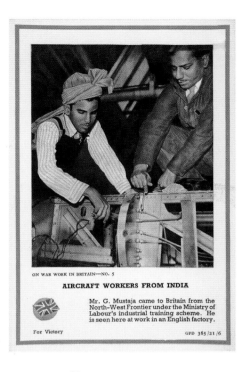

92
From the 'For Victory' series:
Aircraft Workers from India.
(PP/20/24L)

93 (overleaf)
The 'In Freedom – Strength!' series. Pocket-facts postcards proved an effective means of combining dramatic images with detailed information.
(PP/25/1A,3,6,7,10,16)

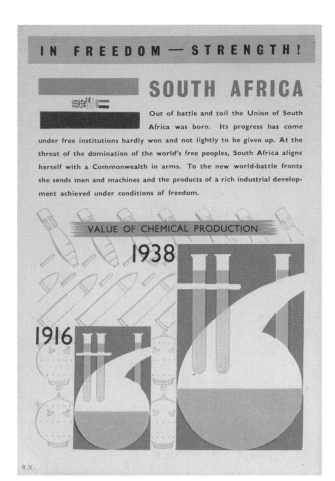

IN FREEDOM — STRENGTH!

SOUTH AFRICA

Out of battle and toil the Union of South Africa was born. Its progress has come under free institutions hardly won and not lightly to be given up. At the threat of the domination of the world's free peoples, South Africa aligns herself with a Commonwealth in arms. To the new world-battle fronts she sends men and machines and the products of a rich industrial development achieved under conditions of freedom.

VALUE OF CHEMICAL PRODUCTION

1938

1916

R.X.

IN FREEDOM — STRENGTH!

BRITISH MALAYA

Sea girt lands that have thrived and developed their resources under the rule of law, where every man has freedom of conscience and freedom of work, now yield to the Commonwealth war effort an abundance of materials to help in the forging of victory. British Malaya guards the Eastern seas, and guarantees the flow of essential commodities to the Empire and Allied arsenals.

EXPORT OF **TIN**

PP/25/10A

1914 · 47,689 TONS   **1940 · 85,384 TONS**

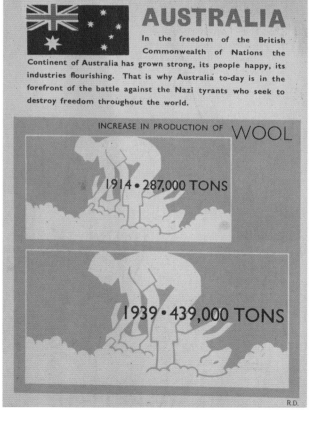

IN FREEDOM — STRENGTH!

AUSTRALIA

In the freedom of the British Commonwealth of Nations the Continent of Australia has grown strong, its people happy, its industries flourishing. That is why Australia to-day is in the forefront of the battle against the Nazi tyrants who seek to destroy freedom throughout the world.

INCREASE IN PRODUCTION OF WOOL

1914 · 287,000 TONS

1939 · 439,000 TONS

R.D.

IN FREEDOM — STRENGTH!

★ INDIA ★

A vast increase has come to India, in production of raw materials and in output of manufactures, under British rule. Economic power is being given now without stint to aid in the Empire's fight against Hitler.

PRODUCTION OF COAL

R.S.

1914 · 15,960,000 TONS   **1939 · 24,815,000 TONS**

IN FREEDOM — STRENGTH!

 ★ **CANADA** ★

is the world's largest producer of nickel. Her vast industrial and food-growing resources have been pledged by her people to aid Freedom's cause in the struggle against Nazi tyranny.

INCREASE IN PRODUCTION OF
NICKEL

PP/25/18A

1914 · 20,000 TONS **1939** · 101,000 TONS

RB

R.Q.

IN FREEDOM — STRENGTH!

 ★**CEYLON**★

The happiness and prosperity of her peoples and the productivity of her soil, ever-increasing through her years of association with the Empire, have shown Ceylon that freedom means strength. That strength is now directed to Freedom's cause in the battle against Nazi tyranny.

EXPORT OF COPRA
(*coconut kernels yielding food oils*)

1914 **1938**
70,598 TONS **194,664 TONS**

IN FREEDOM — STRENGTH!

NEW ZEALAND The prosperity and contentment of New Zealand has come to her through freedom in the British Commonwealth. To-day the people of New Zealand are using their man power and their great resources in the fight against the evil forces of Nazi brutality.

Exports of FROZEN MEAT

1914 · 3,229,973 cwts.

1939 · 5,373,601 cwts.

B I

IN FREEDOM — STRENGTH!

 ★ **CANADA** ★

Modern Canada is a young giant amongst industrial nations as well as one of the greatest food-producing countries. Canada, like the whole British Commonwealth, has grown strong in liberty and to-day is putting forth all its strength so that liberty shall live.

INCREASE IN PRODUCTION OF
WHEAT

PP/25/16A

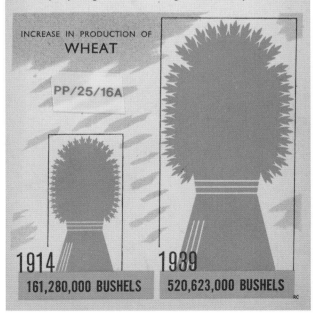

1914 **1939**
161,280,000 BUSHELS 520,623,000 BUSHELS

RC

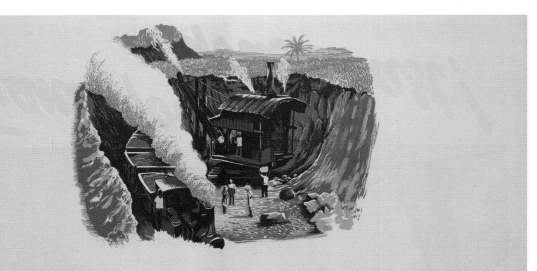

Your Manganese makes STEEL for fighting ships

G.P.D. 265/37/9

Thank you Gold Coast!

94
*Thank You
Gold Coast!*
(PP/BS51/29)

Your Iron Ore makes front-line TANKS and GUNS

95
*Thank You
Sierra Leone!*
(PP/BS51/29)

YOUR 'SPITFIRES' IN ACTION

Subscriptions from Bermuda have bought "Spitfire" fighter aircraft for Britain. These planes protect British homes and industries from aerial attack and harass enemy shipping and transport.

When enemy bombers approach Britain, the fighters go up to drive them away. Here is a Bermuda fighter plane shooting down an enemy bomber over one of Britain's industrial towns.

Bermuda fighter planes also take part in offensive sweeps over enemy-occupied territory and cause much damage to shipping and transport and communications with their machine-gun fire.

Bermuda fighters protect Allied merchant ships from hostile aircraft. Many vital cargoes have reached port only because of the watchful presence of fighter planes.

Other war gifts from Bermuda include contributions for ambulances, scrap metal, Air Raid Relief, Anti-Aircraft Command Welfare, Royal Air Force Benevolent Fund, Aid to Russia, and many other funds.

Thank you, Bermuda!

simple images with detailed statistical information. Striking was a series of postcards entitled 'In Freedom – Strength', which provided succinct summaries of the main contributions from each nation (Fig. 93). For example, one dealt with India and the production of coal: 'A vast increase has come to India, in production of raw materials and in output of manufactures, under British rule. Economic power is being given now without stint to aid in the Empire's fight against Hitler.' It is interesting to compare a colonial country with a Dominion such as Canada (for which these postcards were translated into French) and its wheat production: 'Modern Canada is a young giant amongst industrial nations as well as one of the greatest food-producing countries. Canada, like the whole of the British Commonwealth, has grown strong in liberty and today is putting forth all its strength so that liberty shall live.'

Posters proved a cheap and effective means of making short, powerful visual statements. Such posters were produced by the MOI both for home consumption and for the people of the colonies, showing them the ultimate destination of the fruits of their efforts for the Allied cause. Particularly noteworthy was a series that thanked an individual country for an indigenous product and demonstrated its specific importance in the common cause. Cotton from the Windward Islands played 'a great part in the defence of Britain in making barrage balloons to protect cities from enemy dive-bombers'. Rubber from Ceylon is used for 'army vehicles' tyres and also for rubber dinghies, to save the lives of pilots who bail out of their aircraft over the sea'. In the two examples illustrated (Figs 94, 95), manganese from the Gold Coast makes steel for fighting ships and iron ore from Sierra Leone contributes to front-line tanks and guns. Posters sometimes came in a comic-strip format, when a multiple narrative was required. For example, Empire and Commonwealth countries were encouraged to make financial

96
Your 'Spitfires' in Action. Thank You, Bermuda!
Colonial governments sponsored Bomber Command squadrons rather than having their own personnel involved. They were then entitled to name a squadron. It was good imperial propaganda and both the British and the colonies loved little nuggets of information, such as the fact that the Jamaica-sponsored squadron supplied barrels of rum.
(PP/BS51/29)

97
The Mighty War Effort of the British Commonwealth.
(PP/14/36A)

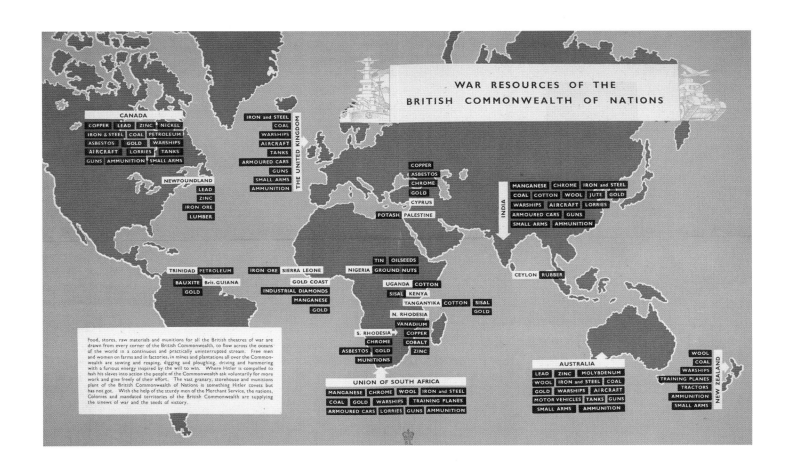

Britain is your friend and
believes in progress for all

Germany is your enemy and believes
in slavery for all non-Germans

VICTORY IS VITAL!

GERMANS WOULD ROB
WEST AFRICANS OF THEIR PRODUCE

98
The 'Victory is Vital' series.
Employing simple imagery and concise
narrative, these booklets offered a stark
contrast between the respective motives
and attitudes of Britain and Germany towards
the African colonies. Such propaganda has to
be seen in the wider context of the Ministry
of Information's 'Empire Crusade'.
(PP/25/108A, 109A)

and other contributions to Britain's war effort. *Your 'Spitfires' in Action* (Fig. 96) tells a series of stories about the impact of Bermuda's contribution to the purchase of a Spitfire: 'Subscriptions from Bermuda have bought "Spitfire" aircraft for Britain. These planes protect British homes and industries from aerial attack and harass enemy shipping and transport.' Another strip shows in graphic detail how 'Bermuda fighter planes also take part in offensive sweeps over enemy-occupied territory and cause much damage to shipping and transport and communications with their machine-gun fire'. These are simple messages designed to demonstrate the gratitude felt by the 'mother country'.

Another approach adopted by the MOI was to show that the combined strength of Empire and Commonwealth would, inexorably, lead to final victory. Pamphlets were more suited to this type of message. Pamphlets and leaflets allowed the MOI to provide detailed information combined with glossy photographs and illustrations that provided a visual punch to the production. In the *British Empire's King and Queen* (see Fig. 38), George VI rallied his people by declaring: 'Wherever else did human idealism and practical sense combine to weld one-fourth of the human race, scattered over a quarter of this globe, into an entity based on respect for individual freedom, and spontaneously generating the willing service of all in the common interest?' In 1942 the MOI produced a stylish forty-nine-page booklet entitled *Sixty Million of Us. The Colonies at War*, which examined in extraordinary detail the magnitude of the Empire's combined resources now

Under Britain you can
buy what you like

Under Germany you would starve
and be made slaves

VICTORY IS VITAL!

GERMANY WOULD MAKE
WEST AFRICANS INTO SLAVES

being co-ordinated to support the British war effort.[3] Equally informative, but more instantly effective, was a fold-out leaflet, *The Mighty War Effort of the British Commonwealth* (Fig. 97), which illustrated the Commonwealth's resources and manpower by using a map of the world to show the extraordinary global effort that was being harnessed in the fight against its enemies. Such publications – which were further supplemented by films, radio programmes, and leaflets dropped over occupied territories – concluded that it was only a matter of time before Fascism in its various manifestations would be defeated. From 1942 onwards, this was a message all the more effective in propaganda terms because it could now be backed up by military victories in numerous theatres of war.

To balance this, the MOI also wished to demonstrate what Britain was doing for its colonial partners. This involved a two-pronged approach: showing how Britain was protecting them against the enemy, while also demonstrating how British know-how and education was facilitating their own development. To this end, a series of pamphlets entitled 'Victory is Vital' concentrated on different aspect of Fascist oppression (Fig. 98). These were very simple documents aimed at a basic level of literacy, and there is, unquestionably, a patronising element to them. The two examples illustrated are directed at West Africa. The first pamphlet claims that Germans 'would rob West Africans of their produce'. The front cover shows German soldiers whipping and clubbing defenceless

BRITISH SHIPS

GUARD AFRICAN SHORES

African peasants and stealing their goods. On the inside page two images are juxtaposed; one shows a British administrator shaking hands with a fully clothed West African, with the caption 'Britain is your friend and believes in progress for all'. This image conveys a sense of equality in terms of stature and dress in a symbolic hand-shake. Below, a Nazi soldier is whipping a virtually naked peasant lying prostrate on the floor, with the caption 'Germany is your enemy and believes in slavery for all non-Germans'. The cover on the other pamphlet shows semi-naked Africans being marched away from their homes in chains ('Germany would make West Africans into slaves'). An illustration inside reveals Africans trading happily in a store, 'Under Britain you can buy what you like'. The contrasting picture is of an emaciated, naked peasant begging for food: 'Under Germany you would starve and be made slaves'. On another page the text states: 'A German newspaper recently said: "A lower race needs less food, less room and less clothing than a higher race." Britain stopped the Germans from ill-treating Africans by beating Germany in the last war. Britain will beat the Germans again with your help.'

The MOI were fully aware that the Nazi propaganda machine was attempting to drive a wedge between the British Empire and its colonies. Part of the Ministry's response was to show the benefits of remaining aligned to the British Empire and Commonwealth. Not only was Britain protecting its Empire by means of its military power and capabilities

99
Two posters showing different ways in which Britain was protecting its colonies. The posters, designed for African consumption, are painted in an extremely bright, colourful style.
(PP/BS51/29)

(Fig. 99), but also the maternalistic 'mother country' was also providing much-needed help for the development of the colonies (Fig. 100). These posters were intended for public buildings such as civic centres, schools, and universities. Such propaganda material is very much a product of its time. Just as the British Empire was forced to change after the war to become the Commonwealth of Nations,[4] so these images of British imperial superiority would now be viewed as arrogant and offensive.

The MOI occasionally produced material for both home and overseas audiences that demonstrated the bravery of the Empire and Commonwealth. One poster from a major propaganda series commissioned by the MOI was entitled *Smash Japanese Aggression!* (Fig. 101). The poster vividly illustrates the fearlessness and bravery of Indian troops fighting the Japanese in the Far East. The second poster depicts African troops in action and is from the same series but with a slightly different twist to the title, *Smash the Japs!* (Fig. 102). Both are rare examples of World War II propaganda that reveals the full horror of warfare. All combatants tended to avoid such explicit images because in psychological terms it should, or might, elicit sympathy for the enemy that is about to be killed (or who has already been slain.) But audiences who were familiar with the atrocities committed by the Japanese would have felt little sympathy for the Japanese soldier at the end of the Indian Lieutenant's bayonet or of the African soldier's rifle butt.

SAVING THE SOIL OF THE WEST INDIES TO GROW MORE FOOD

The West Indies must grow more food for their people, who are increasing rapidly in number. They are mostly farmers. In some of the islands suitable land is not available for many new farms and the old farmland is yielding smaller crops because the soil, which is becoming less fertile, is being washed away. This picture shows West Indians, advised by a British expert, learning how to save the soil, and how to grow more food and more kinds of food.

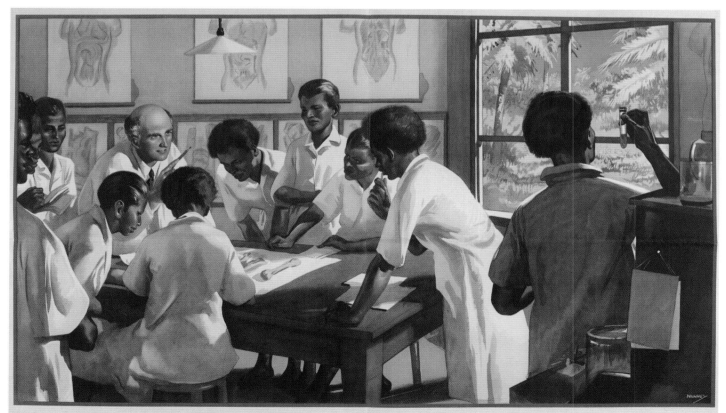

LEARNING TO BE DOCTORS IN FIJI

Throughout the British Colonial Empire much is being done to improve and maintain the health of the people. This important work is carried on not only by Europeans but also by local men and women who are trained to become doctors or nurses. Here are medical students at work under the supervision of a British doctor in the Central Medical School at Suva, capital of the Colony of Fiji. They are not all Fijians; some come from other and far-distant Pacific islands. They will go home to heal the sick, to prevent the spread of diseases, and to raise the standard of health among their peoples.

Although the war with Japan remained peripheral for many British people, it was felt necessary to reassure countries in Asia and in the Middle East, who were either fighting or felt threatened by Japan, that Britain was still waging its own war against the Japanese. Posters and leaflets were the preferred choice of propaganda and one strategy included showing how the recently established United Nations was committed to pursuing the conflict in South-East Asia until Japan surrendered unconditionally. The Chinese nationalist leader Chiang Kai-shek was invariably presented in this context as the Allies' democratic strongman of Asia. The MOI also produced a series of posters in the final year of the war in English, Arabic, and Persian demonstrating Britain's own commitment. The most striking was a poster designed by Sevek for the MOI entitled, *On to Japan!*[5] In this dramatic, minimalist, Art Deco-style poster an archer is using a plane as his bow and aiming it at Japan (Fig. 103). The Rising Sun flag of Japan has been used to create the effect of a target around the islands of Japan.

Towards the end of the war and in recognition of the critical roles played by the British Empire and the Commonwealth, King George VI made an address to 'my colonial peoples'. Part of the speech was reproduced as a leaflet and distributed throughout the British Empire (Fig. 104). In it, the King reflected on 'the promises and loyalty which so many of you sent me in the darkest days of our history (which) have been redeemed many times over'. Although he died shortly after the war in 1952, George VI's reign saw the acceleration of the dissolution of the British Empire.

100
Two examples of the benefits of remaining aligned to the British Empire. The text for *Learning to be Doctors in Fiji* reads: 'Throughout the British Colonial Empire much is being done to improve and maintain the health of the people. This important work is carried on not only by Europeans, but also by local men and women who are trained to become doctors or nurses. Here are medical students at work under the supervision of a British doctor in the Central Medical School at Suvam, capital of the Colony of Fiji. They are not all Fijians; some come from other and far-distant Pacific islands. They will go home to heal the sick, to prevent the spread of diseases, and to raise the standard of health among their peoples.'
(PP/BS51/29)

101 (overleaf left)
Smash Japanese Aggression!
Although it is anonymous, this poster was probably by Harold Forster. It is a rare propaganda depiction of the horror of military combat.
(PP/BS51/29)

102 (overleaf right)
Smash the Japs!
The slogan is in Kiswahili: 'Our Soldiers beat the Japanese'. Like Fig. 101, it is a recruitment poster, in this case appealing to Africans to join the armed forces. More often propaganda aimed at Africa was related to war production rather than the front-line fighting role.
(PP/BS51/29)

104
Leaflet. *King George VI's Address to the British Empire.*
(PP/BS51/29)

"Throughout this bitter and terrible conflict, I have never doubted that the response of my colonial peoples to all calls made upon them would be swift, wholehearted, and complete. It is a wonderful thing for me to reflect that the promises of loyalty and support which so many of you sent to me in the darkest days of our history have been redeemed many times over."
GEORGE R.I.

An Indian lieutenant of the Baluch Regiment led a spirited bayonet charge to capture ammunition from a Japanese dump in the Martaban area. He was awarded the Distinguished Service Order.

SMASH JAPANESE AGGRESSION !

ASKARI WETU WASHINDA WAJAPANI

Smash the Japs!

G.P.D. 365/68   Printed for H.M. Stationery Office by Greycaines, Watford and London. SI-1085

Printed in England by J. Howitt & Son Ltd., Nottm.   51-1344

SEVEK

103
Poster *On to Japan!* (1945).
An extraordinarily powerful,
modernist image of Britain as an
archer backed by a full military
arsenal of planes, tanks, and boats.
The poster was intended to
demonstrate Britain's continuing
commitment to defeating Japan.
(PP/BS51/29)

Britain and the Middle East: Friend or Foe?

More problematic for Britain was its relationship with Muslim nations in the Middle East. During World War II, the Middle East was the site of a propaganda struggle between Britain and its allies, and Nazi Germany and the other Axis powers. Propaganda produced by the Nazis found a receptive ear in some areas of the Persian Gulf. The Nazi regime developed an approach to Muslims that largely ignored the *Protocols of the Elders of Zion, Mein Kampf*, and other European sources in favour of selected passages from the Qur'an. The Nazis portrayed Islam as their natural ally and, accordingly, called for its revival while urging Muslims to act piously and emulate the prophet Muhammad. Radio Berlin in Arabic went so far as to declare: 'Allahu akbar! Glory to the Arabs, Glory to Islam.' The Nazis noted the parallel between sayings from the Qur'an (Sura 5:82, 'You will meet no greater enemy of the believers than the Jews') and the words of Hitler ('By resisting the Jews everywhere, I am fighting for the Lord's work') and helped transform the Qur'an into an anti-Semitic tract whose primary purpose was to call for eternal hatred of Jews.[6]

The British made efforts to counter this German propaganda by radio broadcasts of their own and through the production of printed materials such as posters, leaflets, and pamphlets. The MOI was keen to demonstrate to the Muslim world that Christianity and Islam had much in common and that they needed to show solidarity to defeat what it termed the 'godless evil of Hitlerism'. *The Muslim Attitude to the War* was one of the

105
God Defend the Right.
(PP/10/10A)

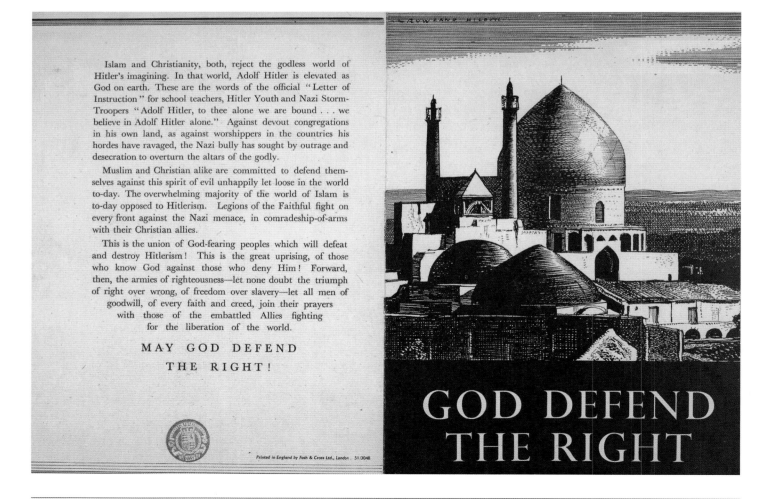

Islam and Christianity, both, reject the godless world of Hitler's imagining. In that world, Adolf Hitler is elevated as God on earth. These are the words of the official "Letter of Instruction" for school teachers, Hitler Youth and Nazi Storm-Troopers "Adolf Hitler, to thee alone we are bound . . . we believe in Adolf Hitler alone." Against devout congregations in his own land, as against worshippers in the countries his hordes have ravaged, the Nazi bully has sought by outrage and desecration to overturn the altars of the godly.

Muslim and Christian alike are committed to defend themselves against this spirit of evil unhappily let loose in the world to-day. The overwhelming majority of the world of Islam is to-day opposed to Hitlerism. Legions of the Faithful fight on every front against the Nazi menace, in comradeship-of-arms with their Christian allies.

This is the union of God-fearing peoples which will defeat and destroy Hitlerism! This is the great uprising, of those who know God against those who deny Him! Forward, then, the armies of righteousness—let none doubt the triumph of right over wrong, of freedom over slavery—let all men of goodwill, of every faith and creed, join their prayers with those of the embattled Allies fighting for the liberation of the world.

MAY GOD DEFEND THE RIGHT!

Printed in England by Fosh & Cross Ltd., London. 51/3048

GOD DEFEND THE RIGHT

first pamphlets dropped over the Middle East by the RAF and urged Muslims to stand firm with Britain and her allies. It was written by M. Najati Sidki ('a Syrian journalist of note') and also translated into English. Writing just before the Nazi invasion of the Soviet Union, the author, having quoted extensive sections from the Qur'an to counter Nazi propaganda, summarises the current position as follows:

> The peoples of the East and Muslims in general are all united in supporting the cause of Democracy, in both word and deed. This they do, not in order to please the Allies, and not out of fear for them as Hitler's agents allege. They support the Allies because Democracy is a vital cause for them, and because the freedom of peoples is the ideal for which they have long struggled.[7]

In the pamphlet, *God Defend the Right* (Fig. 105), which was published in English and Arabic, the Nazi doctrine represents religious intolerance. The front cover shows a mosque with 'God Defend the Right' and the back cover contains the essence of the propaganda message. Unlike the previous pamphlet, which was more of a polemic, this call to arms in the name of 'God-fearing allies' is the authentic voice of the MOI:

> Islam and Christianity, both, reject the godless world of Hitler's imagining. … Against devout congregations in his own land, as against worshippers in countries his hordes have ravaged, the Nazi bully has sought by intrigue and desecration to overturn the altars of the godly. Muslims and Christians alike are committed to defend themselves against this spirit of evil unhappily let loose in the world today. The overwhelming majority of the world of Islam is today opposed to Hitlerism. Legions of the Faithful fight on every front against the Nazi menace, in comradeship-of-arms with their Christian allies. This is the union of God-fearing peoples which will defeat and destroy Hitlerism! This is the great uprising, of those who know God against those who deny Him! Forward, the armies of righteousness… MAY GOD DEFEND THE RIGHT!

The MOI also published an extremely interesting booklet entitled *Alphabet of the War* (Fig. 106). Each page is a letter of the (Arabic) alphabet and depicts something that begins with that letter related to the war. 'Treachery – the favourite weapon of Hitler with which he tries to enslave the world', shows a Nazi stabbing an enemy in the back.[8]

On a more human level several densely illustrated children's storybooks were published, aimed at different target audiences in the Middle East and in Muslim countries in North Africa. They were designed by W. Lindsay Cable, who famously illustrated Enid Blyton's books in 1940 and 1942 as well as working for the MOI. *Hussein & Johnny* (Fig. 107) was translated into Farsi and was intended for an Iranian audience. Hussein is brought to England and enjoys aspects British life, including playing football for his school team and riding on steam locomotives with his friend Johnny, with whose family he is living. The books were intended to show how enlightened and righteous Britain was and how the country had bravely fought against Fascism, which was a threat to both nations. *Ahmad & Johnny* (Figs 108, 109, 110) follows the same format, although here Ahmad is Sudanese and Johnny's father previously lived in Sudan. It is written in Arabic. It is not stated explicitly (in this story at least), but it seems Johnny's father brought Ahmad back from Sudan with him. Ahmad mentions an uncle but no father, so perhaps he is an orphan. There are several attempts to link Sudan and Britain as friends and allies. Ahmad and Johnny go for a walk in the beautiful Kent countryside (after his father has warned them not to go too far because spies and soldiers could be around!) and they bump into a congenial farmer. He says that his son is serving in Sudan and was involved in fighting against the Italians in East Africa. Britain is described as the 'home of freedom and the source of hope of the future'. Ahmad, who is always seen wearing a fez, and the farmer compare milk and yogurt in England and Sudan; the beauty of the countryside is stressed. The two boys and the farmer then meet a British pilot and a squadron of RAF planes flies overhead. Ahmad

106
Booklet. *Alphabet of the War*.
'Treachery – the favourite weapon
of Hitler with which he tries to
enslave the world.'
(PP/1/28L)

says he loves to learn about planes and the pilot starts telling him his story. It starts as a personal reminiscence about learning to fly, his first time flying and so on, and then becomes a simple narrative of the outbreak of war and the Battle of Britain (in which he took part). As the pilot finishes his story, Johnny's father appears and shakes his hand, thanks him and tells him that he and all the pilots will be remembered as 'immortal heroes of truth and justice'. Like *Hussein & Johnny*, this storybook provides a shorthand history of the heroism of Britain in standing alone against Nazism (Dunkirk and the Battle of Britain are the examples used) and they depict the country as the beacon of freedom and (religious) tolerance.

Posters did not often target the Arab world, but were more usually aimed at other overseas areas. There are, however, rare Arabic examples, and two have recently been discovered. Both of the posters seek to promote a strong, progressive image of Britain and stress the involvement of schoolchildren. One poster presents an overtly militaristic image of British youth and has the tag line يتمرن طلبة المدارس بريطانيا اليوم ليكونوا صناع و جنود الغد ('Students of British Schools Practise Today to be the Builders and Soldiers of Tomorrow'). The poster has a large image of a boy in British Army uniform firing a Bren machine gun. Its text discusses military service for youth in the country. The other poster (Fig. 111) emphasises the involvement of schoolchildren (of both sexes) in British society in shaping the future of the country – in this case 're-planning London'. By depicting young people involved in a mock Parliament, the poster alludes not only to Britain's actual Parliament – in contrast to Germany's dictatorial system – but also to the supposedly inclusive nature of a modern Britain that involved young people in broader issues related to society. Both posters contain the slogan 'For the Sake of Freedom', which appears below a picture of the Union Jack.[9]

Pocket-facts postcards in general proved a popular propaganda vehicle with the MOI. They were cheap to produce, they could be dropped by the RAF in large numbers, and the format combined detailed narrative with visual impact. The Director of Middle East Propaganda at the MOI, Professor L.F. Rushbrook Williams, targeted the Middle East region with carefully selected themes. Fig. 112 shows a number of examples of Nazi exploitation and oppression of conquered peoples. More sophisticated were a series of six postcards by the Egyptian-born political cartoonist Kem (Kimon Evan Marengo), who was a prolific creator of propaganda cartoons for the British during World War II.[10] The postcards are based on an episode from the famous Persian epic the *Shahnameh*, or 'Book of Kings'. The Iranian scholar Mojtaba Minovi, who was working for the BBC Persian service during the war, helping to edit the pro-Allied magazine *Rūzgār-i naw* (The New Age).[11] When asked for advice on an effective propaganda campaign for Iran, he suggested using stories and imagery from the *Shahnameh*. The *Shahnameh,* written by Firdawsi (940–1025), tells the history of Iran in verse over the course of 55,000 rhyming couplets, from its mythical origins in prehistory to the end of the Sasanian Empire (AD 650), and includes many of the classic stories that have come to be emblematic of Persian culture. Firdawsi is credited

107 (left)
Two editions of **Hussein & Johnny**. This series of comic books written in Farsi was intended for an Iranian audience.
(PP/ 10/23A, 24L)

108 (below)
Front covers of three editions of *Ahmad & Johnny*.
(PP/1/7)

قي "كلابلاند" وهو مثال لحياة الشباب بريطانيا يجتمع الأعضاء، مرة في الأسبوع لنظر في المسائل المتعلقة بالنادي ولمناقشة ما بين لهم من المسائل العامة. وتراهم بالصورة وهم يتباحثون في مسألة عامة طرحت على بساط البحث ألا وهي إعادة تخطيط مدينة لندن. وبهذه الطريقة يتعلم شباب بريطانيا وأفراد شعب البلد كيفية حمل المسئوليات إلى عاتق على كاهلهم، وبعمل معظم هؤلاء خلال

تدريب الشعب
أولاد وبنات بريطانيا يتباحثون

| | |

111 (above)
For the Sake of Freedom.
Training the People:
British Boys and Girls discussing
the re-planning of London
(تدريب الشعب و الولاد و بنات بريطانيا
يتباحثون في تخطيط لندن).
A small poster in Arabic
demonstrating how British school
children engage, from a young
age, with democracy.
(OR/R/15/1/355 f. 41)

109 (opposite top)
Ahmad and Johnny meet a jovial
farmer in the Kent countryside.

110 (opposite bottom)
Ahmad and Johnny meet a fighter
pilot who fought in the Battle of
Britain.

with saving the Persian language at a time when Arabic had become the paramount language of religion, culture, and power.[12]

Kem's six postcards, which were commissioned in 1942, use the myth of the tyrant Zahhak in an attempt to render anti-German propaganda more relevant to Iranian cultural sensibilities (Fig. 113). The tyrant Zahhak, who features as Hitler in the postcards, epitomises an oppressive and barbaric ruler who brings to an end the enlightened rule of Jamshid. One understanding of Firdawsi's tale is that Zahhak is symbolic of the Arab invaders who brought an end to the Sasanian Empire and supposedly to Persian civilisation. After Zahhak fully displays his capacity for barbarity, Ahriman (that is, Iblis or Satan) causes to grow from his shoulders serpents that require a daily feeding of human brains, with victims chosen from among the youth of Persia (Iran). After years of reigning in terror, Zahhak has a dream of his downfall in which three warriors approach on horseback, one of whom is Feraydun, from whose face *farr* (the light of kingliness and justice) emanates. After this dream, a blacksmith, named Kaveh, arrives at Zahhak's court requesting the release of his son, one of the youths who is to be fed to the snakes on Zahhak's shoulders. In front of his court, Zahhak feigns mercy and releases Kaveh's son, but later asks Kaveh to sign a document attesting to his mercy. Kaveh refuses to falsely affirm the justice of a tyrant and tears up the document. He then raises his blacksmith's banner on a standard, foments a popular rebellion and goes in search of Feraydun, the future king who would rid Iran of Zahhak's injustice and brutality. At the end of this episode, Feraydun dethrones Zahhak but, rather than killing him, binds him in Mount Damavand to be tortured by the snakes on his shoulders until the end of time.

احمد وجانى

كان احمد وجانى يسيران على مهل فى طريق ضيق من طرق الريف المتربة وكان جانى قد جاء الى هذا المكان الهادىء من مقاطعة «كنت» فى سيارته السريعة ليقابل صديقا له عرفه لما كان فى السودان . وقد جاء ليتباحث معه فى بعض الاشغال الخاصة .

ــ «اذهبا يا ولدى وتمشيا قليلا . ولكن لا تذهبا الى ابعد من دار المزرعة فسوف لا اتغيب اكثر من نصف ساعة» . ــ قال والد جانى بعد ان نزل من السيارة واغلق جميع ابوابها بالمفتاح . اذ لا ننس انه لا يجب ان تترك سيارة غير مقفلة بالمفتاح او عربة او خلافه مما يمكن لجاسوس او جندى من جنود المظلات الواقية ان يستولى عليه ويستخدمه لاغراضه . ويدخل فى هذا ايضا دراجات الاطفال .

ثم اضاف والد جانى وهو يبتسم :
ــ «ولا داعى لان احذركما بعدم احداث سوء او ضرر» .

وقف الولدان بجانب الباب الخشبى يراقبان جونسون يراقب المزارع وهو يسوق الماشية الى المرعى .

٢

وكانت الشمس تتألق فوق اجسامها السمينة اللامعة ذوات اللونين الابيض والاسود . وكان يسمع خوارها من آن لآخر بينما تضرب باذنابها الطويلة وتحنى رقابها لتأكل من الحشائش النضرة .

حقيقة لقد كان المنظر جميلا هادئا يزيده روعة وجمالا صوت القابر وهى تغرد فى العلياء، وحفيف اشجار الحور كلما داعب النسيم اوراقها حتى ليكاد يصعب على الانسان ان يتصور وجود حرب وقتال الم وجود معسكرات التعذيب الالمانية والسفاحين الفاشستين الذين يدخلون الرعب الى قلوب الملايين من الابرياء، هذا الرعب الذى لم ير العالم له مثيلا من قبل .

اما هنا فى بلاد انجلترا السعيدة ومصدر آمال المستقبل للرجال بيت الحرية فان كابوس حقيقة اوروبا فى عام ١٩٤١ لا يبدو اكثر من حلم بشع مشئوم .

سار الفلاح متجها نحو البوابة عندما رأى الوجهين الصغيرين يرمقانه بالنظر فى شىء من

٣

112
Six samples of postcards in Farsi. They are representations of different countries (Greece, Romania, Yugoslavia, Hungary, Italy) showing what terrible things happened to them under Nazi occupation – the theft of Hungary's gold, famine in Greece, the breaking up of Yugoslavia. Italy is shown in a pejorative light, since it entered the war as an ally of Germany.
(PP/18/12A)

Right: Kaveh, the symbol of liberation for the Iranian people, coming before Zahhak-Hitler and raising his blacksmith's apron as a banner of rebellion. **Centre:** the arrival of the promised warriors, Churchill leading the way with his cigar, following by Stalin with his pipe, and Roosevelt with his cigarette in its signature holder. The trio are led by the symbol of Iranian national liberation, Kaveh, with his banner, suggesting that an Allied victory would be a triumph for the Iranian people and not an occupation. Zahhak-Hitler is strapped across the horse with the serpents Mussolini and Tojo (who have grown from his shoulders), while Göbbels (with red tong and horns) is dragged screaming by the horse's tail. **Left:** a stripped and humiliated Zahhak-Hitler is nailed to Mount Damavand by the liberated people, with the Mussolini and Tojo snakes on his shoulders looking rather deflated as the trio of Western leaders gaze benevolently at the scene.

The other major weapon in the MOI's arsenal in its propaganda directed at the Arabic world was the BBC. Its Empire Service had started broadcasting in 1933, but it would take Fascist Italy's invasion of Abyssinia (Ethiopia/Eritrea) before the government could be persuaded to start an Arabic service. Following Mussolini's invasion in 1935, Italy opened a short-wave propaganda station in Bari, targeting the Middle East in Arabic to undermine British interests, particularly in Palestine. It proved to be a highly successful campaign, a mixture of entertainment and allegations of British atrocities. The Foreign Office felt it had to respond and the BBC Arabic Service went on-air in January 1938.[13] From the very outset the BBC attracted a dedicated audience in the Middle East, convinced of its veracity and integrity. In this context the increasing importance of the BBC overseas mirrored a trend that was taking place in Britain, where Fleet Street's position as the first point of news declined from 1939 to 1945. This was a paradoxical situation; as more people bought its editions, newspapers were replaced by radio as *the* most trusted source of news. By 1944 the BBC's 9pm radio news programme was estimated to reach up to 50 per cent of the population (at its peak, the BBC recorded its audience at 34 million out of a population of 48 million). The BBC retained the trust of the public, which newspapers had largely lost. A similar belief in the veracity of the BBC also applied to its overseas broadcasts (to the British Empire and to all the other parts of the world). These were an especially important source of news and communication for resistance movements. The BBC provided its own literature describing its role in the world,[14] and the MOI published and distributed pamphlets detailing the extent of BBC coverage and its popularity within the Arabic-speaking world (Fig. 114). Such publications, which rarely contained political propaganda, were also intended to encourage others in the Arabic-speaking world to listen regularly to BBC broadcasts.

113
Kem's postcards depicting the *Shahnameh*.
(PP/13/9L)

114

The BBC and the Arabic World. A strikingly modern
cover design. Inside the pamphlet are numerous
photographs showing that listening to the BBC is a
shared experience. Here we see happy families
listening to their radios and a group of elders
listening intently in a communal context.
(PP/12/27A)

The Soviet Union and 'Uncle Joe'

Even more problematic for the MOI was Britain's changing relationship to the Soviet Union. In the early part of the war the Soviet Union was in alliance with Germany. The majority of Britons regarded Communism and the Soviet Union with deep mistrust. During this period, the *Daily Worker*, the official publication of the British Communist Party, ceased to attack Nazi Germany and advocated policies that some perceived as seeking to undermine the war effort. For this reason in January 1941 the newspaper was suppressed by the (Labour) Home Secretary, Herbert Morrison.[15]

The distrust of the Soviet Union was deepened further by the Nazi–Soviet Non-Aggression Pact of August 1939, the Red Army's role in the partition of Poland just a few weeks later, and then its brutal invasion of Finland. When the Nazi invasion of the Soviet Union began on 22 June 1941, the British Empire discovered that it had acquired a new, and most unlikely, ally. Initially the MOI was unsure how to handle this, especially as the British public appeared pessimistic about Russia's chances of withstanding the Nazi advance.[16] These suspicions of Russia evaporated overnight in June 1941: even the most hostile anti-Soviet critic, Winston Churchill, responded positively, and the Prime Minister's swift and wholehearted declaration of support for the Soviet Union on 22 June made it imperative that the MOI adopt a similar position in domestic propaganda. Anthony Eden's meeting with Ivan Maisky, the Soviet Ambassador to London, gave the Ministry important insight into government thinking. It was agreed to promote better Anglo–Russian understanding, and to this end the British public were to be given more information about the nature of the peoples that made up the Soviet Union, their ways of life, their traditions, and so on. In response the MOI played down Communism and emphasised the nationalist, rather than the ideological, motivation of the Russian people in their struggle against Nazism.

In November 1941, Lord Beaverbrook, a close confidant of Churchill's and briefly Minister for Supply, headed the British delegation to Moscow with his American counterpart Averell Harriman. Beaverbrook was the first senior British politician to meet Joseph Stalin since the German invasion of the Soviet Union. Much impressed by Stalin and the sacrifice of the Soviet people, he returned to London determined to persuade Churchill to launch a second front in Europe to help draw Nazi resources away from the Eastern Front, to aid the Soviets. On his return from the Soviet Union, having failed to persuade Churchill to launch a second front, Beaverbrook published *The Spirit of the Soviet Union*, a book largely made up of Soviet anti-Nazi cartoons and posters that had been presented to him by Stalin. A flavour of the book can be gleaned from the first cartoon by Boris Efimov called 'A Promise Kept'. It shows Hitler saluting a line of graves with SS helmets on top, that stretch as far as the eye can see across the Russian countryside. Hitler proclaims: 'Each one of you, my faithful SS men, will receive "Lebensraume" (living space).' In the Foreword to the book, Beaverbrook wrote:

> *To help the Russians in their immortal struggle we must direct our energies and our will. It must become a passion of the people. From the factories of Britain our help must flow in a mighty stream. Tanks and aircraft and munitions of war. All that we can make and more than we can spare ... The Russians will use all that we can send them. And with what a magnificent fighting spirit they will use them!*[17]

All royalties from the sale of the book were donated to the Soviet Red Cross Fund and some of the illustrations were sold separately as posters; one such was the vicious satirical cartoon, *Maneater* (Fig. 115), which depicts Hitler as a savage ape-man devouring the bones of his victims, with vultures lurking in anticipation in the sky above. The blood drips from Hitler's mouth onto the skulls from France, Greece, Yugoslavia, Romania, Poland, and Belgium that lie strewn on the ground.

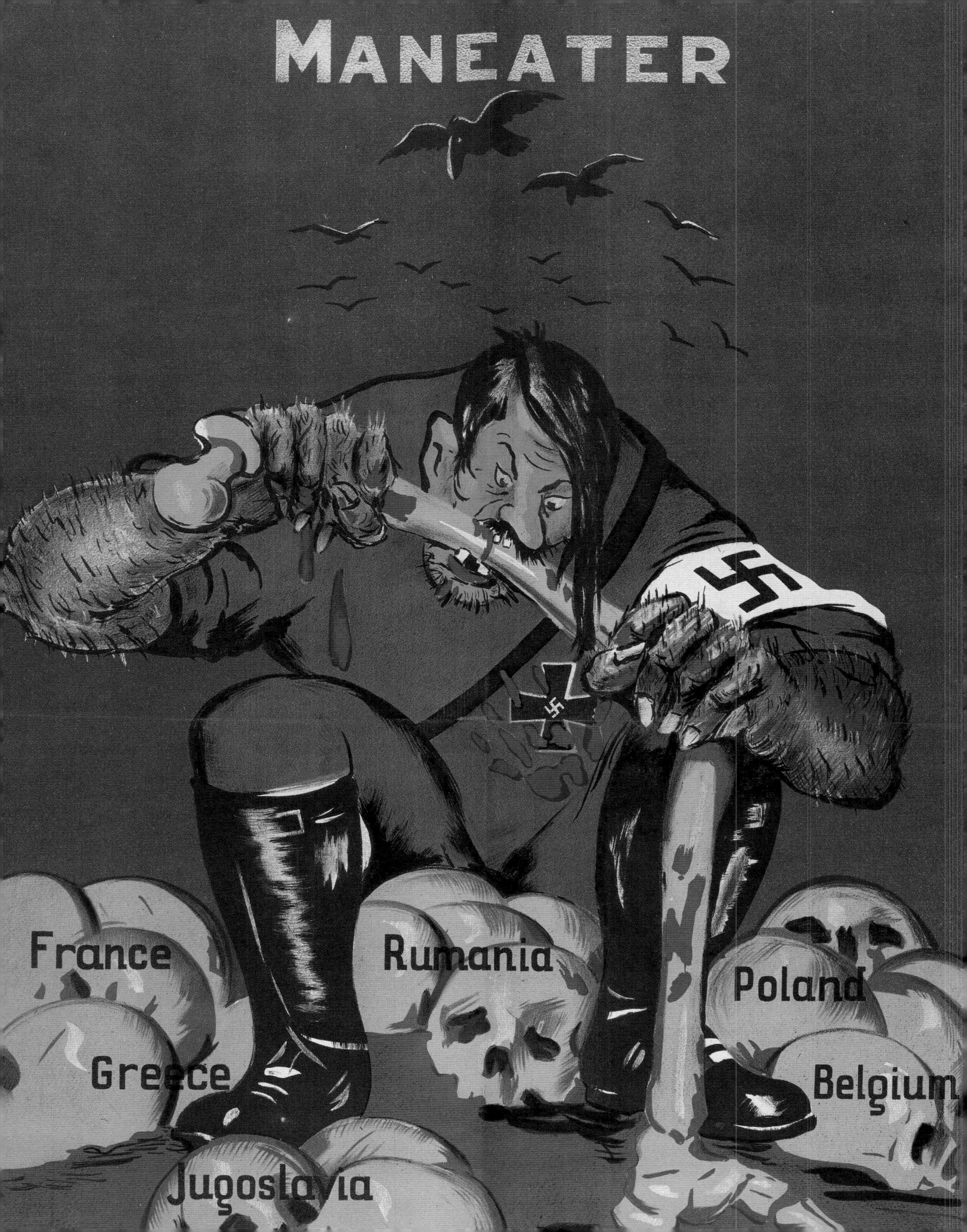
MANEATER
France
Rumania
Poland
Greece
Belgium
Jugoslavia

The response to Beaverbrook's appeal was immediate and extraordinary. The MOI published an illustrated pamphlet called *Comrades in Arms! Britain and the USSR* (Fig. 116). It included the full text of Churchill's speech of 22 June and some of the Soviet cartoons. The front cover conveys the new spirit of comradeship ('Comrades in Arms!') between the two nations and a further appeal from Beaverbrook is included on the back cover. In calling for renewed support for the Soviets, the propaganda message avoided all reference to political ideology, but focused instead on the Russian peoples and the sentiment that 'Their Fight is *Our* Fight'. The renewed appeal prompted the government to send a flow of supplies and armaments via the dangerous Murmansk convoys. The Trades Union Congress (TUC) assisted this through its 'Help for Russia' fund and maintained close contact with Soviet trades unions through the Anglo–Russian Trade Union Council, established in 1941. Until the end of the war, the anti-Communism which had been the hallmark of the TUC leadership since 1926 was temporarily abandoned. Moreover, Russian soldiers and civilians were constantly held up as embodiments of various wartime virtues, such as that depicted in the poster 'Cover Your Hair For Safety. Your Russian Sister Does!', which was injected with a dash of heroic socialist realism. Numerous local and national campaigns organised fund-raising ventures and assisted with the 'Aid to Russia' weeks. Most extraordinarily of all, Joseph Stalin, who had previously been depicted in British propaganda as a deceitful and conniving dictator, was suddenly transmogrified into an avuncular 'Uncle Joe' and appeared regularly on British postcards together with other Allied leaders such as Franklin D. Roosevelt, Charles de Gaulle, and Chiang Kai-shek (Fig. 117).

The MOI, for its part, encouraged publishers to bring out translations of Russian books and the BBC began broadcasting programmes devoted to Russian life and literature. In February 1943, following the retaking of Stalingrad by Soviet forces, the MOI arranged a vast evening of celebration at the Royal Albert Hall, ostensibly to mark the twenty-fifth anniversary of the Red Army (Fig. 118). The event, which was widely covered by the press and radio, was attended by politicians from all parties; it included a mass choir and readings from Laurence Olivier and John Gielgud.[18] To show continuing solidarity, the government declared a 'Red Army Day', which was largely approved by the British people with British cities celebrating with pageants, music, and stirring speeches.[19]

115
Maneater. A cartoon from *The Spirit of the Soviet Union* that was made into a poster in Britain.
(PP/51/29)

116
Comrades in Arms! Britain and the USSR. Although it was commissioned by the Ministry of Information, the message was very much driven by Churchill and Lord Beaverbrook. The appeal for British arms and supplies was based on the joint declaration that 'Their Fight is *Our* Fight'.
(PP/7/16L)

WINSTON S. CHURCHILL

FRANKLIN D. ROOSEVELT

JOSEPH STALIN

CHIANG KAI-SHEK

117
Postcards in the 'For Freedom'
series, which were translated into
many languages. Here they are in
French (*Pour la Liberté*). They
include Franklin Roosevelt, Marshall
Stalin, Charles de Gaulle, and
Chiang Kai-shek (Head of State of
the Chinese Nationalist government). Joseph Stalin's rehabilitation
in British propaganda from
conniving dictator to 'Uncle Joe' is
particularly revealing.
(PP/51/29)

118
*Long Live the Red Army! Greetings
from the British People*. The event at
the Royal Albert Hall was arranged
by the Ministry of Information and
the official programme brochure
was also translated into Russian.
(PP/22/48L)

By 1943, the MOI had overcome its initial concerns about promoting the Soviet
Union in a positive light. By focusing on the courage and fighting spirit of the Russian
people and presenting Joseph Stalin as an avuncular nationalist, British propaganda was
able to sidestep any possible inconsistencies with its treatment of the Soviet Union in the
pre-war period. There is no better illustration of the complex celebration of Anglo–Soviet
friendship in British propaganda than the 1943 feature film *Demi-Paradise*. Directed by
Anthony Asquith, it starred Laurence Olivier as a Russian engineer, Ivan Kutznetsoff,
who comes to Britain to discuss plans for a new form of ship propeller. At first he finds
it difficult to adjust to English customs but eventually comes to respect and like the
people, just as they eventually take to him. By turning Anglo–Soviet relations into a
gentle comedy of manners, the film avoided making any point about profound
differences in political cultures. Henceforth Stalin and the Soviet Union would appear
in British propaganda as a central plank of a renewed Allied war effort in its increasingly
victorious fight against the Axis powers in Europe and Japan.

ДА ЗДРАВСТВУЕТ КРАСНАЯ АРМИЯ !

ПРИВЕТСТВИЕ ОТ
БРИТАНСКОГО НАРОДА

This is London …

By 1941 London had become the seat of government of Norway, Belgium, Holland, Poland, Czechoslovakia, Yugoslavia, and Greece. It was also the headquarters of General de Gaulle and the Free French. The British capital served for the rest of the war as a spiritual rallying point for those opposed to the Nazi occupation of Europe. The MOI spent much of 1940–1 nursing occupied Europe out of its state of shock and rekindling hope and the spirit of resistance. The most notable wartime collaboration is probably that with Charles de Gaulle. Whereas President Roosevelt recognised the Vichy government (in occupied France), Winston Churchill refused to do so and backed de Gaulle as leader of the 'Free French'. In June 1940, shortly after the fall of France, an exiled de Gaulle made his famous BBC broadcast calling for French people to resist the German occupation (Fig. 119).

De Gaulle obtained special permission from Churchill to broadcast a speech via BBC Radio from Broadcasting House over France, despite the British Cabinet's objections that such a broadcast could provoke the Vichy government of Marshal Philippe Pétain into a closer allegiance with Germany. In his speech of 18 June 1940, de Gaulle reminded the French people that the British Empire and the United States of America (although the latter was still not in the war) would support them militarily and economically in an effort to retake France from the Germans. Although the speech subsequently assumed mythic importance, the BBC did not record the speech and few

119
Charles de Gaulle in full military uniform broadcasting to occupied France from the BBC studios in London. This photograph was taken on 30 October 1941 just a year after de Gaulle's famous speech of 18 June 1940, of which no photograph exists.

actually heard it. Another speech, which was recorded and heard by more people, was given by de Gaulle four days later. In August the MOI, together with the Free French in London, produced a poster *À tous les Français* (To All Frenchmen), which was widely distributed over France and was intended to accompany the broadcasts. De Gaulle's broadcast and the leaflets which would become known as *L'affiche de Londres* (The London Poster), are considered to be the founding texts of the French *Résistance*.[20]

The themes of the speech ('Whatever happens, the flame of the French resistance must not be extinguished and will not be extinguished') would be reused throughout the war as a means of inspiring French people to resist German occupation. The MOI also published a series of pamphlets charting the work undertaken by the Free French in London and in North Africa. Pamphlets, such as *Free French Forces* (Fig. 120), together with the posters targeting France, were produced in English and French. Fig. 121 is a typical example of an MOI poster from the middle part of the war, designed to instil hope and encourage the French to resist. Its use of vivid colour – suggesting the south of France, with the coast in the background – is striking and the two peasants appear to be deliriously greeting RAF fighter planes circling in the sky above them. Only a closer inspection of the background reveals that a German supply train has suffered a hit and that a squadron of British planes are homing in to deliver the *coup de grâce*.

An important aspect of British propaganda aimed at occupied France was the need to influence French opinion, while taking care not to offend it. During the early part of the occupation, Marshal Pétain's popularity remained high, so it was important, therefore, not to defame him. It proved more effective to concentrate on what the Allies were achieving in pursuit of the liberation of France. Attacks on Vichy officials, if they did occur, focused on Pétain's subordinates, such as the loathed Pierre Laval. Therefore, as the main Allied landings in northern Europe drew nearer, propaganda continued to

120
Free French Forces. A pamphlet that provided detailed information about the work undertaken by Free French forces. Here General de Gaulle is seen meeting King George VI. Note the Cross of Lorraine at the top of the page. (PP/9/6A)

be concentrated on future liberation rather than a collaborationist past. *Unis Pour La Libération* ('United for Liberation') (Fig. 122) is an MOI poster that anticipates D-Day and provides a clear hint that France will be part of its own liberation and, together with the United States and Britain, will play a leading role in reshaping Europe in any post-war settlement.

It was equally important at this stage of the war to support the emergence of national resistance movements across occupied Europe and to demonstrate that exiled governments based in London were continuing to keep the flame of freedom alive, both symbolically by establishing headquarters in London, and actively by publishing their own newspapers with the support of the MOI. The poster *The Voices of Freedom Live* (Fig. 123) details ten examples of national newspapers that were published in Britain and dropped all over Europe, supplementing the news and information already provided by the BBC European services.

The BBC also had an important role to play in this context. As well as encouraging the French people with *Ici Londres* broadcasts of war news and speeches by Free French leaders, the BBC allowed all the exiled governments to make radio broadcasts to their own peoples. The BBC gradually became an important and trusted source of news – a sort of life raft to which all the occupied nations could cling. It was also increasingly listened to by Germans as the war turned against the Nazi regime. The BBC and MOI even produced a pamphlet for European listeners with tips on 'how to tune into London' and 'how to reduce jamming on long and medium wave bands'.[21] In Denmark the Nazi newspaper *Faedrelandet* conceded: 'Many people have more faith in bulletins from London than in the words of the Bible …' A letter, typical of the time, smuggled from a French village in 1942 stated: 'Out of 150 households there are 110 wireless sets. Out of the 110 owners of these sets, 105 at least listen to the BBC regularly.'[22] The Vichy, Italian, and German authorities confiscated sets and imposed punitive fines and imprisonment upon (even threatened to execute) anyone caught listening to the BBC in all countries under Nazi occupation.

In 1943 a booklet, *Chansons de BBC*, put together by the MOI, was dropped over France. It contained the sheet music of songs together with cartoons that made fun of the Germans and Italians by anticipating their impending defeat.[23] One song entitled 'O La Jolie Defaite' reveals a disgruntled-looking Hitler and Mussolini and behind them the flags of Britain, France, and the United States. The final chorale with the sheet music went:

> *La chose la plus sure,*
> *Vieil Hitler, vieux Musso,*
> *La chose la plus sure*
> *C'est qu' ça s'ra bientôt.* [24]

The song anticipates the final Allied push against Hitler and Mussolini. The theme that Britain was no longer alone and that Allied strength would soon liberate France and occupied Europe figured in a number of posters and leaflets that were dropped by the RAF in this period. One poster (Fig. 124) is particularly interesting because of its restrained design and colouring and the sombre stature of the lone British Tommy (reminiscent of British posters produced in World War I). The caption reads: 'Two years ago the British Empire was alone … Today four-fifths of the world are united against the Axis tyranny.' The configuration of Allied strength continued to be stressed. The MOI was particularly concerned to show the extent of the contribution made by the Allies to the British war effort. Posters and pamphlets again proved an important means of communication for this type of message. Now, however, the Soviet Union could be included. Fig. 125 provides two examples of posters in this genre; both detail the contribution that men and women from many Allied countries were making. The national flags provide the shorthand to the extent of this contribution across Europe.

121
A colourful poster, which was also produced in French, showing French farmers welcoming RAF fighter planes which have been targeting German supply trains.
(PP/51/29)

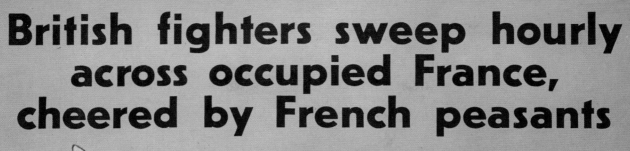

British fighters sweep hourly across occupied France, cheered by French peasants

UNIS POUR LA
LIBERATION

122
Unis Pour La Libération
('United for Liberation'). A British poster
that anticipates D-Day and revealingly
includes France as part of a trio of major
nations involved in national liberation —
a clear hint that, as a major ally, France
would be involved in shaping the
post-war world.
(PP/BS51/29)

123
Two posters showing how leaders of the
occupied nations of Europe were continuing
their liberation struggle from London.
The Voices of Freedom Live is a simple design
with the national flags of the newspapers at
the top of the poster. *Leaders of the Allied
Nations* ingeniously uses the V for Victory
to frame the photographs of the individual
leaders in exile in London. These posters
were translated into many languages and
distributed across occupied Europe for the
various resistance movements to circulate.
(PP/BS51/29)

IL Y A DEUX ANS
L'Empire Britannique
était seul...

AUJOURD' HUI, LES QUATRE CINQUIEMES DU MONDE SONT UNIS CONTRE LA TYRANNIE DE L'AXE

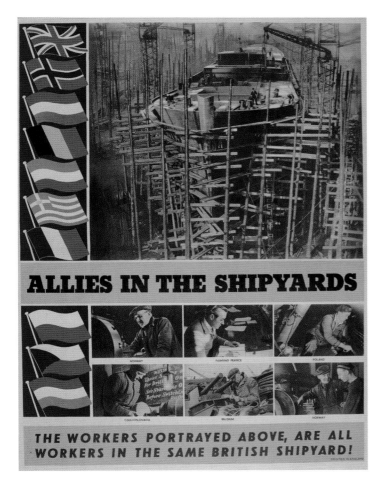

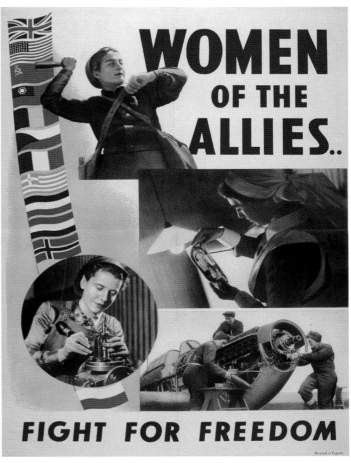

124
Poster *Two Years Ago ...* A somewhat restrained, almost sombre, design juxtaposed with an inspirational message of hope for the future.
(PP/BS51/29)

125
Allies in the Shipyards: Women of the Allies.
Two posters illustrating the contributions made by the men and women of Britain's European allies to the British war effort. Unusually, for Britain at least, it includes a photograph of a Soviet woman soldier in action.
(PP/BS51/29)

The Yanks Are Coming!

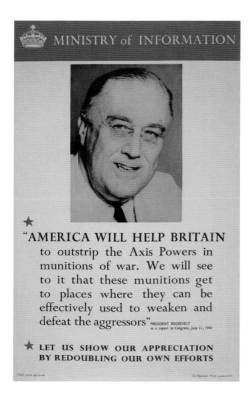

126
A small leaflet and bookmark.
This low-key propaganda anticipates the United States' entry into
the war and focuses on renewed
military provisions to encourage
the British Home Front to
'redouble its own effort'.
(PP/BS51/29)

127
Pictures Are Better Than Words.
A strikingly simple design that
demonstrates the changing tides
of war as the British lion gains
the ascendency.
(PP/BS51/29)

128 (overleaf)
Poster. *The Resources of the
United States.* A map detailing
America's extraordinary
resources, ranging from military
equipment to raw materials
and food production.
(PP/BS51/29)

After 1942, British propaganda took on a more confident, almost triumphalist, tone.
Partly this was due to the exploits of the RAF and the British forces in North Africa, but
even more decisive to the future outcome of the conflict was the entry into the war of
the United States, following the Japanese attack on Pearl Harbor on 7 December 1941.
Prior to this, the US had agreed to 'lend-lease' Britain essential war materiel. It was a
significant decision, in that it meant that the British war effort, even before America
became a combatant, was going to be backed by America's vast industrial power. Initially
the MOI used American assistance to encourage the British Home Front to redouble its
own efforts. A small leaflet and bookmark, published with an official MOI heading,
quotes from President Roosevelt's speech to Congress on 11 June 1941, in which he
pledges support in the fight against the Axis, whom he refers to as 'the aggressors' (Fig.
126). After Pearl Harbor, when the United States was fully engaged in defeating the Axis
powers, the MOI – which had already made much of the new alliance with the Soviet
Union – could now ratchet up its wider propaganda campaigns into overdrive.

Towards the end of 1942 the MOI launched a poster in Britain and overseas that was
intend to reflect the new-found confidence. It was simply entitled *Pictures Are Better Than
Words* (Fig. 127) and used the symbol of the British lion to represent the shifting fortunes
of the nation in the conflict. In 1939, the lion is subdued – almost overwhelmed by the
size and sheer numbers of Hitler's military might. In 1940, as Britain starts to increase its
production of tanks, planes, and ships, the lion is less cowed and begins to rise from the
ground. In 1941 the lion has risen upright and is confronting the enemy who is beginning
to shrink in size and numbers. By 1942 the British lion, sensing it is now in the ascendency,
is roaring ferociously as Hitler is in full retreat and shrinking even further.

However, with the arrival of American troops in Britain after January 1942, the
MOI was handed the responsibility of smoothing relations between a large body of
foreign soldiers (that included black servicemen) and their civilian hosts. To judge from
the responses of the public, the entry of the US into the war was greeted by relief and
gratitude but also by a lingering sense of impatience as to why it had taken them so long
to fight for democracy and freedom. There was almost a 'malicious delight' that a country
'too damned wealthy' would now encounter 'the hardship and suffering of war'. Initially
the public were more favourably disposed to make sacrifices to help Russia than they
were to accommodate American troops flaunting their wealth and provisions.[25]

The MOI decided to set up an American Forces Liaison Division, which
co-ordinated a locally based network intended to enhance relations between the public
and the American forces. Re-orientation programmes were established for new arrivals
and this included an hour-long film *A Welcome to Britain* (1943) directed and devised
by Anthony Asquith and featuring the American actor Burgess Meredith. The film was
made by the MOI for the American Office of War Information (OWI), which showed
it to all American troops on arrival in Britain. Meredith, in military uniform, acts as a
guide and narrator, explaining to his audience of American GIs the etiquette of English
pubs, the currency and rationing system, and the privations suffered by the British. In a
forthright section on racial prejudice, Meredith explains that there are fewer social
restrictions on blacks than in America and that the 'coloured man' would be made more
welcome in Britain than at home. The film met with critical acclaim within Britain
(although it was never shown on the commercial cinema circuit) and in a test poll of
American troops conducted by the OWI it proved highly popular.[26]

By 1943 the number of negative reports about American troops had virtually
disappeared (although there remained grievances) and there was a general consensus that
the Americans were 'settling down well'.[27] This allowed the MOI to concentrate on its
main propaganda task of detailing the overwhelming combined strength of the Allied

1939

1940

PICTURES
ARE BETTER THAN WORDS

1941

1942

THE RESOURCES OF

KEY TO MAP
Figures show value of
Annual Pre-War Output

AIRCRAFT
$ 106,568,000

MOTOR VEHICLES
$ 2,848,786,000

SHIPBUILDING
$ 250,457,000

MACHINERY
$ 5,891,599,000

IRON & STEEL
$ 3,330,491,000

OIL REFINING
$ 2,546,746,000

MUNITIONS & FIREARMS
$ 117,180,000

TEXTILES
$ 7,061,609,000

MEAT CANNING
$ 2,787,358,000

TIMBER
$ 630,000,000

U.S.A. PRODUCTION OF RAW MATERIALS
as percentage of World total

MOLYBDENUM SULPHUR OIL MAIZE COTTON IRON COAL COPPER ZINC PHOSPHATES SILVER LEAD MEAT OATS

The United States of America
the world. Its industrial ca
combined. Today, the U.S.A
playing a decisive part i

THE UNITED STATES

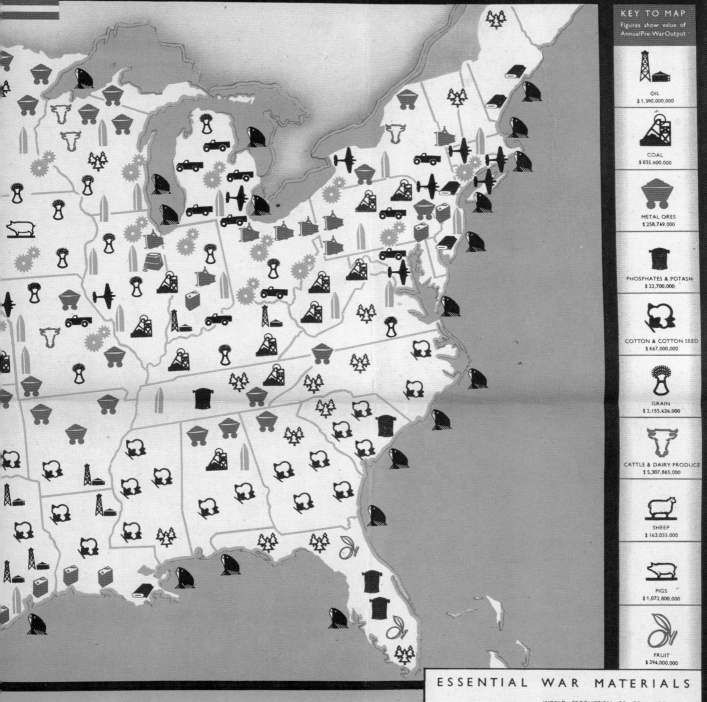

he greatest industrial power in
y exceeds that of all Europe
"the Arsenal of Freedom" is
e war against aggression.

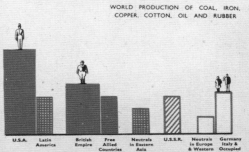

ESSENTIAL WAR MATERIALS

WORLD PRODUCTION OF COAL, IRON,
COPPER, COTTON, OIL AND RUBBER

U.S.A. | Latin America | British Empire | Free Allied Countries | Neutrals in Eastern Asia | U.S.S.R. | Neutrals in Europe & Western Asia | Germany Italy & Occupied Territories

HITLER IS TRAPPED IN EUROPE

The would-be world conqueror is concerned now only to defend. On September 3rd, 1943, Italy, his major ally, surrendered. The Axis begins to crack. The third partner, Japan, nonplussed by the rapidity of the United States' recovery from her heavy blow at Pearl Harbour, has suffered heavy defeats at sea and has already lost some of her gains. British and American sea-power slowly tightens its grip.

Since the magnificent victory at Stalingrad, Russia has already delivered further crushing blows and freed vast regions from the enemy. In the South, the Mediterranean has been reopened to United Nations' shipping. Neither here nor in the Atlantic Ocean have Hitler's U-boats been able to prevent the safe arrival of supplies. From West and East and South alike, the United Nations' bombers are systematically destroying the Nazi power to wage effective war.

34

THIS MAP SHOWS THE SITUATION IN THE WEST, A FEW DAYS PRIOR TO THE UNCONDITIONAL SURRENDER OF ITALY, SIGNED SEPTEMBER 3rd, 1943, EFFECTIVE SEPTEMBER 8th, 1943.

Vainly the Nazis try to sustain morale in their " Festung Europa," their fortress without a roof. At the end of the fourth year of war the position of Hitler is that he is brought at last to bay. Within Europe are countless millions who have waited years for their deliverance. Some eight millions of them are in the Reich itself. The next stages of the war may be long and may see setbacks. But that Hitler's evil plan for the domination of the world by Germany has been defeated is, happily, quite sure.

35

129

Four Years of War
(1943). 'Hitler is trapped in Europe' …
and Japan is 'nonplussed'.
(PP/9/17).

camp now that the US could be included. This was achieved by first showing the mighty resources of the US and then coupling this power with the Allied cause. *The Resources of the United States* (Fig. 128) is an MOI poster intended for both home and overseas audiences: 'The United States of America is the greatest individual power in the world. Its industrial capacity exceeds that of all Europe combined. Today, the USA as the "Arsenal of Freedom" is playing a decisive part in the war against aggression.' The 'arsenal of freedom' was a clever turn of phrase, but it was also meaningful in that the MOI could unequivocally demonstrate that the odds had now turned decisively in favour of the Allies. In a pamphlet called *Four Years of War* (Fig. 129), published just after the surrender of Italy in September 1943, the propaganda message was clear; Hitler 'the would-be world conqueror' is 'trapped in Europe … concerned now only to *defend*' (my emphasis) and Japan is 'nonplussed … suffering heavy defeats'. By means of diagrams and maps it concludes that 'British and American sea-power slowly tightens its grip'. Following the United States' entry into the war, the British made much in their propaganda of the combined strength of their joint sea power. *Two Mighty Fleets* (Fig. 130) is a double-sided leaflet containing, on one side, the icons and symbols of the two fleets with two young sailors, and on the other side, their respective naval strength, including the number of vessels and the potency of their weaponry.

American's entry into the war also gave renewed impetus to the 'V for Victory' campaign which had been launched in early 1941. The campaign continued to gain strength after twenty-six nations, meeting in Washington, established the embryonic United Nations in January 1942. The V for Victory was now widened to embody more than simply a symbol of defiant resistance to Nazism. Instead it became a global push on all fronts in pursuit of ultimate victory for the United Nations. The MOI produced numerous variations on this theme. Perhaps one of the most famous posters and leaflets produced was *Freedom Shall Prevail!* (Fig. 131). In this poster soldiers from the Allied

countries line up on either side of a V for Victory constructed from the flags of the corresponding nations. The nations are: Britain, Canada, Australia, New Zealand, Southern Rhodesia, Newfoundland, South Africa, India, The Colonial Empire, China, USSR, Yugoslavia, Holland, France, Poland, Czechoslovakia, Greece, Norway, and Belgium. The message is simple but effective: 'Freedom Shall Prevail!' Further variations of this theme included the poster *This is the Sign of Victory for the Allies* (Fig. 132), incorporating the flags of some of the nations involved and five compelling reasons outlining why ultimate victory is inevitable, and *The Allies Are Hitting Back* (Fig. 133), a striking design that juxtaposed the solidarity of Allied soldiers, shoulder-to-shoulder, against a background photomontage of recent successes on land, in the air, and at sea. Such propaganda was not exaggerating (for once) when it claimed that the Allies now possessed greater man, air, sea, and machine power, plus greater resources. These posters were translated into many languages and also dropped over Germany in large numbers to undermine the morale of the civilian population.

Finally as D-Day (Operation Overlord) drew closer, posters, leaflets, and postcards dramatising the final land, air, and sea assaults were produced, fuelling expectations of ultimate victory. The Political Warfare Executive (PWE) was the British clandestine body created to produce and disseminate both 'white' and 'black' propaganda, with the aim of damaging enemy morale and sustaining the morale of the occupied countries. It would be the PWE that was largely responsible for liaising with resistance groups and for subterfuge.[28] Nevertheless, the MOI continued to produce propaganda for a wider overseas audience. *29 United Nations Prepare to Deal Hitler's Death Blow!* is an MOI poster which highlights a less glamorous aspect of the overwhelming numerical strength of the Allies (Fig. 134). The poster shows a never-ending stream of supply trucks heading for Germany in support of the Allied land and air squeeze. Victory was near, and Fascism – in its original historical manifestations – was on the verge of extinction.

130
Two Mighty Fleets. A double-sided leaflet. This is the front cover, showing two young sailors with their respective flags and the vessels in action.
(PP/40/18L)

Reading Right to Left—FIRST ROW: Britain, Canada, Australia, New Zealand, SECOND ROW: Southern Rhodesi
Newfoundland, South Africa, THIRD ROW: India, FOURTH ROW: The Colonial Empire

FREEDOM S

131
Poster and
leaflet. *Freedom
Shall Prevail!*
British Empire
and Common-
wealth forces
form up on one
side of the V.
(PP/BS51/29)

Reading Left to Right—FIRST ROW: U.S.A., China, U.S.S.R., Yugoslavia, SECOND ROW: Holland, France, Poland, Czechoslovakia, THIRD ROW: Greece, Norway, Belgium

ALL PREVAIL!

PRINTED IN ENGLAND BY FOSH & CROSS LTD., LONDON.   (51-3035)

5 REASONS WHY THE ALLIES WILL WIN

1. The Allies have greater man-power.

2. The Allies have greater air-power.

3. The Allies have greater sea-power.

4. The Allies have greater machine-power.

5. The Allies have greater resources.

THIS IS THE SIGN OF VICTORY FOR THE ALLIES V

132
This is the Sign of Victory for the Allies, citing five reasons why an Allied victory was now inevitable.
(PP/BS51/29)

133
The Allies Are Hitting Back. A dramatic grand gesture of united strength.
(PP/BS51/29)

By Land, Sea and Air
THE ALLIES ARE HITTING BACK

Printed in England by W. R. Royle & Son Ltd. 51—9769

29 United Nations prepare to deal Hitler's death blow

Postscript: The New Jerusalem

'Happiness was in the air because our own dangers and troubles were clearly over: because the security and stability of our British way of life was now assured with the downfall of the tyrants who would have destroyed it. After five-and-a-half years it was at last safe to allow the mind to dwell on the future.'

SIR RAYMOND STREAT

MANCHESTER INDUSTRIALIST, MAY 1945

In November 1943, a United Nations Relief and Rehabilitation Administration was formed by forty-four nations in Washington. Its purpose was to assist war-devastated areas of Europe and Asia in need of care and rehabilitation. The firm establishment of the United Nations Organisation began at the Bretton Woods Conference in July 1944. Even before the war had ended, organisations and individuals were planning ahead to a post-war world that would have to be rebuilt following the enormous destruction of the war. On 6 January 1941, President Franklin D. Roosevelt (FDR) in his State of the Union Address to Congress outlined four fundamental freedoms that people 'everywhere in the world' ought to enjoy. The Four Freedoms included freedom of speech and worship, and freedom from fear and from want. In essence, the war would be justified as a fight for freedom. American propaganda drew on FDR's 'Four Freedoms'. Winning the war meant defeating the 'new order of tyranny' of the Axis with its dictators, bombs, concentration camps, and 'quick-lime in the ditch'. Winning the peace meant establishing a new world order of 'co-operation of free countries' based on the Four Freedoms. In this context, the MOI was prepared to work with the United Nations Information Office (UNIO) to design and distribute propaganda material offering nations hope for a better and fairer future. The Four Freedoms were explicitly incorporated into the preamble to the Universal Declaration of Human Rights, which reads:

> Whereas disregard and contempt for human rights have resulted in barbarous acts which have outraged the conscience of mankind, and the advent of a world in which human beings shall enjoy freedom of speech and belief and freedom from fear and want has been proclaimed the highest aspiration of the common people ...

The United Nation's Four Freedoms formed the spearhead of a major propaganda campaign in the form of four posters that were distributed throughout the world (Fig. 135). These four UNIO posters, stylistically different but all equally imaginative, are characterised by their overtly Westernised vision of the future. So the war ended with the defeat of Fascism within and outside of Europe and with a restatement of fundamental democratic principles.

The British equivalent of the Four Freedoms expressed itself in themes such as 'Your Country Needs You'. This, in turn, manifested itself in the notion of a shared 'people's war' — a nation working together (as in the slogan 'Let Us Go Forward

134
A highly colourful poster showing the 29 flags of the individual nations that made up the United Nations. The message of combined strength and unity is clear. Note that Great Britain is given special prominence as the Union Jack is separate from the rest of the flags.
(BS51/29)

135
The United Nation's
Four Freedoms.
The poster campaign was
translated into many languages,
and embraced different stylistic
devices, but what the posters had
in common was a quintessentially
white, Westernised narrative.
(PP/BS51/29)

Together') and the putting aside of class, regional, and social differences. This strategy was also applied across the British Empire. As the public wanted to be reassured of the nation's capacity to produce armaments and their effective use, artistic compositions of industrial sites and workers produced a new iconography. Offices and factories were stages for a shifting social order, adjusted and attuned to wartime needs. Propaganda also stressed the new roles undertaken by women for the war effort – from performing menial tasks with the Auxiliary Territorial Service to complex work in armaments factories. Though bearing in mind the un-met promises ('the land fit for heroes') made during World War I, British propaganda also emphasised the possibility of post-war change. After 1942, as defeat gradually became less likely, thought was increasingly given to the shape of post-war Britain. It was a debate in which the MOI was reluctant to engage. The Ministry was more concerned with the Empire, France, wartime healthy eating, and 'make do and mend', than with talk about a new order in Britain. The MOI was further shackled by the Prime Minister's desire for silence on the subject.

For all its reluctance to engage in debate, the MOI could not fail to recognise the emerging public interest in the post-war reconstruction, which had gathered considerable momentum after the publication of the Beveridge Report (on 'Social Insurance and Allied

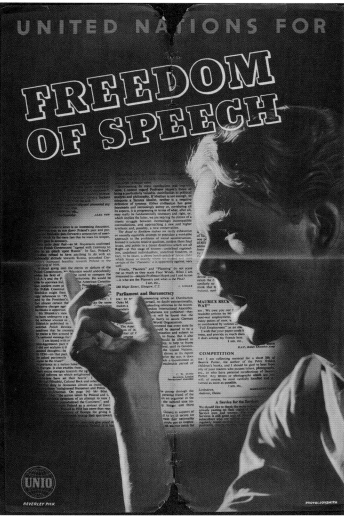

Services') in December 1942. It came out at a crucial moment, just after Britain's victory at El Alamein and just before the Red Army's recapture of Stalingrad. In the months following the report's publication, 650,000 copies were purchased. By identifying five issues that could only be defeated by state action (Idleness, Want, Squalor, Disease, and Ignorance), Beveridge had provided the British people with a domestic focus for victory. Revealingly there is not to be found in the MOI's records a single mention of the report, nor of any preparation of the publicity accompanying its publication.[29] This is hardly surprising given the view expressed in Churchill's Cabinet memorandum in January 1943:

> *Ministers should, in my view, be careful not to raise false hopes as was done last time by speeches about 'Homes for Heroes', etc. The broad masses of the people face the hardships of life undaunted but they are liable to get very angry if they feel they have been cheated. . . . It is for this reason of not wishing to deceive the people by false hopes and airy visions of Utopia and Eldorado that I have refrained so far from making promises about the future.*[30]

Churchill's argument that the nation should concentrate upon winning the war before considering future reconstruction cut little ice with the public. Mass-Observation noted at the time that post-war expectations for a continuation and extension in the state provision of social services were very much governed by wartime experiences.[31] Only a full welfare state appeared to be acceptable as the ultimate prize for victory. Moreover, passions had been aroused by the Beveridge Report that reflected the fragility of the wartime political truce.

However, Churchill was still fixated on wartime grand strategy and was not interested in welfare schemes. Following Beveridge, he half-heartedly put his name to a Conservative document, *Post-War Reconstruction*, in June 1943.[32] Home Intelligence reports suggest that the public saw this as a cynical move to appease public opinion and to postpone debate about substantive economic and social reforms. Perhaps Churchill thought that the encouraging war news at the end of 1942 and during the final half of 1943 would divert public attention away from future reforms. However, the war itself ignited a sense of entitlement that no amount of silence on the part of the MOI could crush. The evacuation of 3 million working-class children from the big cities to the countryside forced people of all backgrounds to recognise the dire state of affairs. People wanted to believe that after the war Britain would be a better place – a 'New Jerusalem' was a phrase of the time – a country worth fighting for. In August 1944, the Coalition's Education Act, which among other things provided secondary education for all, fuelled further the momentum for new order. Although it became known as the 'Butler Act' after R.A. Butler, the Conservative minister who skilfully guided it through Parliament, it would be a reforming Labour government that would implement it after the war.

While the MOI had resolutely attempted to distance itself from all calls for post-war reform, it had not been entirely successful. Even in 'official' MOI literature, an occasional subversive message would slip through its censorship net. In the lovingly detailed *Ourselves in Wartime*, which looked back nostalgically at the 'people's war' and declared it a 'triumph of Britain united in the fight for freedom', there is barely a mention of post-war reconstruction. However, in its conclusion there is this oblique reference: 'If we can only keep in the years of reconstruction, the self-sacrifices and cooperation which has carried us through the years of conflict there can be little doubt that we shall build an England [sic] better than the one we left behind in 1939.'[33]

Generally, however, the Ministry retained a firm control over most of the literature that it commissioned, but film propaganda was another matter. Production timetables and costs dictated the release dates of films and this made it far more difficult to prevent films from being shown once they had been produced. As a result a few films did address the controversy of a 'new order'. In 1941, for example, a short film made by the Boulting brothers for the MOI entitled *The Dawn Guard* contained an explicit reference to British war aims. The film takes the form of a dialogue between two members of the Home Guard (played by Percy Walsh and Bernard Miles) standing sentry duty on a rural hillside, as to what the war was all about. The older man, Bert (Walsh), sees it in terms of defending traditional ways of life. Bert complains about the Nazis 'upsetting the ways and wrecking the lives of millions of people' and he believes that 'it's the liberty we had and never thought about we got to fight for – to get our lives back to where they was'. This was the 'official' line adopted by the MOI at the time. But it is not enough for the younger farmer (Miles) who looks to the future rather than to the past. He expresses the view that a sense of solidarity brought about by the war should be carried over into rebuilding the world when the war was over. 'We've made a fine big war effort, well when it's all over we've got to see to it we make a fine big peace effort.' The farmer wants to see a world free from poverty and unemployment: 'We can't go back to the old ways. … That's gone forever.' *Dawn Guard* is more philosophical than most films commissioned by the MOI and is imbued with a vision of a 'brave new world' arising from the ruins of the old and of war as the 'midwife of social progress'.

There were exceptions (such as *The Shipbuilders* and *Millions Like Us,* both 1943) but most films shied away from such concerns. However, in 1945 Humphrey Jennings directed *A Diary for Timothy*, with a script by E.M. Forster, which interpreted the events of the last winter of the war in the form of a diary for a newly born child. The film was commissioned by the MOI. The four central figures of the film – Goronwy the miner, Bill the engine driver, Alan the farmer, and Peter the fighter pilot – are representative of the 'people's war' and all do their bit with courage and calmness. The film poignantly looks back for Timothy to the events of the war but revealingly it also looks forward to a New Jerusalem. The narrator of *Diary*, Michael Redgrave, starts by warning Timothy that 'you are one of the lucky ones … If you had been born in wartime Holland or Poland or even a Liverpool or Glasgow slum, this would be a very different picture'. There is a significant emphasis on the return to political freedom and liberty which peace would bring, but this in turn meant obligations and responsibilities. While the BBC announces another major assault on the cities of Germany, Redgrave warns sombrely:

> … the danger is over for us, now that the enemy in Europe is breaking … life is going to become more dangerous than before oddly enough … because now we have the power to choose and the right to criticize and even grumble. We're free men, we have to decide for ourselves and part of your bother Tim, will be learning to grow up free.

The film cuts from more bombs being dropped from British and American planes, to Goronwy who is sitting in a nursing home recuperating from a mining accident. His mind drifts back to the 1920s and 30s and we see a young Goronwy (played by his son) walking across the Welsh countryside, which has been scarred by coal tips. The old miner laments: 'I was thinking about the past … the last war, the unemployment, broken homes, scattered families … and I thought "Has this all really got to happen again?"' For Jennings and others this was more than a rhetorical question. The camera zooms onto Timothy, warm and safe in his pram, while an inferno of flames breaks out over Germany. A plaintive appeal to the infant draws the film to its final ethical and moral conclusion:

> Up to now we have done the talking. But before long you are going to sit up and take notice. What are you going to say of it and what are you going to do? You heard what Goronwy was thinking … unemployment after the war, and then another war and then more unemployment. … Will it be like that again? Are you going to have greed for power ousting decency from the world as they have in the past? Or are you going to make the world a different place, you and all the other babies?

Diary for Timothy proved popular with cinema audiences, but its message did not represent the 'official' stance of the MOI or that of the Prime Minister.[34] In December 1944, Churchill permitted himself to appear on Christmas postcards (in the 'For Freedom' series) distributed in Britain and the Empire (Fig. 136). His message was restrained ('Every good wish for Christmas') but the image of defiance and bulldog tenacity was familiar. His appeal, based on a combination of patriotism, insularity, and xenophobia, had helped succour Britain in its hour of greatest need. 'Cometh the hour cometh the man.' In 1945, to mark the ending of the conflict, a commemorative book of photographs of Churchill and transcriptions of his stirring wartime speeches was produced (Fig. 137). Revealingly, the MOI ended the war continuing to look back at the past. Like the Prime Minister it was now patently out of touch with the mood of the British people. While Churchill remained focused on winning the war, the Labour Party began to turn its attention to winning the peace. Its determination not to return to the past led to a landslide election victory on 26 July 1945, shortly after the end of the war in Europe in May.

The MOI's fate was similar to that of Churchill. It lingered on a little longer, but was unceremoniously disbanded in March 1946, with its residual functions passing to the new Central Office of Information. Even its former Minister, Duff Cooper, concluded that a centralised propaganda bureau had no place in a post-war democracy. Writing in his memoirs he noted, 'I believe the truth of the matter to be that there is no place in the British scheme of government for a Ministry of Information.'[35]

136
Postcard: Prime Minister Winston Churchill's Christmas wish for 1944.
(PP/20/83L)

THE RT. HON. WINSTON S. CHURCHILL

With every good wish Christmas 1944

For Freedom

137 (overleaf)
Churchill. His Finest Hour.
A commemorative pamphlet of his wartime speeches: 'They stand to remind us of a great man and an incomparable leader.'
(PP/ 48/32A)

33 | THEIR FINEST HOUR

"'Let us therefore brace ourselves to our
duties,
and so bear ourselves that,
if the British Empire and its Commonwealth
last for a thousand years,
men will still say,
'This was their finest hour'."

JUNE 18, 1940

Made and Printed in England by Wyman & Sons Limited, Reading

1   N. Nicolson (ed), *Harold Nicolson Diaries and Letters 1939–45*, (London, 1970), 1 October 1940. The Lugard system is presumably a reference to Sir Frederick Lugard (1858–1945), who theorised on the 'dual mandate' as an expression of the fundamental principles of European imperialism in British Tropical Africa. Lugard argued that the resources of Africa could be productively marshalled and utilised by the more technologically advanced imperial nations of Europe for the mutual benefit of the coloniser and the colonised.

2   Cf. TNA. INF 1/251, 'Home Front Propaganda', November 1941. This review of 'exhortation propaganda', as it was termed by its author Stephen Taylor, concluded that 'there is little evidence that these campaigns ("Empire Crusade") have had any appreciable effect'. A brief discussion of the Empire Crusade can be found in I. McLaine, *Ministry of Morale. Home Front Morale and the Ministry of Information in World War II* (London, 1979), 223–4.

3   BL. PP/22/44L, *Sixty Million of Us. The Colonies at War* (1942).

4   In April 1949, following the London Declaration, the word 'British' was dropped from the title of the Commonwealth.

5   Sevek's real name was Severin Rajchman. He was born in Poland in 1918 to a Polish father and a Czech–Austrian mother. When he was six months old the family moved to Vienna. Sevek studied at the Art Academy of Vienna and worked with the Austrian branch of the US film-making company MGM (Metro Goldwin Meyer). In 1940, he joined the British Army in the Middle East and later worked for the Ministry of Information.

6   For a detailed analysis of Nazi propaganda directed at the Middle East, see J. Herf, *Nazi Propaganda for the Arab World*, (New Haven, CT, 2011).

7   British Library, (PP/14/28A), *The Muslim Attitude to the War* (undated), 35.

8   The initial letter of the Arabic word does not exist in the English alphabet, but is roughly a 'kh' sound. I am greatly indebted for this and indeed much of this section on the Middle East to Louis Allday (British Library) for his generosity in providing and translating material for me.

9   Louis Allday has produced a brief blog for the British Library on the discovery of these two posters entitled 'For the Sake of Freedom: British World War II Propaganda Posters in Arabic'. See: http://britishlibrary.typepad.co.uk/untoldlives/2014/02/for-the-sake-of-freedom-british-world-war-ii-propaganda-posters-in-arabic.html#sthash.u600ttkh.BpXEqQHO.dpuf (last accessed November 2015)

10 For an analysis of Kem's contribution to the MOI during World War II, see V. Holman, 'Kem's Cartoons in the Second World War,' *History Today* (March, 2002), 21-7.

11 Rūzgā-i naw was published by Hodder & Stoughton in London and Doubleday Doran in New York on behalf of the MOI. It was primarily a cultural and literary magazine which was published quarterly in Persian between 1941 and 1946. The editor was A.J. Arberry (later Professor of Persian at the School of Oriental and African Studies) and the magazine was intended to counter-pro German sentiments in neutral Iran. See Ursula Sims-Williams, 'The New Age (Ruzgar-i naw): World War II cultural propaganda in Persian' at: http://britishlibrary.typepad.co.uk/asian-and-african/propaganda/page/2/#sthash.ORVCmvSh.dpuf (accessed February 2016). See also, Valerie Holman, 'Carefully Concealed Connections: The Ministry of Information and British Publishing, 1939-1946', *Book History*, vol. 8 (2005), 197-226.

12 For a more detailed discussion of the *Shahnameh*, see A. Wynn, 'The Shah-name and British Propaganda in Irn in World War II', *Manuscripta Orientalia*, 16/1 (June 2010), 3-5. See also the post for the British Library by Nur Sobers-Khan, http://britishlibrary.typepad.co.uk/asian-and-african/propaganda/page/2/#sthash.AaDSCa1M.dpuf (last accessed November 2015)

13 It was followed in the same year by Spanish and Portuguese broadcasts to Latin America. The BBC went into the war broadcasting in seven foreign languages and came out of it as the world's largest international station, broadcasting in forty-five. See T. Hickman, *What Did You Do in the War, Auntie? The BBC at War* (London, 1995), 103–27.

14 See an 'official' pamphlet promoting the work carried out by the BBC by A. White, *BBC at War* (London, undated but probably 1943).

15 Most British newspapers supported Morrison's actions. See the *Guardian* (editorial), 22 January 1941. The government's ban on the *Daily Worker* was lifted in September 1942 following a campaign supported by the Dean of Canterbury Cathedral and also by the Labour Party.

16 TNA. H.I. Weekly Reports, INF 1/292, 18–25 June 1941.

17 *The Spirit of the Soviet Union. Anti-Nazi Cartoons and Posters* (London, 1942), 3.

18 The scene of a children's choir on stage against a backdrop of a banner offering 'Greetings to the Red Army and the glorious fighting forces of the United Nations' is captured in Humphrey Jennings's film masterpiece *A Diary for Timothy* (1945).

19 Cf. TNA. H.I. Weekly Reports, INF 1/292, 16–23 February 1943. This was not an entirely

magnanimous gesture on the part of the government, which was determined to prevent the Communist Party from gaining any political impetus from this new alliance with the USSR.

20 At a court-martial by Vichy, on 2 August 1940, de Gaulle was sentenced to death in absentia, for treason. The 70th anniversary of the speech was marked in 2010 by the issuing of a postage stamp and a 2-euro commemorative coin.

21 *Notes for European Listeners*, BL. PP/16/5L.

22 Quoted in Hickman, *What Did You Do in the War, Auntie?*, 127.

23 BL. B.S. 14/1004. For two examples from the song-book, see also D. Welch, *Propaganda, Power and Persuasion* (London, 2013), 172.

24 'The most certain thing, Old Hitler, Old Musso, The surest thing, It will be soon'.

25 TNA. INF 1/292, 'Public Attitudes Towards the U.S.A.', 24 December 1941.

26 For more detailed information, see A. Aldgate and J. Richards, *Britain Can Take It. The British Cinema in the Second World War* (Edinburgh, 1994), 292–3.

27 TNA. H.I. Weekly Reports, INF 1/292, 1–8 September 1942. This and other reports suggested that a residual factor contributing to tension ('considerable indignation') between the civil population and the American troops was the discrimination publicly exercised by white American soldiers against their black compatriots.

28 In the popular view, propaganda is commonly associated with the idea of the 'big lie', but in fact it operates on many different levels. It may be 'black', but it may also be 'grey' or 'white'. And when it comes to conflict, actual warfare may be bolstered by 'psychological warfare'. Broadly speaking these three terms can be defines as follows:
White: truthful and not strongly biased, where the source of information is acknowledged.
Grey: largely truthful, containing no information that can be proven wrong; the source is not identified.
Black: inherently deceitful, information given in the product is attributed to a source that was not responsible for its creation. For a detailed analysis of different 'shades' of propaganda see, Welch, *Propaganda, Power and Persuasion*, 33–38. For an analysis of PWE propaganda disseminated prior to D-Day (Operation Overlord) see D. Welch, 'La propagande britannique et le second front. L'action du Political Warfare Executive', in Leleu Jean-Luc (ed), *Le Débarquement: De l'événement à l'épopée*, (Rennes, 2016).

29 Ian McLaine first made this claim in 1979 and I can confirm the absence of any reference to Beveridge from my own research. See McLaine, *Ministry of Morale*, 171–85.

30 TNA. CAB 66/33 Memorandum by Prime Minister, 12 January 1943. Also cited in McLaine, *Ministry of Morale*, 183.

31 *Political Quarterly*, Mass-Observation, 'Social Security and Parliament', *Political Quarterly*, vol. XIV, 1943.

32 *Post-War Reconstruction*. The pamphlet was published in June 1943.

33 *Ourselves in Wartime* (London, undated but probably 1944).

34 The response from film critics was not, however, overwhelmingly positive and it was accused by some of overt sentimentality. See E.A. Robinson, 'A Critic Has a Good Cry', *Daily Mail*, 25 November 1945.

35 D. Cooper, *Old Men Forget* (London, 1957), 287–8. In fact Brendan Bracken had written to Churchill in March 1945 requesting permission to dismantle the Ministry, arguing that it should no longer be seen to be involved in matters of 'acute controversy' such as post-war reconstruction. The Prime Minister asked Bracken to keep the department in existence until the defeat of Japan. TNA. INF 1/942, Minister of Information to Prime Minister, 2 March 1945. Also cited in McLaine, *Ministry of Morale*, 276.

Further Reading

Addison, Paul,
Churchill on the Home Front 1900–1955.
London, 1992

Addison, Paul & Crang, Jeremy (eds),
*Listening to Britain: Home Intelligence
Reports on Britain's Finest Hours.*
London, 2011

Aldgate, Anthony & Richards, Jeffrey.
*Britain Can Take It: The British Cinema
in the Second World War.*
Edinburgh, 1994

Bank, Jan.
Religion In Europe During World War II.
London, 2012

Calder, Angus.
The People's War.
London, 1969

Chapman, James.
*The British at War: Cinema, State
and Propaganda, 1939–1945.*
London, 1998

Connelly, Mark,
*We Can Take It! Britain and the
Memory of the Second World War.*
Harlow, 2004

Croall, Jonathan.
*Don't You Know There's A War On?
The People's Voice 1939–45.
Voices from the Home Front.*
The History Press, 2006

Cruickshank, Charles.
*The Fourth Arm: Psychological Warfare,
1938–1945.*
Oxford, 1981

Cull, Nicholas J.
*Selling War: British Propaganda and
American "Neutrality" in World War Two.*
New York: Oxford, 1995

Field, Geoffrey.
*Blood, Sweat, and Toil: Remaking the British
Working Class, 1939–1945.*
Oxford, 2011

Grayzel, Susan.
*At Home and Under Fire: Air Raids
and Culture in Britain from the Great War
to the Blitz.*
Cambridge, 2012

Hickman, Tom.
*What did you do in the War, Auntie?
The BBC at War*
London, 1995

Holland, James.
The Battle of Britain.
London, 2011

Jones, Helen.
*British Civilians in the Front Line:
Air Raids, Productivity and Wartime
Culture, 1939–1945.*
Manchester, 2006

Lewis, Peter.
A People's War.
London, 1986

Marwick, Arthur.
Britain in the Century of Total War.
Middlesex, 1965, 2006

McCloskey, Barbara.
Artists in World War II.
Westport, Conn, 2005

McLaine, Ian.
*Ministry of Morale: Home Front Morale
and the Ministry of Information
in World War II.*
London, 1979

Nicholas, Sian.
*The Echo of War: Home Front Propaganda
and the Wartime BBC, 1939–45.*
Manchester, 1996

Overy, Richard. (ed),
*The Oxford Illustrated History
of World War II.*
Oxford, 2005

Smith, Malcolm.
*Britain and 1940. History, Myth
and Popular Memory*
London, 2000

Stammers, Neil.
*Civil Liberties in Britain During
the Second World War.*
London, 1983

Van Creveld, Martin.
The Culture of War.
New York,, 2008

Welch, David.
Propaganda: Power and Persuasion.
London, 2013

Welch, David.
*Propaganda, Power and Persuasion.
From World War I to Wikileaks*
London, 2014

Welch, David, & Fox, Jo. (eds.),
*Justifying War. Propaganda, Politics
and the Modern Age.*
Basingstoke, 2012

Index